LIVINGSTONE

Police Force, Police Service

Police Force,
Police Service

Care and Control in Britain

Edited by

Mike Stephens

and

Saul Becker

MACMILLAN

First published 1994 by
THE MACMILLAN PRESS LTD
Houndmills, Basingstoke, Hampshire RG21 2XS
and London
Companies and representatives
throughout the world

ISBN 0–333–57483–4 hardcover
ISBN 0–333–57484–2 paperback

A catalogue record for this book is available
from the British Library.

8   7   6   5   4   3
03 02 01 00 99 98

Printed in Hong Kong

For Hayley, Christopher, Lauren, and Carys

Thomas and Patrick

Gareth and Alexandra

and

For Jessica and Sophie

Contents

List of Tables

Notes on Contributors

Saul Becker is Director of Studies for the interdisciplinary Master's degree programme in Policy, Organisation and Change in Professional Care in the Department of Social Sciences, Loughborough University. He teaches and writes on policy issues concerned with personal social services, social security and community care.

Trevor Bennett works at the Institute of Criminology, University of Cambridge, where he is a university lecturer. His academic interests include community policing, crime prevention, offending, and drug addiction.

Sue Conroy is a Research Officer at the Thomas Coram Research Unit in London. Her interests include child protection investigations and decision-making, and the joint investigation of child sexual abuse by the police and social services.

Susan S. M. Edwards works at the University of Buckingham, where she is Senior Lecturer in Socio-Legal Studies. In addition to her writing in the field of domestic violence, her academic interests include women and crime, victims, pornography, criminal appeals, and the criminal justice system.

Nigel G. Fielding is a Reader in the Department of Sociology at the University of Surrey, where he pursues his interest in police studies and criminal justice, qualitative research methods, and the development of computer software for qualitative analysis.

Simon Holdaway is Reader in Sociology in the Department of Sociological Studies, Sheffield University. He is particularly interested in the police occupational culture, race relations and equal opportunities, and the probation service.

Robin Oakley was formerly a Senior Research Fellow at the Centre for the Study of Community and Race Relations at Brunel University. He now works as an independent training and research consultant, and as an academic adviser to the Home Office Specialist Support Unit for Police Training on Community and Race Relations. In addition, he is interested in race and equal opportunity issues in Britain and Europe.

Robert Reiner is Professor of Criminology in the Law Department, London School of Economics. In addition to his wide interests in the area of policing, he is also concerned with criminal justice, criminological theory, and media and crime. In 1991 he published *Chief Constables*, and his well-known book *The Politics of the Police* has recently been reissued as a second edition.

Mike Stephens is Lecturer in Social Policy in the Department of Social Sciences, Loughborough University. His academic interests include policing, the criminal justice system, community mental health care, and neighbourhood law centres.

David Thorpe is Senior Lecturer in the Department of Applied Social Science at Lancaster University, where his interests include social work and juvenile justice, substitute care, child protection, and evaluative methodologies in child welfare programmes.

Neil Walker is Senior Lecturer in the Department of Public Law, University of Edinburgh. He is interested in police sociology and the constitutional position of the police, legal and constitutional theory, freedom of expression, local government law, and statutory interpretation.

Introduction: Force is Part of the Service

Saul Becker and Mike Stephens

This book takes us to the centre of the debate about care and control in the police service. The police face new and renewed challenges to their traditional modes of operation, posed amongst other things by a heightened public and media concern with lawlessness and wrongdoing, by the escalation in reported crime, and by an uncharacteristic assault on the police body politic from a government concerned to improve performance, quality and value for money in *all* publicly funded utilities (see, for example, Sinclair and Miller, 1984; Audit Commission, 1990; Home Office, 1993; Sheehy, 1993). A rehabilitation of the care/control debate is urgent – it is at the heart of the matter about the future direction of British policing. The ways in which policy makers, chief constables and rank and file officers address the critical balance between care and control, and engage with the policy and procedural issues, will have major implications for the shape, goals and legitimacy of the police service up to, and beyond, the millennium.

The Limits of Care and Control

It is widely assumed that the major function of the police is to maintain public order – a control function for which normally they alone are responsible. Holdaway (in Chapter 3) shows how the dominant occupational culture amongst the rank and file is certainly very much one of control and enforcement. This views 'real' policing as paramilitary operations to quell disorder and as patrol and specialist work related to crime detection. At the other extreme is the *service function* – the general, often run-of-the-mill, non-crime-related tasks that the police must carry out and which are normally considered to be of low status because these activities rarely constitute 'real' police work. Walker (in Chapter 2) shows how the control ethos is constructed and reinforced through a military–bureaucratic organisational structure. In practice, however, much of this control function is targeted on some of the most marginalised and powerless groups in society. Disturbingly, as Reiner suggests in Chapter 1, control has often been characterised by the use of excessive force and by the abuse or misuse of power. To an extent, this has heralded a crisis of legitimacy for the police, especially among certain groups and communities, whose trust and support for the service has become minimal at very best, and at worst openly hostile. As Holdaway (in Chapter 3) comments in relation to the experience of black people: 'control, an occupational and cultural feature of policing, and racial prejudice and discrimination, which are structural features of society, intermingle to provide a framework within which an encounter between a police officer and a black youth is conducted'. A 1992 Home Office study shows that Afro-Caribbeans are fifty per cent more likely to be stopped in their vehicles than white people and nearly four times more likely to be stopped on foot (Southgate and Crisp, 1992).

The caring functions of the police on the other hand are infrequently discussed and analysed in police texts, despite evidence from activity studies which show that police officers spend more time on service than on crime control, and that this side of their work is popular amongst much of the public (Shapland and Vagg, 1988; Southgate and Crisp, 1992). Recently, however, the police – in particular, the more newly appointed chief constables – have increasingly emphasised the caring nature of their contemporary role. The *Statement of Common Purpose and Values* by the Metropolitan Police, a core part of its programme to improve the quality of the capital's police service, describes the need for officers to provide 'protection and reassurance to Londoners, and to be compassionate, courteous and patient'. Many police forces throughout the country have dropped the word 'force' and have assumed the mantle of 'service', with all the concomitant trappings of corporate identity and image. But, as Holdaway suggests in Chapter 3, this concern for service expressed by chief constables is not universally welcomed: 'Their ideas are in tension and conflict with the ranks' view that places direct crime control by the police and force rather than persuasion centre stage'. Moreover, the organisational structure is still very much one which supports the ethos of control. As a number of contributors to this volume show, the power of the organisational structure and of the police subculture, and their respective influence on the shape of British policing, should not be underestimated.

But neither should we underestimate the power of rhetoric and image in bringing about change. In Chapter 1 Reiner reminds us that the traditional image of the British police officer (the avuncular bobby on the beat) is 'one of a citizen in uniform working within the consensus of the community, relying on popular backing rather than force'. Today, as we have already indicated, chief constables are also attempting to reconstruct police legitimacy through service rather than through force and control. This may have arisen as a consequence of the crisis of legitimacy referred to above – the increasingly frequent image displayed on our screens and in our papers of the police officer as inefficient, even corrupt and criminal – not to be trusted or given support by the public at large. Over time, an emphasis on service, and an accompanying shift in rhetoric and language, may lead to fundamental changes in the direction, identity and image of the police, and, longer term, to changes in what the public *expects* from *its* police service, and the degree to which the public will lend its support. In particular, the police service is attempting to gain greater legitimacy and respect amongst the Asian and black communities. This is no easy task given many of the incidents which are reported concerning police treatment of black people. As Holdaway shows in Chapter 3, the occupational culture of rank and file officers very much views black people with suspicion, and as individuals who require control, and sometimes suppression. Stephens shows in Chapter 7 how this may have led to a disproportionate number of Afro-Caribbean people being detained by the police under mental health legislation. In an effort to address some of

these issues, and to make the service more representative of the
society and communities it serves, the police have been keen
to recruit black officers to the ranks. But again, the power of the
subculture, with its racist banter, has worked against effective
recruitment, and against the retention of black officers who do
join the service. Holdaway (in Chapter 3) suggests that some
black officers are forced to resign because of the culture and
language of many of their colleagues. Oakley (in Chapter 4)
argues that training initiatives can be one important way to
bring about better community and race relations. He suggests
that the new emphasis on service and care 'transforms the
status within policing of "community relations", which moves
from a peripheral concern to being central to the policing role'.

Care through Control

By tracing the changing image of the police through television
fiction, Reiner (in Chapter 1) charts the changing politics of
police legitimation. It is, he argues, a dialectical progression,
from *Dixon of Dock Green* (the symbol of the police as carers)
through *The Sweeney* (the police as controllers) to *The Bill* (the
synthesis of care and control). But Reiner also reminds us that
to see care and control as polar extremes is too simplistic:
control is not pursued simply to control; often hidden behind
the function of control is care and protection – care for the innocent bystander and victims of crime: 'The fundamental motive
of *The Sweeney* is concern for innocent victims, and a drive to
care for them against the depredations of the villains who prey
on them'. Consequently, force is part of the service: 'The police
provide the service of protecting the public by the appropriate
use of legitimate force'. And, as Holdaway confirms: 'Although
care and service can amount to the exercise of control this is
not always the case. The complexity of policing means that in
many situations officers take action that at first sight appears
to be based on control but in fact is established on service and
care . . . care and service to others'.

How then are we to judge whether a particular police action
is predominantly care or control? Holdaway suggests in Chapter 3 that 'the most careful analysis has to be made of the

meaning of situations and of related actions to police officers, victims of crime, complainants and others before the reasons for particular interventions and outcomes from them can be understood'. Whereas, for instance, paramilitary policing is essentially a control function with minimal elements of care, there are other police activities where the balance between control and care is more complex. Community policing in its various forms is one such example. But looked at from a civil libertarian perspective, some commentators have suggested that there are dangers in too close an overlap between these functions. Bennett (in Chapter 5) charts the recent developments in community policing. He expresses concern that because the dominant policing ethos amongst the rank and file is still one of control, innovative schemes such as community policing, which are usually 'bolted on' to the existing system, sit uncomfortably within that system and culture.

In some situations the caring function appears to be in the ascendancy, for example in police handling of victims (women who have been the subject of domestic violence and children who have been sexually abused) or of offenders who also require care or treatment (for example, the mentally ill or the juvenile offender). Edwards (in Chapter 6) argues that 'violence against women, and sexual assault perpetrated by male intimates are two areas of police work where these dual functions of care and control meet, sometimes in a manner complementary, while at other times they co-exist in conflict'. She adds: 'victims are often caught up in the conflicting efforts of the police both to care for them and to control offenders by bringing offenders to trial, at which the victim is expected to give evidence and to support the prosecution . . . In trying to care for victims and empower women, and at the same time control the sexual and violent offender, the police are faced with the difficulty of encouraging victims to prosecute and of enforcing the criminal law'. Edwards argues that prosecution and control ought to be pursued by the police regardless of the apparent wishes of the victim. Again, control is part of the *service*.

Another arena in which police functions of care and control are entwined is that of child sexual abuse. Fielding and Conroy (in Chapter 9) examine the work of police and social services in

child sexual abuse investigations. They confirm that whilst the
police are generally regarded as agents of control, and social
services as agents of care, this simple distinction fails to reflect
the complex reality of the two organisations and their practice:
'There is much in their work and culture that runs against the
grain of the stereotype ... The practice of joint investigation
better reconciled social services to control and made the police
more alert to welfare considerations'. Nonetheless, Fielding
and Conroy also express concern that whilst there was tangible
movement away from their traditional posture, over time there
was a tendency for both organisations to revert to customary
concerns and practices – the police emphasising their role as
controllers and social workers expressing their role as carers.
This suggests that any movement by the police to develop
legitimacy through service, rather than through control, may
be slow and limited, especially if entrenched attitudes win the
day. Fielding and Conroy suggest that 'the case of child protection suggests some of the practical challenges that face efforts to
change the established balance of care and control in the police'.

A further group of people requiring control, but also sensit-
ively applied care, is the mentally ill. Stephens (in Chapter 7)
charts the ways in which people with mental health problems
may come to the attention of the police. In particular, he
outlines police use of section 136 of the 1983 Mental Health
Act: 'When individuals are subject to police attention under
section 136 there is the potential both for a controlling and a
caring outcome'. By drawing on the lessons to be learnt from a
crisis intervention service in Madison, USA, Stephens argues
for the integration of the caring function into police dealings
with the mentally ill in Britain. The use of section 136 can be
an act of care through control: 'those individuals suspected of
being mentally disordered may be removed from a public place
to what is termed a place of safety in order to carry out an
assessment of that person's condition or to make arrangements
for that person's treatment'. Stephens suggests that police involvement in a crisis intervention service would allow for the
proper assessment of people with mental illness, and reduce the
chances of discrimination playing a significant role in the placement and treatment of the mentally ill, in particular, black
people with mental illness. But control can also come through

care: 'The police's primary interest in social control is in no way undermined by the operation of a crisis intervention programme. Indeed, since an efficient programme relieves the police of many time-consuming duties, it actually allows them to focus more strongly on the preferred crime management aspects of their role'.

Holdaway, in Chapter 3, puts a similar argument. He suggests that control may well come through the service function, but that this may also have a backlash: 'police commitment to and involvement in youth work founded on service to the public may lead to a perceived and actual but unintended increase of the control of young people and feelings of distrust among them'. Thorpe in Chapter 8 looks in detail at this police involvement with young people, in particular their handling of juvenile offenders – another arena where the police must maintain a delicate balance between care and control. He suggests that the movement by the police into cautioning schemes, whereby offenders are diverted from prosecution 'was in both theory and practice a shift from control to care by choosing to involve police officers directly in the provision of services to youths'. Thorpe goes on to trace the development and rationale for police diversion work and focuses on the experience of the police service in Northamptonshire. He shows that the scheme was able to reduce significantly the numbers of juveniles facing prosecution, and reduce the use of care and custody. However, an unintended consequence of moving into a caring mode of operation may have been to 'net-widen', bringing into the system (of cautioning and diversion) juveniles who would otherwise have remained outside. Police officers, Thorpe argues, felt at ease in their work – whether one calls it care or control, justice or welfare: 'Once operational instructions relate to the achievement of specific tasks, which are to be performed in specific inter-agency settings, then the context determines the outcome. Since the Northamptonshire scheme was very much a police-inspired enterprise, then its success in a sense was guaranteed'.

In the past some authors have warned against the police moving too far down the road of service and care. Rather, the police should conduct their controlling and enforcement functions with greater effectiveness and fairness (see, for example,

Waddington, 1984). Walker (in Chapter 2) suggests that if either care or control is allowed to dominate in intra-organisational relations, 'then significant problems emerge in terms of the capacity of the organisation to co-ordinate and harmonise its collective efforts and to remain responsive to its public constituencies'. He argues for a 'closer equilibrium' between care and control functions so that 'each could check the excesses and supply the omissions of the other'. Oakley (in Chapter 4) suggests that police training needs to address the relationship between care and control: 'if the concept of service is to be at the centre of the policing role, then issues of "care" and their relationship to "control" need also to become far more central to police training, and to be firmly contextualised within a sound intellectual understanding of communities and "police-community relations"'.

In the final chapter, Stephens and Becker bring together the various threads and strands of the book. They argue that a great deal of the substance of police activity and policy, at a micro and macro level, is the provision of a *matrix* of control and care. Other professions are also involved in these tasks. Within the personal social services there is a traditional concern with care, coupled with essential controlling purposes. So, social work, probation, and other human service professions are, like the police, involved in *policing*. In many examples of police activity (and police policy) both functions are taking place simultaneously. In other instances one role is more dominant than the other. Stephens and Becker argue that there are philosophical and pragmatic reasons for the interlinking of care and control in police work. Citizens have the right to security: security from crime, from violence and from the fear of crime. The police role is not just one of combating crime, but about ensuring decent minimum standards of security – a caring *and* controlling function. The law itself, by defining the boundaries and rules for (legal/illegal) behaviour, is also a mechanism for the care *and* control of citizens. Caring can extend control rather than be its polar extreme. Stephens and Becker suggest that the police may wish to strive for greater legitimation through the caring function, but that first they will have to tackle complex issues concerned with identity, organisation and image. The police need to promote an image of strength through caring: caring is an essential part of British policing, and a means through which, legitimately and fairly, the police can pursue effective measures of control, to provide a more secure existence for all of us.

Bibliography

Audit Commission (1990) *Effective Policing – Performance Review in Police Forces* (London: HMSO).

Home Office (1993) *Police Reform. A Police Service for the Twenty-First Century*, Cm 2281 (London: HMSO).

Shapland, J. and Vagg, J. (1988) *Policing by the Public* (London: Tavistock).

Sir Patrick Sheehy (1993) *Inquiry into Police Responsibilities and Rewards*, Cm 2280.I (London: HMSO).

Sinclair, I. and Miller, C. (1984), *Measures of Police Effectiveness and Efficiency*, Home Office, Research and Planning Unit, Paper 25 (London: HMSO).

Southgate, P. and Crisp, D. (1992) *Public Satisfaction with Police Services*, Home Office, Research and Planning Unit, Paper 73 (London: HMSO).

Waddington, P. A. J. (1984) 'Community Policing: A Sceptical Appraisal' in P. Norton (ed.), *Law and Order and British Politics* (Aldershot: Gower) pp. 84–99.

1

The Dialectics of Dixon: The Changing Image of the TV Cop

Robert Reiner

Policing in Great Britain has always been as much a matter of image as substance. The modern professional police force was only established in the early nineteenth century after nearly a century of abortive attempts by its utilitarian protagonists (Emsley, 1983 and 1991; Palmer, 1988; Reiner, 1992a, Part 1). Sir Robert Peel and the other architects of the 'new police' confronted a wide array of opposition, from the top to the bottom of the social hierarchy. This was couched in a rhetoric of concern for the traditional liberties of the English, which were seen as threatened by a police force that would inevitably be a tool of government, an oppressive agency of political and social control.

A variety of strategies were adopted by Peel and the first two Commissioners of the fledgling Metropolitan Police, Rowan and Mayne, in order to allay popular anxieties and secure a measure of consent for the 'bobbies'. Ultimately these were to prove successful, facilitated by the background context of slow and fitful but gradually increasing social integration of British society after the mid-Victorian period (Reiner, 1992a, Chapter 2). This reached its apogee in the post-Second World War climate of social and political consensus.

Since then there has been a reverse process of increasing dissensus and division, with attendant disorder, particularly

11

since the late 1970s. This corresponds to the advent of Thatcherism, but it has more profound causes than the 1979 Conservative victory by itself. Public acceptance of the police, which was ultimately predicated on a more harmonious and integrated society, has been eroded to an increasing extent (Reiner, 1992a and 1992b).

Popular regard for the police in the 'Golden Age' when the bobby was a prime symbol of national pride owed much to the creation of a particular image, often belied by the substance of policing behind the facade. (For examples from the 'Golden Age' see Mark, 1978, Chapters 2 and 4; Daley, 1986; Woffinden, 1987, Part 1; Brogden, 1991.) The traditional image of the British bobby was of a citizen in uniform working within the consensus of the community, relying on popular backing rather than force, and operating with integrity and impartiality in the task of keeping the peace. Although the police did achieve a high measure of general public support by the middle years of this century – as reflected, for example, in the 'overwhelming vote of confidence' in the police found by the public opinion survey conducted for the 1960 Royal Commission on the Police (Royal Commission, 1962) – there is much evidence from police memoirs and oral histories of behind-the-scenes practices which were a far cry from the rosy image held by the more established social classes. The police have always had as their main work the social control of the most powerless and socially marginal groups in society, which have aptly been dubbed 'police property' (Lee, 1981). The treatment of these has regularly been characterised by abuse of powers, excessive force, and corruption. Nonetheless, until relatively recently the British police were able to preserve their benign image in the eyes of the established, opinion-making classes. The traditional image remains an important reference point, as an ideal for many would-be reformers and as a potent part of professional ideology.

One example of the use of this reference point is the *Operational Policing Review*. This is a recent study that was commissioned in an unprecedented cooperative venture by all the police staff associations (the Police Federation, the Superintendents' Association, and the Association of Chief Police Officers) as a prelude to organisational reform intended to restore public support. It started from the premise that 'traditional British policing is relatively low in numbers, low on power, and high on accountability; that it is undertaken with public consent which does not mean acquiescence but a broad tolerance indicating a satisfaction with the helping and enforcement roles of policing. That its structure allows the public to express their policing wants and needs, and though changes in social attitudes and methods of social control may occur, the culture of policing remains intact. That culture is epitomised by the single constable, close to the community, patrolling his beat with the consent of the general public, armed only with his lawful powers and his use of discretion' (Joint Consultative Committee, 1990, p. 4).

A central aspect of the legitimating myth of the British police has been that they are carers rather than controllers. Law enforcement and order maintenance are only a part of their function. In addition, they provide a host of friendly supportive services to people in need. It is true that the British police have always performed numerous functions of a service kind, the variety of which almost beggars description (Banton, 1964; Punch and Naylor, 1973; Punch, 1979). This is indeed a feature of police forces in most industrial countries, which have always tended to have a broader role than straightforward law enforcement or order maintenance (Cumming, Cumming and Edell, 1964; Monkkonen, 1981; Weinberger and Reinke, 1991). In Britain, however, it was explicitly cultivated by the pioneers of the British policing tradition as a means of gaining legitimacy in the face of the widespread opposition they initially faced (Miller, 1977; Emsley, 1983, pp. 158–9; Reiner, 1992a, pp. 68–9).

The tactic would appear to have been highly successful, as the image of the bobby came to be predominantly the helpful provider of services. In the middle years of this century this image came to be summed-up by the familiar cliche 'if you want to know the time, ask a policeman'. The history of this phrase is itself a succinct history of the fluctuating fortunes of police legitimation through the service myth. Its origins were far removed from the connotations of the benign bobby which it came to acquire. Its roots lie in a popular Victorian music-hall song, in which it was the punch-line sung by a policeman whose uniform opened to reveal a glittering array of precious watches, the 'perks' of the peace-keeping trade. 'The popular catch-phrase . . . reflected not so much the confidence of the Victorians in the reliability of the police, as their assumption that any policeman who did not quickly "win" a watch from the pockets of a drunken reveller was unnaturally honest or dull' (Rolph, 1962, p. 52). More recently, as the image of the police has become tarnished, the phrase seemed to have dropped out of common usage, until revived in a *Guardian* cartoon published after the Birmingham Six's successful appeal in March 1991. This featured a man who turns up late for a date. He offers his girl-friend the excuse: 'I asked a policeman the time, and he lied!'. The meaning of the catch-phrase, like the legitimacy of the police which it encapsulates, has come full circle.

The service role played a great part in the initial legitimation of the British police. It is therefore scarcely surprising that in a period in which this is perceived to be under threat (Reiner, 1992b, pp. 762–4) the police elite should attempt its resuscitation. Following the 1990 *Operational Policing Review*, which the police staff associations had sponsored to assess the sources of their difficulties, the response of the police leadership has been to recreate the idea of the police as primarily a service. A 'Quality of Service' initiative was launched by the Association of Chief Police Officers, following the trail of the earlier Plus Programme in the Metropolitan Police, which had similar roots in an appraisal by management consultants Wolf Olins. The initiative rests upon a 'Statement of Common Purpose and Values' defining the mission of the police explicitly in service terms. The police elite are clearly convinced that the idea of policing as a service to the public, conceived in consumerist terms as 'customers', is the way to seeking a restoration of public support (see, for example, the articles in the special issue of *Policing* on 'The Way Ahead' (Autumn 1991), as well as my interviews with chief constables in Reiner, 1991, Chapter 6). Police stations now feature prominently mounted versions of the mission statement, letter headings have been changed in most forces to the 'X Police *Service*', and phones are answered as X Police *Service*. Use of the term police *force* is no longer 'politically correct' language for constabularies.

The majority of the public have little regular contact with the police. According to a recent survey only about 40 per cent of the population had approached the police for any reason over the previous year (Southgate and Crisp, 1992). It is particularly rare for middle or upper class people to have any adversary contact with the police other than in a traffic context. For these groups – the more powerful in society – images of the police are primarily acquired through the media, and this is likely to be the case for women and older people in all social strata. This makes the question of the content of media images of policing very important in understanding the degree of legitimacy accorded the police in a society.

This chapter will focus on one particular aspect of the mass media presentation of images of policing: television fiction about the police. It will be especially concerned with the shifting balance between images of the police as carers or controllers in TV police fiction, and how this relates to the changing politics of police legitimation. It will first consider the development of fictional images of the police before the TV era.

The Origins of Police Fiction

Crime and law enforcement have always been staple parts of the mass media of entertainment. Detective story writers are wont to trace the roots of their craft back to the Bible or Greek mythology, claiming Cain and Abel or the Oedipus myth as crypto-crime stories (Sayers, 1928). Some of the earliest modern novels, like the works of Defoe or Fielding, portray the exploits of the *demi-monde* and thief-takers. In the eighteenth century there was a flourishing trade in broadsheets, ballads, 'memoirs' and novels about the exploits of legendary highwaymen like Dick Turpin or Jack Sheppard, and thief-takers like Jonathan Wild. The supposed final statements of the condemned were a flourishing literary genre (Rawlings, 1992).

The real take-off in crime and detective fiction occurs with the formation of modern police forces in Europe and North America in the early nineteenth century (Ousby, 1976). Fictionalised memoirs of ex-detectives proliferated, recounting their exploits in all their supposed glory. The prototype was the 1828–9 publication of the *Memoirs* of Vidocq, a thief turned thief-taker who became head of the Paris detective bureau in 1817.

Modern detective fiction is usually traced back to Edgar Allan Poe's trilogy of short stories about C. Auguste Dupin, the archetypal ratiocinative sleuth, beginning with *The Murders in the Rue Morgue* in 1841 (Symons, 1972; Binyon, 1989). The birth of detective fiction thus coincides roughly with the emergence of modern police forces in Britain and the USA. Both can be traced to anxieties of similar kinds amongst the respectable literate strata, fears about the threat to social order represented by the 'dangerous classes' (Palmer, 1978; Knight, 1981; Porter, 1981; Mandel, 1984). They embody similar models of the solution to these respectable fears about subversion, conspiracy and crime. Protection will be provided by the rational and unfailingly resourceful individual symbolising above all the power of reason and right over brutish might. The heroic individual is, however, symbiotically related to a well-ordered social organisation, and dependent upon it for the provision of his mundane needs.

Since the mid-nineteenth century crime and detective fiction have been prominent parts of the output of all the mass entertainment media. The most popular heroes, like Sherlock Holmes, Charlie Chan, The Saint, Dick Tracy, Sam Spade, Philip Marlowe or Batman, seem to remain perennially popular. Whatever medium they originated in, whether novels, pulp magazines, comics, cinema, radio or television, they seem to possess the power to transmigrate successfully to most of the other mass media as well. It has been estimated that about a quarter of the fictional works sold in Britain and America are crime stories, and that up to a third of all prime time TV shows feature crime and law enforcement as their central themes (Dominick, 1978).

One remarkable feature of this huge volume of crime fiction is the absence until comparatively recently of the professional police officer as a heroic figure. The institution which is mandated with the specialist task of preventing and detecting crime in a modern society is the police force. Yet until the end of the Second World War detective fiction was dominated by heroes who are most definitely not professional police officers. The two principal subgenres have been those about classic great mind sleuths in the Sherlock Holmes mould, or private eyes in the Sam Spade or Philip Marlowe style. Many of the fictional detectives have been amateurs who do not earn their living from investigating crime (like Miss Marple for example), or they have been self-employed private practitioners. In these stories professional police forces figure peripherally, and largely in an unflattering light. They are either of limited intellect, often butts of humour, requiring the great amateur detective to show them the way, or they are brutal, corrupt characters obstructing the private eye's fight for justice. There are a few notable exceptions to be sure, but they tend to prove the rule. The handful of 'Golden Age' heroes who are professional police detectives, like Ngaio Marsh's Roderick Alleyn, Josephine Tey's Alan Grant or Michael Innes's John Appleby, are socially and individually quite unlike the ordinary police officer in reality (or in their own novels). They are highly educated upper class gentlemen, little different in style from their amateur sleuth counterparts in other contemporary detective stories. They are in the police force because of the opportunities it provides for the pursuit of their passion – the investigation of crime – not because it delivers a secure if not overgenerous pay packet. They are often remarkably socially mobile in the force, soon ending up as chief constables or Metropolitan Commissioners (like Appleby or Sir Basil Thompson's PC Richardson who rose to being chief constable in the record time of four years!).

Police detectives in the great sleuth mould remain popular in current fiction in all media. Quintessential examples are P. D. James's Dalgleish, Colin Dexter's Morse, and Ruth Rendell's Wexford (although the latter two are more middle class and characteristic of the police career than their 'Golden Age' counterparts). Indeed it would be rare nowadays to find detective stories, even if they are of the classic whodunnit, great sleuth variety, which did not feature a professional police hero. The brilliant amateur is rare in contemporary crime fiction, other than in revivals of 'Golden Age' classics.

The reason is the birth in the postwar period of a new subgenre of detective fiction, the police procedural. This appeared simultaneously in the leading mass media of the late 1940s and early 1950s, on both sides of the Atlantic. The police procedural features mystery plots in which the investigation is undertaken by a professional police detective, portrayed as functioning as one of a team, not as an exceptionally gifted individual. The image is the policeman as bureaucrat, not as genius or knight-errant.

Pioneering examples are Jack Webb's *Dragnet* (on radio, TV and film), *Naked City* (originally a 1947 feature film, later a long-running TV series), the novels of Laurence Treat, Hillary Waugh, Ed McBain and others in the USA and John Creasey's Inspector West and Commander Gideon in Great Britain, and such 1950s TV series as *Highway Patrol* in the USA or *Murder Bag* (later *No Hiding Place*) in Britain.

The birth of the police procedural variant of the detective story coincides with the rise to pre-eminence of TV as the dominant medium of entertainment. Although detective heroes of the classic sleuth and private eye kinds have remained common on TV as well, it is only on TV that police series have been at least equally prominent from the outset (Meyers, 1981 and 1989). In literature and the cinema the police procedural marked a qualitatively new development in crime fiction of the late 1940s (Dove, 1982 and 1985; Dove and Bargainnier, 1986; Reiner, 1978, 1981 and 1992a, Chapter 5). In the next section we will examine the changing images of the police in British TV fiction, where police heroes have been commonplace since the early 1950s when TV first became the dominant medium of entertainment.

Carers or Controllers? Proceeding in a Dialectical Direction

Whilst TV is evidently watched primarily as a means of entertainment, it is not innocent of profound ideological effects in the images it constructs and conveys. The mass media in general have constantly been the centre of acute, anxious debate about their possible pernicious effects. Conservatives, from Patrick Colquhoun in the eighteenth century – who was concerned about the influence of 'bawdy ballad singers' on public morals (Reiner, 1988, p. 143) – to Mary Whitehouse today, have fretted about the media undermining respect for authority and virtue. Crime fiction, perceived as tending to glorify criminals and denigrate law enforcement, because of commercially-driven pandering to the basest aspects of mass taste, is supposed to be part of this process.

Radicals for their part have tended to analyse the media as important apparatuses in the maintenance of the ideological hegemony of the dominant social and political order, incorporating the population into an unjust, oppressive *status quo* . One crucial element in this is the role of crime fiction in intensifying fear of crime and thus bolstering popular support for a criminal justice system and police force which has the prime function of repressing opposition.

These debates about the supposed pernicious effects of the mass media and their depiction of law and order matters have intensified since the advent of television (Sparks, 1992). Television has aroused particular anxiety because of its insidious penetration of the citadel of wholesome family values, the domestic hearth, and because its audiences may consume it in the most passive, private and hence manipulable way. Even more than the cinema, which had itself aroused considerable moral furore earlier in the twentieth century, television has been the target of sustained attempts to monitor and control its content. One flourishing aspect of this has been the development of a minor research industry concerned to measure and analyse the precise content of media images, and to consider their possible effects. Contrary to the fears of conservatives and law enforcement officials, the consensus of this content analysis research has been that media images tend to portray crime as a menacing evil thus bolstering support for the police and other criminal justice agents who are depicted as valiant public protectors. Media images of crime, criminals and criminal justice differ systematically from the 'real' picture, as conveyed by official statistics or criminological research, in ways which magnify the threat and exaggerate the protective contribution of the police (Gerbner, 1970; Gerbner *et al.*, 1980 and 1984; Hall *et al.*, 1978; Pandiani, 1978; Graber, 1980; Garofalo, 1981; Ditton and Duffy, 1983; Reiner, 1992a, Chapter 5). This is not primarily the result of any explicit ideological bias, but the largely unintended effect of a variety of organisational and occupational pressures and processes affecting those who produce the output of the mass media (Rock, 1973; Chibnall, 1977; Ericson *et al.*, 1987, 1989 and 1991; Ericson, 1991; Schlesinger, Tumber and Murdock, 1991; Schlesinger and Tumber, 1992; Sparks, 1992). These processes are illustrated by a consideration of the changing fictional representation of the police on British television.

There have been countless series on British TV featuring leading characters who are police officers. This huge array can, however, be summarised by three dominant moments each encapsulated by a hugely popular and mould-breaking example, carrying in its wake numerous more or less successful epigones in the same style. These are the moments of *Dixon of Dock Green*, *The Sweeney*, and *The Bill*. Linking these three distinct phases in the unfolding fictional representation of the police are some important series, which for all their particular significance, can be seen as transitional episodes in the transformation of the dominant image. *Z-Cars* (and its offshoots *Softly, Softly* and *Barlow*) was an extremely influential point in the transition from the image of policing conveyed by *Dixon* to the dramatically different *Sweeney*. Similarly, *The Gentle Touch* and *Juliet Bravo*, each highly regarded in its own right, represent the shift from *The Sweeney* to *The Bill*, which in ratings terms has proved to be the biggest blockbuster of them all. Each of these three moments represents a different balance between an image of the police as carers or controllers, and corresponds to different contexts in the politics of policing since the Second World War.

This can be captured as a dialectical progression. The thesis, represented by *Dixon*, presents the police primarily as carers, lightning rods for the postwar consensus climate. Its antithesis, *The Sweeney*, portrays the police primarily as controllers, heralding the upsurge of a tough law and order politics in the late 1970s. The synthesis, *The Bill*, suggests that care and control are interdependent, reinforcing each other. As one recent episode title put it, 'Force Is Part Of The Service'. Care is for control, and vice versa (as the earlier discussion of the deliberate cultivation of the service role as a means of police legitimation suggested). This corresponds to a phase in which the law and order policies of the early 1980s have been transcended by a more sophisticated synthesis in which conceptions of crime prevention and community policing have become dominant across the political spectrum (Reiner and Cross, 1991).

The Thesis: Dixon

Dixon of Dock Green was a remarkable broadcasting phenomenon, and a momentously significant symbol for British policing, which still resonates powerfully today (Reiner, 1992b, p. 761). Jack Warner's portrayal of the eponymous hero, PC George Dixon, has become the quintessential image of the traditional British bobby, and debates about the police still regularly provoke nostalgic calls for a return to the 'Dixon' style of policing, as if he had been a real person not a fictional character.

Dixon first appeared in the 1950 Ealing film *The Blue Lamp*, in which he was shot after twenty minutes, the rest of the story concerning the police chase for his killer (played by a young Dirk Bogarde). Jack Warner's portrayal of the kindly, avuncular bobby struck so deep a chord as the embodiment of the consensus mood of Britain in its finest hour (as the decade which began with the Battle of Britain gave way to the one opened by the Festival of Britain) that he was revived six years later for BBC TV. When the series began in 1956 Jack Warner was already over sixty years old, past the age when most chief constables, let alone patrolling constables, have long retired. Yet the series (with Warner in the title role) lived on until 1976, beyond the period of the iconoclastic *Z-Cars* and well into the heyday of *The Sweeney*.

By that time Dixon and the cosy, communal, foot-patrol style of policing he personified seemed vastly anachronistic, at least in terms of TV heroics. What is hard to remember from the perspective of an age in which the Dixon series came increasingly to be seen as cosy and complacent, a model of policing as kindly community carers set in timeless aspic, was that it began life heralded as a new departure in realism. This is true of each new departure in the TV image of the police. TV police series have always adopted a realist style, incorporating evolving techniques to convey a feel of documentary authenticity. Thus the police procedurals which preceded *Dixon* emphasised that their stories came straight from the headlines or police files. *Dragnet* episodes always told us that the story they told was true: 'Only the names have been changed to protect the innocent.' The hero Sergeant Joe Friday's catch-phrase was 'just give me the facts, ma'am', conveying the concern with telling it like it is . . . or was supposed to be. The 1950s cinema series *Scotland Yard*, much revived on TV, opened with presenter Edgar Lustgarten – 'the world's foremost authority on crime and criminals' – reaching for a file inside a record room at the

Yard, and beginning to read from it as the narrative began. The kitchen-sink style of *Dixon* was in its turn seen as a further deglamourising step towards verisimilitude, as were *Z-Cars* and *The Sweeney* with their iconoclastic puncturing of the goody-goody portrayal of *Dixon* and its progeny. *The Bill* for its part reaches new heights in the extent to which its producers emphasise the research incorporated in it, and the deliberate immersion of its writers, actors and creative personnel in the world of real policing, with attachments to police stations and the like (Lynch, 1992).

The author of *Dixon*, Ted Willis, like the writers of most subsequent series were to do, claimed to have delved deeply into the world of the real police through observation, and to be presenting a less glamorous image than other fiction. What *Dixon* debunked was the great detective myth of the TV sleuths of that time, conveyed in such series as *Colonel March of Scotland Yard* or *Dial 999*. *Dixon of Dock Green* was a novel departure in focusing on the comparatively humdrum routine of the foot-patrolling uniform constables and divisional CID of a local police station, not the serious crimes tackled by the elite squads that were the traditional grist of the TV cops-and-robbers mill.

Dixon featured typical working-class policemen who were part of an East End working-class community. They had family and personal connections with people outside the force, and were presented as more rounded personalities than the cerebral supersleuths. Above all, the series presented a much wider conception of the police role, dealing with a host of problems experienced by the local public, and not just crime. The crimes which did occur were ones with their roots in social problems, not an asocial and unexplained original capacity for sin. Even when dealing with the relatively petty crimes which formed his daily round, Dixon was as much a carer as a controller.

The image of police officers as carers rather than controllers persisted in *Z-Cars*, for all that the series was seen initially by many as a shocking new exercise in debunking the police image. The story has often been quoted of how the Chief Constable of Lancashire was so incensed by the portrayal of a PC in a row with his wife in the first episode that he immediately went to London to register a personal protest at the BBC (St Johnston, 1978, pp. 181–4). The iconoclasm of *Z-Cars* lay in its warts-and-all portrayal of the police as adults with personal weaknesses and defects, rather than the Dixonesque superannuated boy scout image, as well as in its documentary visual style. It remained the case that the police were portrayed as working closely with local community problems of a complex kind, and that crime was seen as a product of social problems. As Laing puts it in discussing an episode concerning two twelve year old boys who engage in a spree of petty theft: 'Here the police . . . take on the role of the absent father – mixing authority and care . . . This view of the police as a paternalist institution recurs when, after John Watt has attempted to explain the boys' actions in terms of the "rotten world" they live in, Barlow comments that Watt "should have had three sons, since he would make a good father" . . . The idea of the police as the agency for restoring (or substituting for) broken family and community structures remained a recurring topic throughout the whole series' (Laing, 1991, p. 133).

Z-Cars is thus a transitional series between the *Dixon* and *Sweeney* eras. It retains the sense of police as carers, dealing with a complex array of community problems including crime as an aspect of these, rather than merely as repressive controllers of unequivocal evil. On the other hand it moves away from the one-dimensionally benevolent and virtuous portrayal of the police world. Individual officers are portrayed as fallible, and tensions and conflicts within the organisation are highlighted. As Troy Kennedy Martin, its first scriptwriter put it: '*Z-Cars* began as a reaction against Dixon' (Martin, 1978, p. 126), and it prefigures the subsequent developments of *The Sweeney* in its profanation of the police image. Nonetheless, with the perspective of hindsight, it is the conception of the police as carers not merely controllers, situated in a complexly structured community, that stands out.

The Antithesis: The Sweeney

The image of the police as controllers rather than carers becomes paramount in the early 1970s with *The Sweeney* and its ilk (like *The Professionals, Special Branch, Target,* and *Dempsey and Makepeace*). As summed-up succinctly by one reference work, *The Sweeney* was 'a rough, tough, kick-'em-in-the-teeth crime

series . . . with Detective Inspector Jack Regan and Detective
Sergeant George Carter continuing to make life difficult for
villains – two gangbusters from the Sweeney (underworld slang
for the Flying Squad)' (Rogers, 1988, p. 534).

The depiction of the police world in *The Sweeney* was the
Dixon image stood on its head. This was quite self-conscious, as
the following passage from an early publicity article shows:
'He's not the sort of copper you'd ask for directions, not Jack
Regan. Not as his super-charged Ford slews to a halt spraying
gravel and burning tyre rubber like he owns shares in Pirelli.
He's not the sort of copper you'd ask to find your dog. Not as
the car door bursts open and he leans over it pointing a Police
.38, so big it needs two hands to hold it. He's not the sort of
copper you'd even ask for a warrant. Not as he grinds his knee
into the pit of the villain's back as an added refinement to a
half-nelson, spitting out: "The Sweeney! You're nicked!" But
isn't he lovely?' (cited in Clarke, 1986, p.219).

The Sweeney characterises the police as tough, relentless cru-
saders against crime. They are pitted against criminals who are
not rooted in a broader community, nor presented in even a
partly sympathetic light as the result of social problems. They
are vicious and evil, 'villains' who must be fought and stamped
out, and can only be combated successfully by police officers
who are equally ruthless. To fight crime the police must themselves resort to tactics which appear to mirror those of their
foes, using violence and guile for just ends.

The respectable public, naïve and sheltered from the urban
jungles which the cop must control on their behalf, are squeam-
ish and do not approve of the methods the police must use.
The police organisation itself is a house divided. The uniform
branches, depicted as plodding woodentops, are largely sheltered from the serious villainy which is *The Sweeney's* stock-
in-trade, and are incapable of comprehending or dealing with
it. The organisational hierarchy are too concerned with public
relations and are there to paint a sanitised gloss of correctness
on the real street cops' shenanigans as they do the dirty work
of suppressing villains. They collaborate with the politicians
and lawyers who force the police to operate with 'one hand tied
behind their backs' by due process of law restrictions. *The
Sweeney* are thus doubly marginalised, from the community and

their own bosses. They are driven into being a close-knit brotherhood of working partners, misunderstood by those whose interests they are seeking to protect in the only way possible. The image of the police in *The Sweeney* and its progeny is thus of the police officer as vigilante, breaking the rules of law to achieve true justice and protect a public unable or unwilling to countenance what is necessary for its own preservation.

Regan himself summed it up thus to his driver in a 1975 episode: 'I sometimes hate this bastard place. It's a bloody holiday camp for thieves and weirdos . . . all the rubbish. You age prematurely trying to sort some of them out. Try and protect the public and all they do is call you "fascist". You nail a villain and some ponced-up, pinstriped, Hampstead barrister screws it up like an old fag packet on a point of procedure and then pops off for a game of squash and a glass of Madeira . . . He's taking home thirty grand a year and we can just about afford ten days in Eastbourne and a second hand car . . . No, it is all bloody wrong my son' (cited in Clarke, 1986, p. 222).

The change in the police image conveyed by *The Sweeney* had two principal sources, one in the internal evolution of the crime film as a genre, the other in the developing politics of law and order. *The Sweeney* develops on British TV the characterisation of the cop as vigilante which had been pioneered in the late 1960s and early 1970s by a new, blue wave of American films which themselves reflected a somewhat similar conjuncture in law and order politics as Britain was to experience nearly a decade later (Reiner, 1978 and 1981). Stylistically and thematically the roots of *The Sweeney* are such films as *Dirty Harry* and *The French Connection*, and TV series like *Kojak* and *Starsky and Hutch*. The vigilante theme of *The Sweeney* also resonates with the advent of law and order as a major political issue, championed by the Conservatives and the police themselves in the build-up to Mrs Thatcher's election victory in 1979. The law and order campaigns of the late 1970s feature the same conception of crime as the vigilante cop shows on TV. Crime is the product of evil not social problems, and must be cracked down upon by the state, with the police as its thin blue line of defence which must be toughened and unleashed (Hall *et al.*, 1978; Reiner, 1992a).

The main image of the police on TV in the late 1970s thus was as controllers not carers. However, the hidden dimension of this was a sort of care, and a continuation of the Dixon theme in one crucial respect. The fundamental motive of *The Sweeney* is concern for innocent victims, and a drive to care for them against the depredations of the villains who prey on them. It is this passion for true justice that legitimates bending what are seen as petty legal restrictions hampering the control of crime. As Charles Bronson, a doyen of American vigilante cop movies, voiced it in the 1983 *10 To Midnight*: 'Forget what's legal! Do what's right!' *The Sweeney* and the other vigilante cops are fundamentally as moral as Dixon, and their integrity is unimpeachable, even if they swear, drink, fornicate, and are insubordinate to their bosses. They may not be the boy scouts any longer (Clarke, 1986), but that is because they are fighting a tough war on behalf of vulnerable victims who cannot defend themselves. This hidden face of care by the vigilantes, prompting their control of villains, is made manifest in the synthesis of *Dixon* and *The Sweeney* which becomes the style of cop series in the 1980s, above all in *The Bill* .

The Synthesis: The Bill

Starting in 1984, after a 1983 prototype 'Woodentop' in the Thames TV *Storyteller* series, *The Bill* was originally in the orthodox format of a weekly sixty-minute programme. In 1988 it changed to a pattern of twice-weekly half-hour shows (Lynch, 1992), and in 1993 to three shows a week. In ratings terms it is the most consistently popular of all TV police series in Britain, watched by over twelve million viewers for each episode (Mason, 1992, p. 2).

In essence *The Bill* is the soap opera of the police community and community policing, telling everyday tales of constabulary folk. In this it resembles *Dixon* and *Z-Cars*, being set in a working-class area, and featuring the whole gamut of policing roles, not merely the control of serious crime by elite CID units. However, the depiction of both public and police is much less cosy and incorporates some of the hard edges of *The Sweeney*. The CID are depicted as largely sharing the tough vigilante culture made familiar by *The Sweeney*, albeit tackling more mundane sorts of crime. However, their degree of alienation from their colleagues in uniform and the organisational hierarchy is less pronounced. They are fundamentally symbiotic parts of the division of policing labour, even though there is constant tension in style, culture and working practices.

Crime is also presented in a much more complex and ambivalent way, sometimes rooted in social problems and perpetrated by those needing care as much as control, sometimes the product of greed or brutality which seems beyond explanation and calling only for suppression. The twice-weekly format extended over many years, and latterly the thrice-weekly scheduling, has allowed the continuous introduction of themes reflecting the most recent developments in the policing world, from the impact of the Police and Criminal Evidence Act 1984 (PACE) to sector policing. These not only provide a sense of verisimilitude and topicality, but also allow the constant exploration of social issues like racism and sexism in the force which have never before been the subjects of primetime police series.

The continuing format also allows a much more pessimistic approach to the problems confronting the police. These are seldom wrapped up neatly at the end of the episode, but recur repeatedly in developing ways. They defy simple solutions, whether the boy scout decency of Dixon or the no-holds-barred, tough law and order of *The Sweeney*.

This synthesis of the caring and controlling elements of the police role has frequently been expressed explicitly in the series itself, most succinctly by a recent episode title: 'Force is Part of the Service.' The police provide the service of protecting the public by the appropriate use of legitimate force, although at the same time police forces perform a variety of non-forceful and simply helpful services to people in trouble.

The synthesis of care and control in the police image presented by *The Bill* was again the product both of developments in the cop show genre, and in law and order politics. The more complex demographics of police forces produced a whole wave of British shows featuring leading characters who were not white Anglo-Saxon Protestant males. The way was paved by female leads (*The Gentle Touch* and *Juliet Bravo*), and followed by ethnic minority police (from *The Chinese Detective* to *Sam Saturday*) and young novices (*Rockcliffe's Babies*). Growing awareness of the complexity of police organisations was reflected in series looking at policing from a management rather than street perspective (*Waterfront Beat*, *The Chief*). The nostalgic hunger for a return to the supposed golden days of Dixon-style community policing was reflected in such ultra-pacific series on predominantly service-style policing as *Specials* and *Heartbeat*. The sense of the world outside the police being much more messy, intractable and essentially anarchic than these cosy evocations of community was conveyed in an influential American series, *Hill Street Blues*, which in many ways paved the stylistic path for *The Bill*.

All these changes in the cop show genre echo developments in the politics of law and order. In the mid-1980s the Conservative government implicitly began a U-turn away from its reliance simply on a tough law and order approach, in the face of its apparent failure as manifested by record increases in recorded crime (Reiner and Cross, 1991). Crime prevention in which the public had to figure as key partners with the criminal justice professionals became central to policy. This was congruent with changes that had already begun to affect the police world internally, from the impact of the 1981 Scarman Report on the Brixton disorders to the 1983 application of the Financial Management Initiative on the police, which imposed a greater concern with the rational management of resources on the police hierarchy (Reiner, 1991). The politics of policing moved beyond the simple confrontation between tough law and order and liberal restraints on police power that was the stuff of *The Sweeney*.

The format and style of *The Bill* has become the ideal vehicle for the presentation and exploration of this much more complex sense of contradiction, ambivalence, messiness, and intractability as the very essence of the police world. The Janus-faced conception of police as carers and controllers simultaneously is presented as an uneasy synthesis, unlike the more straightforward foregrounding of only one aspect of the duality in *Dixon* and *The Sweeney*. However, in a fundamental way *The Bill* continues the most basic legitimating message of the earlier series. Whilst there may be bad apples in the organisation, and warts on even the most virtuous of the characters, the force as a whole performs a vital service, and does so with as much integrity and effectiveness as is humanly possible.

Conclusion: The Dixonian Dialectic

This survey of the changing TV fictional presentation of the British police through an assessment of the three key phases in its evolution has suggested both flux and constancy. Changing exigencies both in the crime fiction genre and the politics of law and order outside the media have resulted in varying fore-grounding of first a caring then a controlling face of the police. The synthesis of these two is apparent in *The Bill*, which current-ly dominates the genre.

Underneath the superficial flux is a constant underlying legit-imating theme. The police, caring and controlling, perform a vital social function in the best possible way. They are a neces-sary evil, the moral street-sweepers of the urban jungles in which most people now live, symbolising the quixotic pursuit of order and security through their guardianship of the legitim-ate force which the state seeks to monopolise. As Raymond Chandler put it more expressively in *The Long Goodbye*, using the cops to control crime and other complex social problems is like taking aspirin to cure a brain tumour, but 'No way has yet been invented to say goodbye to them.'

Bibliography

Banton, M. (1964) *The Policeman in the Community* (London: Tavistock).

Binyon, T. J. (1989) *Murder Will Out: The Detective in Fiction* (Oxford: Oxford University Press).

Brogden, M. (1991) *On the Mersey Beat: An Oral History of Policing Liver-pool Between the Wars* (Oxford: Oxford University Press).

Chibnall, S. (1977) *Law and Order News* (London: Tavistock).

Clarke, A. (1986) 'This Is Not the Boy Scouts: Television Police Series and Definitions of Law and Order' in T. Bennett, C. Mercer and J. Woollacott (eds) *Popular Culture and Social Relations* (Milton Keynes: Open University Press).

Cumming, E., Cumming, I. and Edell, L. (1964) 'The Policeman as Philosopher, Guide and Friend', *Social Problems*, 12, 3.

Daley, H. (1986) *This Small Cloud* (London: Weidenfeld).

Ditton, J. and Duffy, J. (1983) 'Bias in the Newspaper Reporting of Crime News', *British Journal of Criminology*, 23, 2.

Dominick, J. (1978) 'Crime and Law Enforcement in the Mass Media' in C. Winick (ed.) *Deviance in the Mass Media* (Beverly Hills: Sage).

Donajgrodski, A. P. (ed.) (1977) *Social Control in Nineteenth Century Britain* (London: Croom Helm).

Dove, G. (1982) *The Police Procedural* (Bowling Green: Popular Press).

Dove, G. (1985) *The Boys From Grover Avenue: Ed McBain's 87th Precinct Novels* (Bowling Green: Popular Press).

Dove, G. and Bargainnier, E. (eds) (1986) *Cops and Constables: American and British Fictional Policemen* (Bowling Green: Popular Press).

Emsley, C. (1983) *Policing and Its Context 1750–1870* (London: Macmillan).

Emsley, C. (1991) *The English Police: A Political and Social History* (Hemel Hempstead: Wheatsheaf).

Ericson, R. (1991) 'Mass Media, Crime, Law and Justice: An Institutional Approach', *British Journal of Criminology*, 31, 3.

Ericson, R., Baranek, P. and Chan, J. (1987) *Visualising Deviance: A Study of News Organisation* (Milton Keynes: Open University Press).

Ericson, R., Baranek, P. and Chan, J. (1989) *Negotiating Control: A Study of News Sources* (Milton Keynes: Open University Press).

Ericson, R., Baranek, P. and Chan, J. (1991) *Representing Crime: Crime, Law and Justice in the News Media* (Milton Keynes: Open University Press).

Garofalo, J. (1981) 'Crime and the Mass Media: A Selective Review of Research', *Journal of Research in Crime and Delinquency*, 18, 2.

Gerbner, G. (1970) 'Cultural Indicators: The Case of Violence in Television Drama', *Annals of the American Academy of Political and Social Science*, 338.

Gerbner, G., Gross, L., Morgan, M. and Signorielli, N. (1980) 'The Mainstreaming of America: Violence Profile No. 11', *Journal of Communication*, 30.

Gerbner, G., Gross, L., Morgan, M. and Signorielli, N. (1984) 'Political Correlates of Television Viewing', *Public Opinion Quarterly*, 48.

Graber, D. A. (1980) *Crime News and the Public* (New York: Praeger).

Hall, S., Critcher, C., Jefferson, T., Clarke, J. and Roberts, B. (1978) *Policing the Crisis* (London: Macmillan).

Joint Consultative Committee of the Police Staff Associations (1990) *Operational Policing Review* (Surbiton: Police Federation).

Knight, S. (1981) *Form and Ideology in Crime Fiction* (London: Macmillan).

Laing, S. (1991) 'Banging in Some Reality: The Original "Z-Cars"' in J. Corner (ed.) *Popular Television in Britain: Studies in Cultural History* (London: British Film Institute).

Lee, J. A. (1981) 'Some Structural Aspects of Police Relations With Minority Groups' in C. Shearing (ed.) *Organisational Police Deviance* (Toronto: Butterworth).

Lynch, T. (1992) *The Bill: The Inside Story of British Television's Most Successful Police Series* (London: Boxtree).

Mandel, E. (1984) *Delightful Murder* (London: Pluto Press).

Mark, R. (1978) *In the Office of Constable* (London: Collins).

Martin, T. K. (1978) 'Four of a Kind?' in H. R. F. Keating (ed.) *Crime Writers* (London: BBC).

Mark, R. (1978) *In the Office of Constable* (London: Collins).

Mason, P. (1992) *Reading the Bill: An Analysis of the Thames Television Police Drama* (Bristol University: Centre for Criminal Justice).

Meyers, R. (1981) *TV Detectives* (San Diego: Barnes).

Meyers, R. (1989) *Murder on the Air* (New York: The Mysterious Press).

Miller, W. (1977) *Cops and Bobbies* (Chicago: Chicago University Press).

Monkkonen, E. (1981) *Police in Urban America 1860–1920* (Cambridge: Cambridge University Press).

Ousby, I. (1976) *Bloodhounds of Heaven: The Detective in English Fiction From Godwin to Doyle* (Cambridge: Harvard University Press).

Palmer, J. (1978) *Thrillers* (London: Arnold).

Palmer, S. H. (1988) *Police and Protest in England and Ireland 1780–1850* (Cambridge: Cambridge University Press).

Pandiani, J. (1978) 'Crime Time TV: If All We Knew Was What We Saw', *Contemporary Crises*, 2.

Porter, D. (1981) *The Pursuit of Crime* (New Haven: Yale University Press).

Punch, M. (1979) 'The Secret Social Service' in S. Holdaway (ed.) *The British Police* (London: Arnold).

Punch, M. and Naylor, T. (1973) 'The Police: A Social Service', *New Society*, 24.

Rawlings, P. (1992) *Drunks, Whores and Idle Apprentices: Criminal Biographies of the Eighteenth Century* (London: Routledge).

Reiner, R. (1978) 'The New Blue Films', *New Society*, 30.

Reiner, R. (1981) 'Keystone to Kojak: the Hollywood Cop' in P. Davies and B. Neve (eds) *Politics, Society and Cinema in America* (Manchester: Manchester University Press).

Reiner, R. (1988) 'British Criminology and the State', *British Journal of Criminology*, 28, 2.

Reiner, R. (1991) *Chief Constables* (Oxford: Oxford University Press).

Reiner, R. (1992a) *The Politics of the Police*, 2nd edn (Hemel Hempstead: Wheatsheaf).

Reiner, R. (1992b) 'Policing A Postmodern Society', *Modern Law Review*, 55, 6.

Reiner, R. and Cross, M. (1991) (eds), *Beyond Law and Order* (London: Macmillan).

Rock, P. (1973) 'News As Eternal Recurrence' in S. Cohen and J. Young (eds) *The Manufacture of News* (London: Constable).

Rogers, D. (1988) *The ITV Encyclopedia of Adventure* (London: Boxtree).

Rolph C. H. (1962) (ed.), *The Police and the Public* (London: Heinemann).

Royal Commission on the Police (1962) *Final Report*, Cmnd.1728 (London: HMSO).

St Johnston, E. (1978) *One Policeman's Story* (Chichester: Barry Rose).

Sayers, D. (ed.) (1928) *Tales of Detection* (London: Everyman).

Schlesinger, P., Tumber, H. and Murdock, G. (1991) 'The Media Politics of Crime and Criminal Justice', *British Journal of Sociology*, 42, 3.

Schlesinger, P. and Tumber, H. (1992) 'Crime and Criminal Justice in the Media' in D. Downes (ed.) *Unravelling Criminal Justice* (London: Macmillan).

Southgate, P. and Crisp, D. (1992) *Public Satisfaction With Police Services*, Research and Planning Unit Paper 73 (London: Home Office).

Sparks, R. (1992) *Television and the Drama of Crime: Moral Tales and the Place of Crime in Public Life* (Milton Keynes: Open University Press).

Symons, J. (1972) *Bloody Murder* (London: Penguin).

Weinberger, B. and Reinke, H. (1991) 'A Diminishing Function? A Comparative Historical Account of Policing in the City', *Policing and Society*, 1, 3.

Woffinden, B. (1987) *Miscarriages of Justice* (London: Coronet).

2

Care and Control in the Police Organisation
Neil Walker

Let me describe two organisations. One has a committed workforce . . . driven by common values and beliefs towards a common objective – the provision of the best possible service to the public. The second is one in which it would appear that control of the workforce is achieved by way of a strict, militaristic code of conduct. . .
Clearly these two organisations can have little in common. Their objectives, management systems and desired outcomes must be different. That, sadly, is not the case. They are the same organisation, the modern police service (O'Byrne, 1991, p. 2286).

Even if it owes something to dramatic license, the diagnosis of institutional schizophrenia recently offered by one serving senior officer strikes a chord with many professional and academic analyses of the internal organisation of British police forces. Just as the care and control dimensions of police work co-exist uneasily in relations with various public constituencies and with other professional groups, so there would seem to be a similarly stark contrast of themes in relations within the police service. The present chapter attempts to explore and develop this line of thought by addressing a set of interrelated questions. In the first place, why and in what form have care and control dimensions developed within the anatomy of the police organisation? Secondly, how do these two dimensions typically relate to one another, and with what consequences for the internal harmony and external effectiveness of police institutions? Finally, in the light of recent reforms in police organisation and current trends in the politics of policing, how, if at all, is the balance of care and control likely to develop in the foreseeable future?

Care and Control in Historical Perspective

As control is viewed by most commentators as the more insistent theme in the historical development of police organisations, it would seem appropriate to start with this dimension (Bittner, 1971; Bradley *et al.*, 1986, Chapter 5; Brogden *et al.*, 1988, Chapter 5). Since its inception, the 'new police' has availed itself of a 'military–bureaucratic' method of internal regulation (Bittner, 1971, p. 52). Police organisations have traditionally been characterised by a clear division of labour, an extended hierarchy of ranks, a common training regime, an elaborate internal career structure, a distinct occupational status, an extensive set of standard operating procedures and a severe internal discipline code, together with many of the symbolic paraphernalia of the armed forces such as uniform, drill and muster. The cumulative effect has been to create a 'managerial structure' (Burns, 1981, p. 3) which, both in terms of the broad array of control mechanisms it allocates to organisational elites and also the ethic of disciplined obedience it embodies, is orientated towards strict top-down direction. There are a number of reasons for this emphasis. Some are functional, concerned to address concrete problems of co-ordination and control affecting the police task, while others are ideological, concerned with the legitimation of police institutions before external audiences.

In functional terms, the most immediate rationale for modelling the police organisation on the military archetype is the apparent analogy between the two institutions. As 'the specialist repository domestically of the state's monopoly of legitimate force'(Reiner, 1992a, p. 49), the police, like the military, require their personnel to use coercive power in unpredictable and perilous circumstances. In light of this, the pattern of everyday discipline within the organisation may be defended as 'a permanent rehearsal for the real thing' (Bittner, 1971, p. 52). The unique police capacity to threaten or apply coercive power in their public dealings also entails that they become disproportionately implicated in the 'dirty work' of society (Harris, 1973, p. 3). Police work may sometimes be dangerous, but is more often demeaning and sordid. Whether dealing with sudden deaths, touring 'skid-row' (Bittner, 1967), investigating the dark underside of domestic or commercial relations, or seeking to keep the lid on hostile pockets of urban deprivation, police officers are regularly engaged in shielding the 'respectables' within a particular social order from the distasteful tasks that are essential to the maintenance of their privileged social position and sanitised self-image. Precisely because they are required to defend the 'culture of contentment' of the majority (Galbraith, 1992), yet are discouraged from disturbing the complacent world-view which lies at its core by advertising the less palatable details of their work, police officers perform a role that they perceive to be both difficult and underappreciated. In such circumstances, it may be reasoned that a *general* ethic of unquestioned obedience to institutional norms is necessary to counter the unattractiveness of *particular* work demands, and that a military–bureaucratic structure of control is best able to instil such an attitude.

If these arguments focus on the nature of the police role, the other set of functional reasons which supports a rigid control structure concerns the considerable practical autonomy that operational police officers enjoy in the enactment of their role. To begin with, the sheer range of problems which may require coercive force as a solution or as a negotiating resource is such that the received mandate of the police is a highly differentiated one, and the work of the individual officer typically episodic and non-routine (Manning, 1977, Chapter 6). Moreover, those problems for which coercion provides an ultimate solution also typically demand prompt and decisive action to achieve, mitigate or avoid such an outcome (Bittner, 1974, p. 30). Thus, there are both theoretical and practical limits upon the extent to which the contextually appropriate course of action for operational officers attending a particular incident can be informed by prior policy guidelines or instructions. Such officers are, in consequence, 'street-level bureaucrats' (Lipsky,

1980). The police's monopoly of key decisions therefore allows them considerably greater leverage within the framework of collective endeavour than is typically the case with lower participants in large commercial organisations. Finally, underlining their scope for 'strong discretion' (Dworkin, 1978) still further, operational officers perform many of their tasks 'in regions of low visibility' (Van Maanen, 1983, p. 377) removed from direct supervisory oversight.

There is, therefore, considerable opportunity for working officers to depart from the official institutional script, or to add their own particular gloss where the authoritative text is unclear or ambiguous. In addition, cultural considerations suggest a degree of willingness to avail themselves of this opportunity. Across an impressive range of police organisational settings (Reuss-Ianni and Ianni, 1983; Punch, 1985; Grimshaw and Jefferson, 1987), it has been contended that there is 'a major schism between the work cultures of upper and lower ranks' (Punch, 1981, p. 26). Management cop culture, according to this analysis, is concerned with the police mandate on a 'systemwide' basis (Reuss-Ianni and Ianni, 1983, p. 258). Its major audiences are external, including the courts, local and national politicians and other powerful interest groups in whose eyes the police must legitimate themselves. Street cop culture, by contrast, is marked by unit-based concerns and is more inward-looking and pragmatic. For operational police officers, the danger, uncertainty and contextual variety of police work tends to bind them to their immediate work group and leads them to eschew the generalised indices of probity and success preferred by their seniors in favour of specific, episodic measures. Further, the insularity and defensive solidarity of the immediate work group amplifies a number of other cultural characteristics which emerge from the specific demands and pressures of operational police work. These include an action orientation, a machismo-centred self-image, a binary moral code, generic suspiciousness, conservatism and a prejudicial attitude towards minority groups with whose members police officers are disproportionately involved in adversarial encounters (Reiner, 1992b, Chapter 3; see also Oakley in this volume). In turn, each of these self-perpetuating characteristics may, on occasion, run counter to managerial imperatives designed to inculcate an attitude of disinterested professionalism and to encourage a sensitivity to the demands of disparate external constituencies.

As is evident from later discussion, the schism thesis caricatures inter-rank relations and obscures or neglects more subtle influences. Like all caricatures, however, it indicates some salient features of the object which it purports to represent. It suggests at the very least that there is no guarantee that the practical autonomy of the operational ranks will be consistently utilised in a manner which accords with notions of optimal performance endorsed by organisational elites. Arguably, this places an additional onus on the package of measures made available through the military–bureaucratic model to secure dedication to the official mission.

Let us, finally, look at the ideological factors underpinning reliance upon the military–bureaucratic model. Policing histories ranged across the intellectual spectrum have stressed the scale of the task required of the new police to legitimate themselves in the new industrial conurbations of the early nineteenth century (Reiner, 1992b, Chapter 1; Brogden *et al.*, 1988, Chapter 4). A key requirement was to assuage the fears of those who felt that a full-time police force would provide a powerful weapon in the hands of dominant political and economic groups seeking to entrench a 'specific order' tied to their own partial interests (Marenin, 1982, p. 258). In this respect, the development of the military–bureaucratic model was significant in exploiting and perpetuating a 'rational institutional myth' deeply embedded in the public culture of many Western societies (Meyer and Rowan, 1977). The essence of this mythical vision is that bureaucracy and rationality are isomorphic, and that in this correspondence between institution and idea lies the promise of the most virtuous and effective organisation of the public realm. Transposed onto the policing domain, the adoption of the bureaucratic template conveyed the message that the police organisation represented a disciplined, impartial body of men, a rational machine for the establishment of 'general order' (Marenin, 1982, p. 258).

Of course, it should not be forgotten that the choice of organisational form on the part of early police institution-builders was as much a matter of necessity as of design. The bureaucratic–military model may have been ideologically alluring, but at the point of time in question it was also the only feasible option available (Bittner, 1971, p. 54). Despite the development of a more sophisticated range of organisational theories in the twentieth century, the comparatively primitive early model has until recently remained substantially unaltered. This is in part due to the durability of the rational institutional myth and its adaptability to new circumstances and problems. In particular, the promise of a singular and coherent commitment to officially preordained ends implicit in the model has not only continued to provide a symbolically reassuring shield against the dangers of illicit political pressure and other corrupting influences, but has also helped to justify the preservation of decision-making autonomy against demands to increase the public accountability of policing (Kinsey *et al.*, 1986, Chapter 8).

An additional ideological explanation for the persistence of the classic bureaucratic model lies in the more general fact that the public image of contemporary policing is of a 'profoundly old-fashioned' institution (Manning, 1977, p. 118). Its commitment to the conservation of social order and its association with a moral vision reified as an absolute, timeless standard of right and wrong (Manning, 1977, p. 5) invests the police institution with a sense of tradition which is itself a significant source of public respect and veneration. For policy makers and image-managers of policing in the modern age, this symbolic legacy has long provided a weighty consideration against innovation and in favour of tried and tested design and practice.

Superficially, it might seem that the historical centrality of the control-oriented military–bureaucratic model to the formal organisation of the policing enterprise would have left little scope for any other framework of intra-organisational relations to assert and sustain itself. However, this would be to assume mistakenly that the official version of organisational reality is faithfully reflected in practice. The former undoubtedly has an important structuring effect, but the pattern of everyday relations also betrays the influence of an informal 'collaborative system' (Burns, 1981, p. 3) within which the organisation and its members display more intimate and caring attitudes.

As with the control dimension, a series of interconnected strands accounts for the development of the care dimension. To

begin with, there is the 'internally self-sufficient career structure' within the British police (Bradley *et al.*, 1986, p. 134). In
the post-Trenchard age, all senior officers have been obliged to
rise through the ranks and to undergo training regimes and
processes of operational socialisation similar to those of their
juniors (Parker, 1990). This provides a sizeable fund of common
experience and knowledge of working the streets and, thus,
of exposure to an operational subculture, which, as noted, is
marked by its encouragement of group solidarity and its maintenance of a sharp division between insiders and outsiders.
Paradoxically, therefore, the very cultural forces which establish intra-organisational divisions, also mark out the boundary
between officers and citizenry, and so ensure at least a residual
symbolic unity across ranks (Bradley *et al.*, 1986, p. 198). In some
cases also, the common entry point produces not only similar,
but shared, background operational experience, certain lower and
higher participants possessing a 'specific particularistic knowledge' of each other which may cement cultural bonds rooted
in the common work experience (Manning, 1977, p. 148).

Further, and somewhat ironically, the practical autonomy
of lower ranks which provides such an important functional
rationale for the development of a bureaucratic control structure
may also be the seed-bed of a more caring, mutually accom-
modating strain of relations. Control of knowledge and monopolisa-
tion of key skills and tasks on the part of junior officers ensures
a more intimate task interdependence and a more even balance
of mutual influence between ranks than the highly stratified
organisational command structure would suggest. Accordingly,
in practice managerial and operational working methods have
to be closely co-ordinated, while the setting of working goals is
best depicted as a 'negotiated order' (Strauss *et al.*, 1963), involving a continuous process of explicit and implicit bargaining
between parties. In turn, the more intensive the patterns of
co-operation and negotiation, the greater the exposure to the
interests and pressures of other ranks, and the more likely it is
that a certain level of mutual empathy will be reached.

For all that these strong cultural undercurrents encourage
a caring ethos within the organisation, it lacks the official
imprimatur and structural entrenchment which the military–
bureaucratic model provides for the control ethos. This is not to

deny, however, that there is significant, and increasing, recognition of the importance of the care dimension within police policy-making circles. Before we discuss these changes and evaluate their significance, however, we need to develop a more general framework for understanding and assessing the relationship between care and control in the police organisation.

The Relationship between Care and Control

If two such apparently contrasting themes as care and control each represents a potentially important dimension in intra-organisational relations, the investigation of the precise relationship between them assumes a key significance. This inquiry has both an explanatory and an evaluative aspect. First, what is the actual pattern of relationship between the two dimensions, and how is it to be accounted for? Secondly, what is the optimal framework of relations between them?

In order to investigate these questions, however, we need sharper and more incisive tools than have been utilised thus far. In particular, we need a unified conceptual language which will allow us to elucidate and compare care and control dimensions of intra-organisational relations in accordance with common criteria. The development of this new vocabulary involves the identification of an analytical distinction which is even more fundamental than that of care and control, but which remains closely linked to our original conceptual proposition.

Two Species of Power Relations

At this deeper level of analysis, it is possible to conceive of the pattern of police organisational activity as determined by the interaction between two different situational logics or operating dynamics, each of which is expressed in terms of a different network of reciprocal influences, or species of power relations, between organisational actors. These are, respectively, the *instrumental power relation* and the *normative power relation* (Walker, 1991, Chapter 3). With one major proviso, which is considered below, the instrumental power relation is more closely associated with the control dimension of intra-organisational practice, whereas the normative power relation is more closely associated with the care dimension.

So called because it contemplates the utilisation of some actors by other actors as means, or 'instruments', to the ends endorsed by the latter, the instrumental power relation encompasses the various ways in which, regardless of any identity or compatibility of perspective, some actors seek to exploit the capabilities inherent in their formal organisational position to exert influence over or constrain other actors. Its outcome reflects the balance of material resources available to each party and how these are strategically deployed. The normative power relation, on the other hand, is so called because it contemplates the establishment of norms, or agreed standards of conduct, in social life. It encompasses the various ways in which an identity or compatibility of perspective may or may not be constituted between different actors. Its outcome reflects the balance of symbolic resources available to each party and how these are strategically deployed. In summary, while the instrumental power relation presupposes the possibility of conflict and struggle between parties over the pursuit of different preferences, the normative power relation presupposes the possibility of the sharing or harmonisation of preferences.

Each power relation can, in turn, be divided into a number of subspecies. Instrumental power relations operate through two main modalities, namely *threat and inducement*, and *control of the allocation of key resources*. The former is the more refined and exact, but also the more complex. It allows detailed control of the actions of another party, but only if a two-stage strategic process is successfully negotiated. This involves not only a capacity and preparedness to impose positive sanctions (inducements) or negative sanctions (threats) so as to encourage or deter certain actions on the part of another party, but also having access to reliable information in order to verify whether the relevant actions have taken place. In turn, such access may be through any of four media, singly or in combination: personal monitoring, telecommunications, third party sources, and documentary sources. For its part, control of the allocation of key resources is a cruder device, but within its limits, more easily executed. To ration or deny key resources, whether petrol, or firearms, or the means to acquire new skills, can only operate as a very broad veto on the actions of others, but, unlike threat or inducement, its effectiveness does not depend upon the capacity for retrospective verification.

The internal groupings of normative power relations are more complex. In the first place, there is *persuasion*, the tested acceptance of another's judgement; secondly, and of much greater significance in the recursive patterns of intra-organisational relations, there is *authority*, 'the untested acceptance of another's judgement' (Wrong, 1979, p. 35). Authority may be *personal, competent or institutional*. Personal authority arises where one party obeys the other due to the existence of an interpersonal bond or the personal qualities of the latter. Competent authority involves deference to the judgement of the other party in recognition of his or her expertise in the matter in question. Institutional authority arises where the subservient party perceives his relationship with a putative authority-holder to fall within a socially established, or institutionalised category with regard to which the command/obedience model of exchange is generally regarded as appropriate. This may to some extent be a simple matter of the occupation of a formally defined social position, such as rank, but institutional status may also be a more elusive and constructed quality, its attribution depending upon the putative authority-holder acting in a manner considered to be in keeping with a particular social position. A final subspecies of the normative power relation is where both parties are independently persuaded of the correctness of a particular course of action on account of *underlying normative consensus*, which in turn derives from common exposure to various forms of formal and informal socialisation, or shared or similar work experience. This subspecies is not only significant in its own right, but also provides a supportive context within which the generation of the other types of normative power relations is facilitated.

This categorisation of instrumental and normative power relations should not be understood as a simple taxonomy of empirical relations within police organisations, but rather as a heuristic device which illuminates a more complex reality. In the first place, as is evident from a cursory examination of the most important subtypes of both species, it would be wrong to view the implication of power relations in the day-to-day life of the organisation in terms of a set of discrete episodes, each consciously enacted. In the case of threats or inducements, an appreciation by one actor of the capacity of another to make use of such techniques may, in accordance with the 'rule of anticipated reactions' (Friedrich, 1937, p. 16), be as effective in ensuring the compliance of the first actor with the wishes of the second as a more overt strategy. So too with authority relations, since the acquisition of authority is in part a function of prior reputation, there is an irreducible element of latency. As in the case of instrumental sanctions, the existence of a resilient context which is highly suggestive to both parties both permits and encourages a strategic economy in intra-organisational exchanges. Underlining their significance, therefore, our two species of power relations are best seen as deeply embedded in recurrent patterns of action within the organisation.

Secondly, even if we allow that power relations often operate at a deep structural level rather than as surface phenomena, there is in any case typically no neat one-to-one correspondence between a subspecies of power relation and a particular relationship between actors. Rather, the various subspecies of power relation are in practice fused or linked in various combinations. However, their prior analytical separation remains crucial for explanatory purposes, since it is only through the establishment of general patterns of combinations between subspecies that it may be possible to develop broad propositions about the relationship between instrumental and normative power relations, and thus between care and control dimensions in intra-organisational relations.

Care and Control: Their Relationship in Practice

The present writer sought to develop this framework of inquiry in a study of managerial ranks in four subdivisions in two Scottish forces. The study employed a combination of interview and questionnaire methods (Walker, 1991, Chapter 4). Two general conclusions about the relationship between normative and instrumental power relations emerged (Walker, 1991, Chapter 5).

In the first place, it was found that in particular inter-rank relationships, power relations within each species tend to operate together and develop a self-perpetuating dynamic to the exclusion of power relations of the alternative species. The emphasis upon indirect and episodic monitoring and upon the use of sanctions and techniques of resource-rationing, which have a peremptory effect, entail that within instrumental relations there is little incentive for the initiator to develop a caring and sympathetic understanding of the circumstances and aspirations of the other party. Nor, likewise, are the actions of the initiator likely to stimulate a more generous reciprocal attitude. The exclusionary and self-perpetuating quality of this species of power relation is further enhanced by the fact that bureaucracy provides a currency of instrumental power that organisational elites can conveniently mint for their own use. Bureaucratic methods, therefore, tend to be offered as solutions to problems of their own making. Rule infractions are met by new rules, sanction avoidance by net-widening, and disinformation by more claustrophobic surveillance in an instrumental cycle which meets failure with a policy of 'more of the same' (Manning, 1977, pp. 193–7).

In contrast, most subspecies of normative power relations imply a more intimate association between the parties. The involvement of persuasion, personal and competent authority, or an underlying normative consensus in intra-organisational relationships tend to presuppose or encourage a climate of favourable interpersonal relations. If we concentrate upon the vital areas of personal and competent authority, respect and trust are two key overlapping components of such relations which tend to operate in a self-propagating manner. The attribution of personal or professional respect reveals and reinforces an openness to persuasion as to the estimable qualities of the other party, and thereby encourages a measure of reciprocity. For its part, the element of trust in personal and professional bonding may have strategic origins, but harbours significant transformative potential. To attain a position where one can trust one's associates is a 'device for coping with the freedom of others' (Gambetta, 1988). Conversely, to win the trust of others allows one to maximise one's own freedom of action. However, in the longer run, the advantages of trust may also serve as 'an instrument of obligation' (Luhmann, 1979, p. 64). Over time, the presentation of self as trustworthy and the demonstration of trust in the other party tend to escape their instrumental roots and to embrace both parties in a genuinely normative structure. In a nutshell, the self-propagating dynamic of normative relations rests both upon objective grounds – the importance of accumulating and preserving a capital fund of mutual confidence which facilitates transactions between the parties, and upon subjective grounds – the affective investment of both parties.

Conspicuous by its absence from this neat conceptual division is institutional authority, which lacks the intimacy associated with the other normative power relations. Instead, the bureaucratic principle, with its emphasis upon hierarchy and impersonality, provides a bridgehead between the symbolic message of institutional authority and the instrumental emphasis upon strategic distance and asymmetry of resources. Indeed, the divisional study suggested the affinity between these power bases to be so strong that their conjunction provided the foundation for one of two generic *authoritative styles* (Walker, 1991, Chapters 3 and 10) through which promoted police officers attempt to marry personal image to a particular profile of power strategies, namely the *autonomous style* (Sennett, 1980, Chapter 2). Remote, authoritarian and proclaiming an indifference to the personal needs and concerns of the authority-subject, the autonomous style stands in direct contrast to the other main 'top-down' authoritative style in the police organisation, namely *paternalism*, which is tied to the more intimate normative power bases and proclaims a deeper concern with protecting and nurturing the interests and aspirations of the subject (Sennett, 1980, Chapter 3).

However, rather than dilute the claim that care and control provide divergent themes in the police organisation, the example of institutional authority in fact reinforces it. This is simply because institutional authority is best conceived of as falling within the control dimension, and so provides the one key exception to the relationship of correspondence between normative power and care, and between instrumental power and control. Indeed, to highlight this point, our two diametrically opposed authoritative styles, autonomy and paternalism, which presuppose this same exception, may be viewed as the paradigmatic instances of control and care in inter-rank relations.

A second relevant conclusion drawn from the divisional research was that the greater the distance between ranks, the lesser the tendency to rely upon the more personalised normative power relations and the greater the tendency to rely upon instrumental power relations and institutional authority (Walker, 1991, Chapter 5). Due to their elevated status, wider functional and territorial responsibility, and different shift arrangements, officers of more senior rank often lack the intimacy of social and work contact with the operational ranks from which personal authority might flow. Also, in an occupation with such a strong tradition of on-the-job discretion and craft expertise, the value of managerial work as a separate area of expert knowledge is persistently questioned (Bradley *et al.*, 1986, Chapter 2), and so senior officers may have to rely excessively on the depreciating fund of their own operational reputation in order to earn competent authority (Walker, 1991, Chapter 8). Further, any underlying normative consensus will become more marginal as the gulf in rank increases, with shared or similar contemporary work patterns reduced to a minimum and pre-occupational and occupational socialisation experience separated by a generational gulf.

On the other hand, officers of more elevated rank are by definition more likely to receive the vicarious benefits of institutional authority, and are better placed to access and deploy the resources through which instrumental strategies are developed. Senior officers hold most of the 'carrots' and wield most of the 'sticks' supplied by the bureaucratic machine. Between the potent extremities of formal discipline and promotion, they can threaten or promise a range of more subtle negative and positive sanctions such as undesirable transfers, fastidious paperwork demands, strict timetables, placement on attractive courses or secondments, and scheduled overtime.

Conversely, more junior managers, in particular sergeants, tend to emphasise in their relations with constables the importance of personal and professional respect and of the development of a harmony of working objectives within the shift team. This is partly because of their close and interdependent working relationship with their juniors, and also because, relative to their seniors, they are dealt a poor instrumental hand. They may be able to dispense certain 'small favors' (Van Maanen,

1983, p. 305), including indoor jobs, desirable beats, reliable partners and unobtrusive supervision, but their ambition in this field tends to be limited to securing within their shift what one respondent described as the 'minimum groan factor' (Walker, 1991, p. 223).

A State of Disequilibrium

If we can infer from the above analysis that a traditional feature of the internal dynamics of British police forces in general has been a lack of equilibrium between control and care dimensions, which is in turn reflected in a marked variation of emphasis in different inter-rank networks, what implications does this have for the overall health of intra-organisational relations? The answer lies in assessing what benefits and drawbacks are associated with each dimension, and whether the tension between them might preclude the development of a more integrated framework of internal relations, which would draw on the strengths and negate the disadvantages of both.

In accounting for the development of the control dimension of British policing, I have already rehearsed a number of the arguments in favour of its central steering mechanism, namely the bureaucratic principle. The emphasis upon a top-down chain of command and upon an elaborate structure of internal regulation, designed to promote uniformity and continuity, underscores the bureaucratic claim to provide a rational model for the control and co-ordination of large-scale collective endeavour. In particular, in a social and occupational milieu where a degree of cultural pluralism is inevitable, the capacity of the bureaucratic system to harness powerful instrumental means in order to encourage conformity to the official mandate involves a crucial recognition of the indispensability of sanctions to the systematic ordering of social relations.

Against this, however, there are a number of entries in the debit column (Argyris, 1968, p. 315; Bradley *et al.*, 1986, pp. 125–6). Police bureaucracy can encourage a rule-based pedanticism, a reluctance or inability to adapt to new circumstances, an unduly narrow policy-making base and an autonomous style of personnel management which, by neglecting the human dimension of a job with high 'stress potential'

(Ainsworth and Pease, 1987, p. 145), may encourage loss of motivation (Jones, 1980), absenteeism (Home Affairs Committee, 1991) and extensive 'easing behaviour' (Cain, 1973).

Furthermore, it is perhaps less well appreciated that even in terms of its primary claim to provide a social technology for the control and harmonisation of collective effort, bureaucracy may prove self-defeating. Accurate feedback on events occurring in a highly dispersed working environment is an indispensable resource for bureaucratic elites, but one which is threatened by defensive accounting on the part of operational ranks (Chatterton, 1979). In turn, information from reliable third party sources offers the most promising means of neutralising this threat: accordingly, as first-line supervisors, sergeants are viewed by many senior managers as their 'eyes and ears' – the key agents of their instrumental control strategies (Walker, 1991, Chapter 5). Yet, this sits uneasily with the fact, already remarked upon, that in terms of the structural opportunities and constraints attached to their position, sergeants have a strong propensity towards developing a normative framework of relations with their juniors. Consequently, they occupy a difficult 'buffer' role (Chatterton, 1987) in which they must win the confidence of juniors in order to provide the detailed knowledge of the 'sharp-end' required of them by their seniors. At the same time, they must also win the confidence of seniors in order to be conceded the autonomy necessary to protect the interests of the operational ranks with whom they retain a strong cultural affinity (Walker, 1991, Chapter 5). This double-edged imperative involves sergeants in a paradox of trust. Their strategic capacity to mediate between instrumentally opposed constituencies and to strike a balance between their respective interests and priorities depends upon their being trusted by both. But this may place incompatible demands upon them in an instrumental climate where each major constituency, street cops and management cops, tends to perceive loyalty to its own interests as inconsistent with a similar commitment to the other. In short, sergeants may have to betray the trust of each constituency in order to win the trust of both. The elements of duplicity and skilful impression management required within this 'balanced approach' test not only the tactical acumen of its exponents but also their sense of social identity and of the appropriate foundations of peer relations. For some sergeants, the moral and strategic perils involved in a career as a high-wire artist may be such that they seek a different career route (Walker, 1991, Chapter 10) – as 'artisans', superior workmen defining their interests as being at one with the constable rank; as 'aspirant executives', nailing their colours equally firmly to the managerial mast; or as mere 'stripes-carriers', disillusioned cynics 'burned out' in the cauldron of operational and supervisory demands (Maslach and Jackson, 1979, p. 59). Whichever alternative solution is chosen, it weakens the already tenuous capacity of a predominantly instrumental structure to generate the candid upward flow of information required for it to succeed.

At first glance, the contrasting prospect of the care dimension assuming pre-eminence in intra-organisational relations would not appear to have similarly dangerous or counterproductive consequences. Ideally, a normative culture would embody the values of autonomy, individual utility and nurturance, and rational consensus. Its product would be an organisation of highly motivated individuals, each contributing to the setting and realisation of corporate goals within a climate free from the wasteful excess of bureaucratic controls and the disinformation strategies characteristic of an instrumental culture.

In practice, however, a working culture pervaded by sentiments of reciprocal concern and normative unity also harbours the capacity to develop along pathological lines. A first possibility is that a false or unreflective consensus is manufactured across the organisation as a whole, supplying internal legitimation for a policing style or policy which is publicly unacceptable. A second possibility, the mirror opposite of the first, is that the trust placed in the rank and file through a more caring and indulgent management system is abused, and certain working groups operate beyond any effective system of organisational control. In the first case, management wields too much influence of the wrong kind; in the second, it wields too little influence of any kind.

As the more radical vision, the former is the less plausible model for interpreting particular organisational developments, at least in political systems where public accountability of the police is both a widespread cultural expectation and a matter of institutional fact. However, the exposure of the conduct of the Los Angeles Police Division (LAPD) through the notorious events surrounding the beating of Rodney King provides an instructive recent exception to this (Dunne, 1991). Arguably, the development of a deviant occupational culture on an organisation-wide basis requires a convergence of various factors: first, a framework of personal authority in which the charismatic leadership style of the chief inspires uncritical loyalty rather than reasoned compliance; second, a leadership philosophy which attempts to run with the grain of the relatively intransigent occupational culture and so to establish normative consensus on terms favourable to the rank and file; and third, a strong mutually corroborative framework of professional authority, where the sense of pride and solidarity engendered by membership of a *corps d'élite* creates orthodoxies of knowledge strongly resistant to external influence. In the case of the LAPD, Daryl Gates fitted the frame as a chief with a well-developed sense of the prejudices of his wider occupational audience. As the Christopher Commission (1991) indicated in delivering a telling indictment against Gates's management, his outspokenly articulated vision of society as embracing a rigidly dualistic moral order was reflected both in a fastidious attitude towards police corruption and a preparedness to defend the use of coercive means by his officers to uphold this moral order, frequently against ethnic minority populations. The result was to give a green light to street officers infused with a strong sense of moral self-righteousness and fired with missionary zeal to adopt an enforcement style that caricatured the normal behaviour of the rank and file.

While the documented history of British policing reveals no cases as stark as the LAPD, it is notable that in an era in which chief constables have become highly politicised figures, the evidence suggests a similar link between the operational style and image of the force on the one hand, and the policing philosophy of top management on the other (Jones and Levi, 1983). And although the philosophy of the British policing elite has tended to coalesce around a broad, service-based 'post-Scarmanist' perspective (Reiner, 1991b, p. 118), there remains a significant minority of old-style 'bosses' whose apocalyptic vision echoes some of the themes favoured by Gates (Reiner, 1991b, p. 307).

However, the dangers inherent in an insular occupational perspective assume a more immediate relevance domestically in relation to our second problematic scenario, in which a permissive managerial style allows free rein to a particular department or working group to pursue unit goals inconsistent with the broader organisational mandate. For example, the series of corruption scandals surrounding the Metropolitan CID and associated squads in the 1960s and 1970s, against which Sir Robert Mark waged war with the symbols and resources of the military–bureaucratic model, have been viewed as a function of an indulgent managerial ethos in harmony with the protective solidarity of detective culture (Hobbs, 1988, Chapter 4). A decade later in London, a quite different managerial approach provoked similar complaints. The Holloway incident of 1983 saw a closing of ranks in the face of an investigation into the police assault of a number of black youths, thereby provoking an unparalleled confluence of criticism from within and outwith the force. The whole affair was persuasively diagnosed by one commentator as an extreme and unintended consequence of an innovative managerial culture which stressed the virtues of delegation and the self-regulation of work groups within a broader framework of rational goal-setting (Holdaway, 1986). More recently still, the belated recognition afforded by the Court of Appeal to a string of miscarriages of justice in Irish terrorism cases and other major criminal convictions has led to an identification of slack police management as a contributory cause alongside a partisan forensic service and a loaded adversarial trial system. In particular, the West Midlands Serious Crime Squad, which emerged as one of the major culprits in fabricating evidence and was consequently disbanded by its then Chief Constable, Sir Geoffrey Dear (Kaye, 1991), was criticised by both the Inspectorate and the Police Complaints Authority in 1991 as 'lacking the firm hand of management' (Kirby, 1992). Despite the scale of the acknowledged problem, however, a further, poignant indication of the scope for deviance where weak management meets a buoyant and self-protective squad mentality lay in the subsequent decision of the Director of Public Prosecutions not to prosecute any officers from the discredited squad on account of insufficiency of evidence (Kirby, 1992).

The importance of the above analysis is that neither the control dimension nor the care dimension represents an unqualified good in intra-organisational relations. If either is allowed to dominate, then significant problems emerge in terms of the capacity of the organisation to co-ordinate and harmonise its collective efforts and to remain responsive to its public constituencies. This is more obviously so of the control dimension, given the traditional hegemony of the military–bureaucratic model, but is also the case with the care dimension in those organisational pockets where it is in the ascendancy.

If, by contrast, control and care dimensions were in closer equilibrium, then each could check the excesses and supply the omissions of the other. A commitment to the development of relations based upon reciprocal concern and common cause can provide a corrective to a bureaucratic reductionism, which understands social relations only in terms of narrow self-interest or group-interest. Equally, however, bureaucratic hierarchies and sanctioning systems can provide a safeguard against the development of misplaced loyalties and 'patterns of indulgency' (Gouldner, 1965), and against the incubation of a complacent insularity within the organisation.

Towards a New Balance?

While the balance principle can be affirmed with relative ease, profound difficulties remain at the level of detailed contextual application. First, given the tendency of care and control dimensions to develop in a mutually exclusive manner, there may be practical impediments to the establishment of a new balance within the organisation. Secondly, the mechanisms adopted to achieve the optimal balance between the two dimensions must also be appropriately matched to the substantive concerns of police work. Thirdly, and most crucially of all, conditions within the wider political and social environment must favour the application of a new blend of normative and instrumental mechanisms. In this concluding section the significance of these three difficulties is discussed in the course of an analysis of the efforts which have been made over the last decade within the British police to transform the climate of internal relations.

It is widely agreed that one of the major innovatory themes in the British police in the 1980s and 1990s has been the development of a new 'managerialism' (Holdaway, 1986; Walker, 1991, Chapter 8; Reiner, 1992a). As we shall see, the full ramifications of this managerialism can only be understood against a broader political canvas. However, its more immediate purpose has been to correct the very imbalance diagnosed earlier, providing a vehicle for challenging the long-standing ascendancy of the military–bureaucratic model through the introduction of more normative structures.

'People' factors and 'system' factors have provided dual components of the reform strategy (Sherman, 1983). As regards the former, the Scarman Report (1981) provided an early impetus with its recommendations for improved management and supervisory training for sergeants and inspectors (Stephens, 1988, Chapters 5 and 6). In 1985, the Special Course for upwardly mobile junior ranks was reorganised to include a greater emphasis upon the development of both personnel and strategic management skills. Similarly, by its focus upon job-related assessment exercises, the new Objective Structured Performance Related Examination (OSPRE), which was introduced into the promotion assessment system for sergeants and inspectors in 1991 (HMCIC, 1991, p. 19), underlines the importance of good interpersonal management skills. At a more senior level, across the entire range of command courses offered by the Police Staff College, Bramshill and the Scottish Police Training College, there has been a marked increase in the attention devoted to forms of management theory and practice which question military–bureaucratic orthodoxies (see, for example, Oakley in this volume). More generally, a Home Affairs Committee inquiry into higher police training, which reported in 1989 (Home Affairs Committee, 1989), sparked a lively debate within political and professional circles about the training and career development needs of senior command officers (Symposium on Higher Police Training, 1990). The upshot of this has been a more systematic emphasis upon 'fast streaming' – the early channelling of officers of high management potential via the Special Course or the newly reorganised Accelerated Promotion Scheme for Graduates, followed by structured progress through the various command courses

(HMCIC, 1991, pp. 19–20 and 1992, pp. 36–7). By cultivating the idea of a separate managerial cadre subject to a specialist educational and career development regime, these developments signal an intention to take management seriously as a sphere of work with its own distinctive ethos, and, by implication, serve to discourage adoption of alternative role models available through close acquaintance with the extant instrumental culture of inter-rank relations.

If we turn to the 'system' factors, the major structural reform that the early 1980s heralded was Policing By Objectives (PBO) (Butler, 1984). PBO promised a radical overhaul of the bureaucratic system, focusing upon two features in particular. First, the inward-looking procedural preoccupations of a bureaucratic organisation, continuously struggling to find a sense of direction amidst a dense foliage of regulations, would be overcome by the setting, in consultation with external bodies, of tangible and realisable objectives to guide action. Secondly, the hierarchy of objectives would extend from the force mandate down to the more concrete level of subdivisional priorities, and the establishment and maintenance of this would be expedited by a continuous management cycle of planning, organising, implementing and evaluating, with all organisational tiers participating. PBO, in short, offered the prospect of a more rational pursuit of legitimate aims within a more harmonious climate of internal relations, which recognised the important contribution to be made to the policy process at all levels.

While the conceptual vocabulary and the detailed vision of PBO may have been modified over the years, it is unquestionable that the general aim of developing a more effective and methodical system for identifying and monitoring organisational aims and achievements within a less centralized decision-making structure has gradually attained a higher profile. Since the early application of the Conservative government's Financial Management Initiative to the police (Home Office Circular, 114/1983) in order to secure closer monitoring of the efficiency with which resources were deployed, a formidable range of bodies including the Home Office and Treasury (Treasury, 1992), HM Inspectorate of Constabulary (Woodcock, 1991), the National Audit Office (1991) and the Audit Commission (Davies, 1990) have encouraged the development of the new framework of managerial accountability. By 1989, all forces in England and Wales could report some interest in PBO-type ideas (Ackroyd and Helliwell, 1991). In its Plus Programme launched that year, the Metropolitan Police committed itself to a major programme of change, the internal components of which included the establishment of more effective performance indicators and a fundamental review of command structure, the organisation of specialist support systems, and the effectiveness of rewards, sanctions and communications systems (Rose, 1990). Such developments have been echoed in many provincial forces. Since the adoption of the Inspectorate's Matrix of Police Indicators in 1987 and the development of its support staff and regional structure and enhancement of its own leadership profile, forces have been obliged to provide more rigorous evidence of their efficiency and effectiveness in meeting specified objectives (Reiner, 1991b, Chapter 2). Also, several have adopted a simplified organisational structure and a flatter command pyramid, with the divisional level replaced or modified and a significant devolution of managerial and financial responsibility to local command units (Audit Commission, 1991; HMCIC, 1991, p. 12 and 1992, p. 14; Hilliard, 1992). Against this substantial backdrop many of the recommendations of the Inquiry into Police Responsibilities and Rewards under the direction of Sir Patrick Sheehy, with its remit to consider rank structure, pay arrangements, working patterns and career development, appear not as radically innovatory but merely as the next stage in an incremental reappraisal and reform of the basic tenets of the bureaucratic control system (Campbell, 1992a; Police, 1992).

Do these changes promise a new synthesis of care and control in the police organisation, and a sophisticated means of matching a high level of internal cohesion and efficiency with a developed sense of responsibility to its public audience? While it would be imprudent to form a conclusive judgement in a period of considerable flux, all three areas of potential difficulty identified above raise doubts about the likely direction of present trends.

In the first place, the legacy of a strong instrumental culture has proven hard to displace. Reforms of the training system to promote greater awareness of alternative management philosophies are dismissed by some students, either in advance or in

retrospective disillusionment, as a somewhat fragile set of exhortations mounted against the prevailing current of organisational practice (Walker, 1991, Chapter 8). Apparently more
robust 'system' reforms may fare little better. For instance, the
service's own *Operational Policing Review* concluded in 1990 that
beneath the institutional façade there had developed scant
commitment to the rationalistic, participative ethos of PBO
(Joint Consultative Committee, 1990). Likewise, a survey of
Metropolitan officers almost two years after the introduction of
the Plus Programme revealed the familiar litany of complaints
from the shop floor directed against management as too distant,
slow to praise, insufficiently supportive and unwilling to consult (Judge, 1991, p. 4). Further, it has been averred that even
at senior command level enthusiasm for Plus has in many cases
been distinctly tepid (Judge, 1991, p. 5).

A number of factors may underlie the relative impotence of
the caring reforms of a normative culture to break the self-
perpetuating cycle of instrumentalism. Having subscribed to
them throughout their career, some officers may be unwilling to
jettison the values implicit in the military–bureaucratic model.
They may feel that, on account of the changing attitudes of
recruits and earlier relaxations of internal controls, discipline
has already declined to a critical level (Reiner, 1991b, p. 244).
Indeed, as noted earlier, they may equate the growth of an
alternative normative culture with its more pathological manifestations in recent high-profile scandals (Roach, 1992). Less
nobly, as beneficiaries of its impressive fund of instrumental
resources, they may have a vested interest in maintaining intact
the prevailing bureaucratic system (Walker, 1991, Chapter 8).

Alternatively, even if not personally opposed to reform, some
officers may be wary of the motives of the initiators and agents
of the new managerialism. Paradoxically, as demonstrated by
the negative reaction of the Police Federation to recent sugges-
tions in favour of an 'officer class' as a logical extension of fast
streaming (Reiner, 1991b, p. 34), one unintended consequence
of a new managerialist approach committed to its own distinctive ideology, discourse and career structure may be to exacer-
bate the very gap between ranks and subcultures which it seeks
to bridge (Holdaway, 1986). In turn, incomprehension may
shade into cynicism. Like the military–bureaucratic approach,

the new managerialism has an ideological as well as a functional significance (Reiner, 1992a, pp. 43–5). Its espousal sends a message to external audiences that the quality of management personnel and practice is the key to improving the effectiveness and probity of contemporary policing, and by inference, that more radical political solutions need not be entertained. Awareness of this may persuade some insiders that for many of its exponents the new managerialism is only window-dressing, disguising an abiding commitment to a more traditional command orientation. Whatever the reasons for suspicion of the sponsors of the new managerialism, this may be heightened by the fact that within a predominantly instrumental regime the structural mechanisms associated with apparently normative reforms may be exploited to reinforce rather than transform the existing balance of power. PBO and similar approaches retain a fundamentally top-down model of policy making, and although greater consultation and participation is promised, the more exacting system of performance monitoring which informs the new policy process may erode the traditional capacity of junior ranks to defend their autonomy through controlling information about the conduct of operations (Walker, 1991, Chapter 11).

A second difficulty associated with present reforms is that, despite their normative underpinnings, they may simply be inappropriate to the nature of police work, and so may provide inadequate vehicles for any change in management philosophy and practice. Again, PBO-type reforms provide the main focus for criticism (Waddington, 1986a and 1986b; Walker *et al.*, 1987; Johnson, 1988). It has been argued that an activity as diverse and demand-led as policing is not amenable to clarification and classification in terms of separate objectives. Further, the process of quantification required to measure attainment of objectives is ill-adapted to policing. It ignores the fact that the value of much police work is symbolic – providing general reassurance of society's commitment to orderly values – and so not easily subjected to tangible measures. It also fails to acknowledge that even those aspirations which can be measured, such as reductions in crime and public disorder, are the outcome of such complexly overdetermined social processes that it is impossible to isolate the significance of the policing input.

While it might be conceded that too rigid and unreflexive an application of PBO methods could result in the misrepresentation, and ultimately, the misdirection of the policing enterprise, the basic thrust behind the effort to subject police performance to accurate measurement and rational critique can still be defended as essentially worthwhile (Davies, 1992). The issue then becomes one of whether the new methodology can be successfully harnessed to the particular demands of policing. At this point we begin to intrude upon the third area of difficulty, since the precise pattern of development of the substantive policies associated with the new managerialism is largely dependent upon broader socio-political considerations.

In this regard, it has recently been argued by a long-time exponent of PBO that rational management and performance appraisal techniques in the police service have reached an important crossroads (Butler, 1992a and 1992b). One available course of action, supported by the police staff associations themselves in their 1990 Statement of Common Purpose and Values and subsequent Strategic Policy Document on Quality of Service, and also by the Inspectorate, is to develop methodologies for promoting and assessing service quality and consumer satisfaction. The other route, championed most prominently by the Audit Commission, is to develop methodologies for promoting and assessing productivity and value-for-money. The former route, with its emphasis upon qualitative rather than quantitative indices, and upon effectiveness as well as efficiency, would appear to be more closely attuned with both public and professional conceptions of the nature of police work. It is also, therefore, the route by which rational management techniques are most likely to succeed in promoting a more normative culture within the service. However, whether the qualitative approach will in practice prevail in the long run or at least be developed in synthesis with the quantitative approach is difficult to foretell. Certainly, the present trend is towards a closer working relationship between the Inspectorate, the Audit Commission and other agencies concerned with the finessing of police performance indicators, and a consequently increasing cross-fertilisation of ideas (HMCIC, 1992, pp. 14–15; Weatheritt, 1993, forthcoming). On the other hand, it may be argued that this policy trend is but one manifestation of the 'new public management' (Hood, 1991) currently fostered at the highest level of government, most notably through the Citizen's Charter, and that it shares with the latter a failure to appreciate and address adequately the tension between quality of service goals and financial efficiency, opting instead merely to hedge its bets in seeking to accommodate a strong version of both.

Finally, and compounding this uncertainty, there is a broader sense in which the volatile socio-political environment of policing bears upon the prospects of a more prosperous balance between care and control dimensions in internal relations. The 'golden age' of the immediate postwar period when the police enjoyed high levels of public legitimacy and were rarely embroiled in controversy has long gone (Reiner, 1992b, Chapter 2). Historically, the police have been given an 'impossible mandate' (Manning, 1971), required to deal with intractable social problems using only the limited means allowed them by law, but it is only in recent years that the police institution has been sufficiently demystified for awareness of the extent of the gulf between ideal and reality to begin to seep through to the collective public conscience. An increase in police scandals and an apparent declining capacity to deliver effectively in terms of crime prevention and detection, married to a public culture which has grown generally less deferential to powerful social institutions, have gradually eroded confidence in the police (Reiner, 1991a).

Accordingly, the overarching question about the future direction of policing towards the end of the present century is whether the process of demystification will continue apace until the police are squarely settled on 'a much lower pedestal' (Reiner, 1991a) with a more modest but attainable mandate to pursue. Alternatively, it may be that an attempt will be made to regain the symbolic 'high ground' and repair the police's image as sacred guardians of the moral essence of society, which previously served to obscure the profane reality of their daily grind. If the former option is pursued, transparency and feasibility will be the ordering principles of the new settlement. The achievement of acceptable levels of legitimacy will depend upon the degree of candour with which the problems of policing are publicly exposed and the success of attempts, through rational management techniques, to attain realistic objectives. If the latter option is pursued, the need for assiduous impression management will continue to inform police actions and decisions before an increasingly demanding and sceptical public audience. Ideological considerations will hold sway, and may outweigh functional considerations in decisions concerning the retention and development of particular organisational structures and policies. Rather than a genuine attempt to provide an optimal balance for the generation of efficient, effective and harmonious internal relations, the sponsorship of a broad range of both instrumental and normative management techniques might simply reflect pressures to supply ever more elaborate external proof of a well-oiled internal engine. The danger then exists of regulatory overkill, where the sheer scale of the exercise cancels out any benefits which might otherwise have been derived from the substance and relative weighting of care and control measures.

Of course, such a pessimistic scenario may not unfold. It is, nevertheless, worth bearing in mind that even if it is generally recognised that the better long-term future for the police lies in the first option, as a mundane institution perceived in a more 'matter-of-fact' manner (Reiner, 1991a, p. 236), policy makers often lack the luxury of a long-term perspective or a clean slate on which to develop it. Legitimacy is, above all, an issue in the here and now, and must be sustained against immediate problems with the tools closest to hand. Accordingly, if both the military–bureaucratic model and the new managerialism have nurtured useful myths about the integrity and effectiveness of police organisations, there will be a reluctance to upset these assumptions by discarding their supporting structures. Further, if a particular short-term crisis can be defused by resort to one type of solution, then considerations of overall balance and volume in the regulatory system are unlikely to prevent this. In this regard, it will be instructive to monitor how the politics of police policy making unfold in the near future as problems of legitimacy and associated reform agendas crowd in from various directions. Most pressingly, the government will be required to address seriously the findings of the Runciman Royal Commission on Criminal Justice, appointed in the wake of the release of the Birmingham Six in 1990. Charged with examining, *inter alia*, abuses of police investigative powers and working against a background of regular disclosure of similar malpractice, the Commission's recommendations inevitably included reforms of the legal and internal disciplinary frameworks which will increase bureaucratic controls over operational officers. Whether and how such initiatives might complement or be complemented by the broader contemporary programme of managerialist reform, including the findings of the Sheehy Inquiry and the new ACPO-inspired 'Operational Code of Ethics' (Boggan, 1992; Campbell, 1992b), is another matter and one which, in the light of their different immediate concerns, none of the various policy making communities may be inclined to consider too closely. Moreover, the White Paper on reforming the police, which is the product of the Home Office's review of the institutional structure and accountability of the police, presents further problems in terms of finding the appropriate balance of care and control functions within the service (Home Office, 1993). The thrust of the White Paper to alter the framework of *external* democratic and financial controls will also inevitably influence the care and control orientations of actors *within* the police organisation (Travis, 1993; see also Stephens and Becker, Chapter 10, in this volume). At least in the short-term, therefore, British police organisations can expect to face an ever more demanding and diverse set of external regulatory pressures. In light of this, it will be no surprise if for the foreseeable future they continue to display schizophrenic symptoms in the way that they conduct their internal relations.

Bibliography

Ackroyd, S. and Helliwell, C. (1991) 'What Happened to Objectives?', *Policing*, 7, 132–43.

Ainsworth, P. B. and Pease, K. (1987) *Police Work* (London and New York: Methuen).

Argyris, C. (1968) 'Organisation: Effectiveness' in *International Encyclopaedia of the Social Sciences*, vol. 2 (New York: Wiley).

Audit Commission (1991) *Reviewing the Organisation of Provincial Police Forces*, Audit Commission Police Papers, No.9, February.

Bittner, E. (1967) 'The Police on Skid Row: A Study of Peace-keeping', *American Sociological Review*, 32, 699–715.

Bittner, E. (1971) *The Functions of the Police in Modern Society* (Washington D.C.: U.S. Government Printing Office).

Bittner, E. (1974) 'Florence Nightingale in Pursuit of Willie Sutton: A Theory of the Police' in H. Jacob (ed.) *Potential for Reform in Criminal Justice* (Beverly Hills: Sage), 11–44.

Boggan, S. (1992) 'Police Draw Up Code Of Ethics', *The Independent*, 13 August.

Bradley, D., Walker, N. and Wilkie, R. (1986) *Managing The Police: Law, Organisation and Democracy* (Brighton: Harvester).

Brogden, M., Jefferson, T. and Walklate, S. (1988) *Introducing Police Work* (London: Unwin Hyman).

Burns, T. (1981) *A Comparative Study of Administrative Structure and Organizational Processes in Selected Areas of the National Health Service* (SSRC Report HRP.6725).

Butler, A. J. P. (1984) *Police Management* (Aldershot: Gower).

Butler, A. J. P. (1992a) 'Developing Quality Assurance in Police Services', *Public Money and Management*, Jan–March, 23–7.

Butler, A. J. P. (1992b) 'Police and the Citizen's Charter', *Policing*, 8, 40–50.

Cain, M. (1973) *Society and the Policeman's Role* (London: RKP).

Campbell, D. (1992a) 'Clarke to Modernise Police Role', *The Guardian*, 21 May.

Campbell, D. (1992b) 'Ethics Code Launch Upsets Police Union', *The Guardian*, 9 December.

Chatterton, M. (1979) 'The Supervision of Patrol Work under the Fixed Points System' in S. Holdaway (ed.) *The British Police* (London: Edward Arnold) pp. 83–101.

Chatterton, M. (1987) 'Front-line Supervision in the British Police Service' in G. Gaskell and R. Benewick (eds) *The Crowd in Contemporary Britain* (London: Sage) pp. 123–54.

Christopher Commission (1991) *Report of the Independent Commission* (Los Angeles).

Davies, H. (1990) 'Effectiveness through Delegation', *Policing*, 6, 596–606.

Davies, H. (1992) *Fighting Leviathan: Building Social Markets That Work* (London: Social Market Foundation).

Dunne, J. G. (1991) 'Law and Disorder in LA: Part Two', *New York Review of Books*, 38, 17, 24 October, 58–66.

Dworkin, R. (1978) *Taking Rights Seriously*, rev. edn (New York: Wiley).

Friedrich, C. J. (1937) *Constitutional Government and Politics* (New York: Harper and Brothers).

Galbraith, J. K. (1992) *The Culture of Contentment* (London: Sinclair-Stevenson).

Gambetta, D. (1988) 'Can We Trust Trust?' in D. Gambetta (ed.) *Trust: Making and Breaking Co-operative Relations* (Oxford: Blackwell) pp. 213–37.

Gouldner, A. (1965) *Wildcat Strike* (New York: Harper).

Grimshaw, R. and Jefferson, T. (1987) *Interpreting Police work: Policy and Practice in Forms of Beat Policing* (London: Allen & Unwin).

Harris, R. N. (1973) *The Police Academy: An Inside View* (New York: Wiley).

Hilliard, B. (1992) 'Local Heroes', *Police Review*, 7 February, 258–59.

HMCIC (1991) *Report of Her Majesty's Chief Inspector of Constabulary for the year 1990*, HC 412, (1990–91) (London: HMSO).

HMCIC (1992) *Report of Her Majesty's Chief Inspector of Constabulary for the year 1991*, HC 21, (1991–92) (London: HMSO).

Hobbs, D. (1988) *Doing The Business: Entrepreneurship, the Working Class, and Detectives in the East End of London* (Oxford: Oxford University Press).

Holdaway, S. (1977) 'Changes in Urban Policing', *British Journal of Sociology*, 28, 119–37.

Holdaway, S. (1986) 'The Holloway Incident', *Policing*, 2, 101–13.

Home Affairs Committee (1989) *Higher Police Training and the Police Staff College*, Third report 1988–89, HC 110, (London: HMSO).

Home Affairs Committee (1991) *Police Sickness*, Fifth report, 1990–91, HC 370, (London: HMSO).

Home Office (1993) *Police Reform. A Police Service for the Twenty-First Century*, Cm 2281 (London: HMSO).

Hood, C. (1991) 'A Public Management for All Seasons?', *Public Administration*, 69, 3–20.

Johnson, L. (1988) 'Controlling Police Work: Problems of Organisational Reform in Large Public Bureaucracies', *Work, Employment and Society*, 2, 51–70.

Joint Consultative Committee (1990) *Operational Policing Review* (Surbiton: Police Federation).

Jones, J. M. (1980) *Organisational Aspects of Police Behaviour* (Farnborough: Gower).

Jones, S. and Levi, M. (1983) 'The Police and the Majority: The Neglect of the Obvious?', *The Police Journal*, 56, 351–64.

Judge, T. (1991) 'The Ivory Tower', *Police*, 23, 6, 4–5.

Kaye, T. (1991) *Unsafe and Unsatisfactory: Report of the Independent Inquiry into the working practices of the West Midlands Police Serious Crime Squad* (London: The Civil Liberties Trust).

Kinsey, R., Lea, J. and Young, J. (1986) *Losing the Fight Against Crime* (Oxford: Blackwell).

Kirby, T. (1992) 'Detectives to escape charges', *The Independent*, 20 May.

Lipsky, M. (1980) *Street-Level Bureaucracy: Dilemmas of the Individual in Public Services* (New York: Russell Sage).

Luhmann, N. (1979) *Trust and Power* (Chichester and New York: Wiley).

Manning, P. K. (1971) 'The Police: Mandate, Strategies and Appearances' in J. D. Douglas (ed.) *Crime and Justice in American Society* (Indianapolis: Bobbs-Merrill) pp. 149–93.

Manning, P. K. (1977) *Police Work: The Social Organization of Policing* (Cambridge, Mass.: MIT Press).

Marenin, O. (1982) 'Parking Tickets and Class Repression: The Concept of Policing in Critical Theories of Criminal Justice', *Contemporary Crises*, 6, 241–66.

Maslach, C. and Jackson, S. (1979) 'Burned-out Cops and Their Families', *Psychology Today*, 12, 26–40.

Meyer, J. M. and Rowan, B. (1977) 'Institutionalized Organizations: Formal Structure as Myth and Ceremony', *American Journal of Sociology*, 83, 340–63.

Michels, R. (1962) *Political Parties* (New York: Free Press).

National Audit Office (1991) *Promoting Value for Money in Provincial Police Forces*, Report by the Comptroller and Auditor General, HC 349, 1990–91 (London: HMSO).

O'Byrne, M. (1991) 'Scrap the Discipline Code', *Police Review*, 15, November, 2286–7.

Parker, K. A. L. (1990) 'The Police Service After the War: Structure and Administration', *Public Administration*, 68, 453–76.

Police (1992) 'Editorial: The Five Just Men?', *Police*, 24, July, 4.

Punch, M. (1981) *Management and Control of Organizations: Occupational Deviance, Responsibility And Accountability* (Leiden/Antwerp: Stenfert Kroese).

Punch, M. (1985) *Conduct Unbecoming* (London: Tavistock).

Reiner, R. (1991a) 'A Much Lower Pedestal', *Policing*, 7, 225–38.

Reiner, R. (1991b) *Chief Constables* (Oxford: Oxford University Press).

Reiner, R. (1992a) 'Fin de siècle Blues: The Police Face the Millennium', *The Political Quarterly*, 63, 37–49.

Reiner, R. (1992b) *The Politics of The Police* (Brighton: Wheatsheaf).

Reuss-Ianni, E. and Ianni, F. (1983) 'Street Cops and Management Cops: The Two Cultures of Policing' in M. Punch (ed.) *Control in the Police Organization* (Cambridge, Mass.: MIT Press) pp. 251–74.

Roach, L. (1992) 'Salute for Democracy', *Police Review*, 1 April, 637–9.

Rose, D. (1990) 'Forces of change', *The Guardian*, 21 February.

Scarman. The Rt. Hon. The Lord (1981) *The Brixton Disorders, 10–12 April, 1981: Report of an Inquiry by the Rt. Hon. The Lord Scarman, OBE* (London: HMSO).

Sennett, R. (1980) *Authority* (New York: Random House).

Sherman, L. (1983) 'After the Riots: Police and Minorities in the US 1970–1980' in N. Glazer and K. Young (eds) *Ethnic Pluralism and Public Policy* (London: Heinemann) pp. 212–35.

Stephens, M. (1988) *Policing: The Critical Issues* (Brighton: Wheatsheaf).

Strauss, A., Schatzman, L., Bucher, R., Ehrlich, D. and Satshin, M. (1963) 'The Hospital and its Negotiated Order' in E. Friedson (ed.) *The Hospital in Modern Society* (Chicago: Free Press) pp. 147–69.

Symposium on Higher Police Training (1990) *The Howard Journal*, 29, 199–219.

Travis, A. (1993) 'Clarke Winning Fight Over Police Revamp', *The Guardian*, 23 January.

Treasury (1992) *Minute on the Eighth Report from the Committee of Public Accounts 1991–92*, Cm 1856 (London: HMSO).

Van Maanen, J. (1983) 'The Boss: First-Line Supervision in an American Police Agency' in M. Punch (ed.) *Control in the Police Organisation* (Cambridge, Mass.: MIT Press) pp. 275–317.

Waddington, P. A. J. (1986a) 'Defining Objectives', *Policing*, 2, 17–25.

Waddington, P. A. J. (1986b) 'The "Objectives" Debate', *Policing*, 2, 225–34.

Walker, N. (1991) *Police Culture and Organisation* (PhD thesis, Glasgow: University of Strathclyde).

Walker, N., Bradley, D. and Wilkie R. (1987) 'Beyond Managing By Objectives', *Policing*, 3, 68–74.

Weatheritt, M. (1993 forthcoming) 'Measuring Police Performance: Accounting or Accountability?' in R. Reiner and S. Spencer (eds), *Police Decision-Making and Accountability* (London: Institute for Public Policy Research).

Woodcock, J. (1991) 'Overturning Police Culture', *Policing*, 7, 172–82.

Wrong, D. (1979) *Power: Its Forms, Bases and Uses* (Oxford: Blackwell).

3

Recruitment, Race and the Police Subculture

Simon Holdaway

Police Cultures – Care and Control

> ... nations stumble upon establishments which are indeed the result of human action, but not the execution of any human design. (Ferguson, 1767)

Sociology includes the study of unintended consequences of action. This is no less the case for the sociological study of the police than it is for the study of any other institution. An unintended consequence of placing more officers on foot patrol in response to perceived public need to allay fear of disorder, for example, can lead to more opportunities for people to report incidents of crime and disorder and a consequential inflation of recorded crime rates. Similarly, police commitment to and involvement in youth work founded on service to the public may lead to a perceived and actual but unintended increase of the control of young people and feelings of distrust among them. In many different areas of policing it is possible for a sociologist to describe and analyse the unpredictable flux and flow of change.

From this perspective, sociology is primarily diagnostic rather than prescriptive. It would be a foolhardy sociologist indeed who attempted to predict the consequences of policy changes implemented on the basis of research findings. This is not to say that sociology cannot and in the past has not successfully been prescriptive but, rather, to remind us that human creativity (and intransigence), thankfully rears its head in imaginative ways. We can envisage some but not all the consequences of change.

Creativity and adaptation to change within organisations, resistance being just one of its manifestations, can be fostered and supported by the values and related strategies of action that are held dear by groups of people sharing similar interests. The shared, core values and related strategies and tactics of police work accepted by officers working in urban Britain – the so-called occupational culture – remains such a source of support. Institutional change is therefore never one-directional but always moulded through the assumptions that are lodged in the minds of those who implement policies in their day-to-day work, whether it be concerned with management or another type of activity. There are now within the literature of the sociology of the police various studies of the ways in which the rank and file have moulded policies based on variant values and ideas about the objectives of police work so that they accord with their own preferences (Chatterton, 1979; Manning, 1980; McConville *et al.*, 1991; Holdaway, 1979 and 1991).

In 1974, as part of a wider study of the police occupational culture, I documented the work of members of a small, plain clothes squad of officers who patrolled an inner city area (James, 1979). The squad's brief was to arrest people committing street robberies ('muggings' in popular language), and snatch-thefts and to do so after the observation of streets and other locations where the offences were occurring. This meant that members of the squad had to spend long periods of time in unmarked vans while, from their perspective, little or nothing happened.

In the meantime some robberies occurred in other streets that were not under observation and the victims of the crimes consistently reported that their assailants were young black men. Nevertheless, the officers were told by the superintendent in charge of them that they were to remain in their observational positions because they would eventually witness an offence and so secure the evidence necessary to obtain a sure conviction. This was a strategy that contrasted with the officers' preferred *modus operandi* of stopping black youths in streets near to the location of an offence and questioning them about their movements in the hope of getting some relevant verbal or other evidence to secure a confession of guilt.

The superintendent's brief was very soon changed as it was put into action by the squad. Observation vans became, in a sense, emergency vehicles, responding to 999 calls by speeding through the streets to many different types of incidents. Officers from the squad began to arrest offenders for all manner of offences. Black youths were stopped and in some cases brought to the station for questioning about robberies. These were the unintended consequences of attempting to change the ways in which the squad's members routinely worked, of attempting to change the way they preferred to work. The officers changed their mandate to harmonise with the values and strategies of the police occupational culture, which supported them and validated their actions as, from their point of view, they commonsensically translated policy as it is written into policy as it is put into action. The unintended consequences of senior officers' action led to a very different style of policing from the one they anticipated.

There are many factors that need to be taken into account if a full explanation of the reasons for the squad's change of senior officers' directives is undertaken. However, one long-standing lesson from research about many aspects of policing is evident from this example. Formal organisational rules, enshrined in law, policy or some other prescriptive, managerial instrument, are changed as they are used within the context of policing the streets. Studies of police training, the use of information technology, the handling of 'domestic disputes' and the implementation of the Police and Criminal Evidence Act indicate that the ideas and associated actions that inform the practice of routine policing are at least as important and at most the key determinant of how an officer will act when dealing with a situation (Fielding, 1988; Chatterton, 1989; Manning, 1988; Hanmer, 1989; McConville *et al.*, 1991).

A clear objective can be written into any prescriptive directive but it is not safe to assume that the same clarity of purpose will be affirmed by those who implement it. The views of many senior officers about the purpose of police work and how it should be practised are rather different from those found among the ranks. Summing up his study of police socialisation, Nigel Fielding makes clear an implication of this point: '. . . no reform can hope to succeed that does not enlist the support of the ordinary constables who construct the reality of the policing we experience' (Fielding, 1988, p. 205).

A Caring Police Service

Since the 1981 riots in Brixton, police reform has certainly been at the forefront of a good number of chief constables' minds. Although there is evidence to demonstrate that the trend is far from secure (Reiner, 1992), a number of younger chief officers, and a smaller number of older ones, are developing policies that emphasise service and care rather than force and control as the key notes of their work. The Commissioner of the Metropolis, for example, now formally commands (or manages, more like), the Metropolitan Police *Service*. The Met's Plus Programme followed a report from a management consultancy firm that concluded the force should 'feel more united', 'be clearer about what it is there for', 'improve leadership and management systems' and 'become less defensive and isolated' (Metropolitan Police, 1992, p. 2). Echoing Fielding's words, the introduction to the publicly available literature about the Plus Programme, which incorporates the various elements of reform, puts it that:

> These are not superficial issues. They call into question many of the fundamental ways we have been doing things. They give a very clear signal that we must change. But change is a very difficult process. It takes a long time. To be effective it must involve everyone – involvement which shares the reasons for change, the process that is being undertaken, the recognition and praise as results are achieved. The ultimate aim of this process of change is to improve the level of service we provide to the public. (Metropolitan Police, 1992, p. 2)

Senior officers in many police forces where the 'total quality' management perspective has been adopted would endorse these sentiments. However, although senior officers who are developing policies based on this and other, similar managerial systems will feel confident about the outcome of their plans, there is always the likelihood that, from their perspective, unintended consequences of action will be realised. Many of these unintended consequences will be shaped as proposals for change meander through the commonsensical assumptions of the ranks' occupational culture. Here the dominant notions of policing as action, as challenge, as concerned with crime, of people as unworthy of trust, of the need to keep at bay the encroachments of societal disorder will translate managerial intentions into rather different outcomes.

The entrenched ideas of the rank and file differ from those of many chief officers appointed within the last five years. Offering service to and nurturing care of the public are at the centre of their reforms. Their ideas are in tension and conflict with the ranks' view that places direct crime control by the police and force rather than persuasion centre stage. There is little evidence of a corporate culture within any of the 43 constabularies in England and Wales. A definition of 'real' police work is highly contestable.

Ideas about service to the public, about conciliation as the objective of dispute settling, about offering help to people in difficult and vulnerable situations, about minimal intervention, and more, are found in the vocabulary and actions of the ranks. It is rather too easy, and in part the fault of those of us who have written about the occupational culture as if it is one-dimensional, to characterise the hedonism, crime-searching and arrest-seeking aspects of the occupational culture to the neglect of features that could be called those of 'care' (Holdaway, 1989). Police officers practice a variety of styles of policing.

Further, although care and service can amount to the exercise of control this is not always the case. The complexity of policing means that in many situations officers take action that at first sight appears to be based on control but in fact is established on service and care. It is all too easy to equate arrests as straightforward examples of police control. I have in mind situations like that where a man who has committed a minor assault on his partner is taken into custody because she and their children are protected from their vulnerable position by this kind of intervention. The arrest and crime control focus of the occupational culture could in this situation offer care and service to others (see Bittner, 1967; Kemp *et al.*, 1992).

A decision about whether or not police action in a particular situation amounts to care or control is, therefore, by no means straightforward. The most careful analysis has to be made of the meaning of situations and of related actions to police officers, victims of crime, complainants and others before the reasons for particular interventions and outcomes from them can be understood. Notwithstanding these points the *emphasis* on control and force is paramount within the occupational culture.

Service and Care – Definitions

A definition of police service or care as opposed to control is very difficult to formulate. One feature of it would be that an officer dealing with a situation where police action is requested or required attempts to appreciate the constraints that limit opportunities for people to take an alternative course of action. In the case of a domestic assault, for example, a police policy and practice based on service will among other points emphasise the view that the power of women is less than that of men and that the financial and other resources available to move from home are likely to be very limited, and so on. To offer a service is in the first instance to understand the context within which someone who asks for police intervention is acting. Furthermore, it is to understand that within a public service like the police, not least when much of its authority and power are vested in the law, an officer's actions can have wider, serious repercussions that reflect on the police as an institution located within a particular social structure. The so-called isolated domestic assault is committed within societal boundaries. The ways in which such incidents are handled symbolise and instrumentally reconstruct the structural position of women within contemporary Britain. To deal with 'domestics' in innovative ways by offering a service – that may indeed involve an arrest and subsequent restriction of liberty – is to reconstruct and thereby change the structures of constraint that limit the opportunities open to women who are disadvantaged. The change may be minimal but it is change nevertheless. The occupational culture of the rank and file tends to orientate officers to their own rather than 'client-defined' definitions of need and appropriate action. The shorthand recipes for appropriate action found in the occupational culture do not encourage the more reflective, analytical appreciation to which I have alluded (see Chapter 6 in this volume by Susan Edwards).

There is a further aspect to this point that has raised important, largely unexplored questions for researchers. This is about the extent to which wider social structures of inequality constrain police action. Women are vulnerable to physical harm inflicted by men rather than teenagers or whoever. Large-scale structures of social inequality establish this context within which men can control women more readily than women can control men. It would be remarkable if male police officers were not to some extent also influenced by these transcendent structures of gender and therefore worked from the view that we live in a world where to some extent men will dominate women.

This does not mean that all is rosy for the sociologist with an interest in policing and gender relations. A reading of the social structural position of women cannot straightforwardly tell us why an officer has acted in a particular way when dealing with a domestic assault. Social structures are always in flux and flow, dynamic therefore, and open to change (Berger and Luckmann, 1966). There are, nevertheless, flexible social structural boundaries that frame the manner in which officers can resolve conflict. The occupational culture is not free-standing but part of a wider social structure. The meaning of police care and control is not infinitely malleable.

Race Issues

Police service and care is not just confined to people who are in trouble, seek information or whatever; it is not confined to relationships between the police and the public that it serves as officers move out from their organisation into a wider public terrain. There is now a view that the composition of the police workforce, for example, should in some way reflect the ethnic diversity of British society. This perspective will enable constabularies to offer a more sensitive service to minority ethnic groups, to foster an appreciative view of the context within which the members of these groups are situated and so improve the quality of their relationships with them (Scarman, 1981; Home Office, 1982). Addressing a conference on equal opportunities in the police service, the chair of the Commission for Racial Equality, Michael Day, reminded officers that they had made little progress in this area and that 'fuller involvement of ethnic minorities and women enhances the quality of policing that a force would provide' (*The Guardian*, 1992). This is an attractive proposition to a number of chief officers who realise that tense relationships with black and Asian people present them with one of the most difficult problems they face.

An improvement in the quality of police service is just one of a number of objectives to justify efforts to recruit people from minority ethnic groups into the police. Another is the realisation of equality of access of all citizens to police employment, irrespective of its consequences. Another is more symbolic and 'political'. When black and Asian people are recruited they demonstrate a high level of confidence in the police in particular and British society in general. A cynical variant of this view is that the image of the police is enhanced when black and Asian officers are seen on the streets. And another version is that 'ethnics' do not have the qualifications to enter the police so standards are lowered to let them in.

All of these opinions and more can be found among serving police officers. The former views tend to be the currency of senior officers, the latter of the ranks. Their intention to recruit from minority ethnic groups may be to increase the quality of service or to improve equality of access to employment. An unintended consequence of the same action may be to raise questions about tolerance towards black and Asian potential colleagues within the police workforce. The rank and file have rather different views about minority ethnic recruitment than the senior officers who have developed policy.

As recruitment policy is implemented within a constabulary, the commonsense assumptions about the ways in which black and Asian people are addressed and discussed may not change, and the routine use of racist language may lead a number of recent black and Asian recruits to resign. In the longer term this situation may, on the one hand, lead to a spoiling of senior officers' well-constructed and well-intentioned recruitment drives targeted on minority ethnic groups and, on the other, raise the racial consciousness of those black and Asian officers who remain in police service and mould them into a group with shared and recognised characteristics and interests. Black and Asian officers then become a politicised group within the police.

Recruiting from Minority Ethnic Groups

Studies of the police occupational culture have revealed the prevalence of racist language as routine (Smith and Gray, 1985; Holdaway, 1983). During a study of black and Asian officers working in seven constabularies, it was found that they frequently faced racist banter from colleagues and, before applying to a force, prejudice from future colleagues was cited most frequently as the factor that may prevent recruitment from their ethnic groups. Over half the officers interviewed in this study said that they had been the subject of racist name-calling, which they accepted as part of the general banter of canteen conversation (Wilson *et al.*, 1984).

In their study of the Metropolitan Police, Smith and Gray observed over a period of time how six constables of Afro-Caribbean origin were treated by colleagues: 'Overall, it is clear that for most black and brown people, being a police officer puts them under considerable strain. They have to take abuse from the public and put up with racialist language and jokes from their colleagues, and they are subject to a conflict of loyalties' (Smith and Gray, 1985, p. 154).

More generally, black and Asian people have been found to have less confidence in the police than their white peers, but the evidence does not indicate a general rejection. Black youths, for example, seem more critical of the police than their elders. Gaskell found that a sample of black youths living in inner city boroughs held generally positive views towards British society. They nevertheless also held consistently critical views of the police (Gaskell and Smith, 1981). In a recent survey in the Metropolitan Police area – a so-called customer survey – it was found that black people were markedly less satisfied than white people when asked about the service offered to them by the police. Levels of satisfaction, however, tended to be high for both groups (Research Services, 1990). Black and Asian people's views of the police are therefore somewhat varied, but the general conclusion to be drawn from the available evidence is one of an attitude characterised by reservation rather than either clear support or contempt.

Within this setting senior officers need to do all they can to monitor the consequences of their policy making and implementation. In particular they need to weigh the effects of the occupational culture on policies like those concerned with recruiting black and Asian people.

To explore this issue data from two projects about the recruitment of black and Asian people into the police will be discussed. The first was conducted in 1984, the second in 1988. During the 1988 project, which will be given most attention, intensive research was completed in three forces where the rationale underpinning strategies to recruit from minority ethnic groups was diverse, but based on the notion that the police workforce should in some sense be representative of the general population. Service to the public is thereby reflected in the representation of the dominant minority ethnic groups within the police ranks. Recruitment from minority ethnic groups, black and Asian groups in particular, was in this sense indicative of police service *per se*.

Over a decade ago Lord Scarman argued that special resources should be allocated to secure recruitment from minority ethnic groups.

> At a time when there is no difficulty in attracting well-qualified white recruits, it may appear an unnecessary use of resources to engage in such a drive. But securing a police force fairly representative of the community as a whole requires that the effort be made. (Scarman, 1981, p. 77)

In one force a year-long recruitment drive involving media presentations, street-to-street leafleting campaigns, the planned use of a recruitment caravan, school visits and many other activities was sustained with considerable vigour. In another, similar initiatives were introduced and in addition an excellent access course was offered to potential recruits from all ethnic groups. The third force had undertaken some planned initiatives in a rather half-hearted way but their intention to recruit black and Asian people into their ranks was nevertheless clear. These recruitment initiatives, at least those in two of the forces, had the clear, public commitment of the chief constable. The recruiting officer had a plan to pursue and an outcome to realise. From their perspective a policy for implementation was in place.

Control

Studies of the occupational culture have stressed the ranks' emphasis on and importance of control of territory and people. 'The ground' belongs to them, they possess it and have first claim to ownership. They control the area policed and the people who inhabit it. In corresponding vein, control extends to people who are stopped by the police for one reason or another: they become police property. The demeanour of people stopped is especially important, particularly in so far as it indicates to officers an assent to police control. Here a 'care and service' perspective is relegated to a secondary status: control is paramount.

When a perspective like this underpins police work, feelings of frustration about the opportunities afforded to black youth within British society feed into routine encounters with officers. Distrust and suspicion rather than hostility are their keynote. Manifest or latent racial prejudice and discrimination may enter such an encounter, linking the actions of an individual officer to wider structures of ethnic inequality. However, control, an occupational and cultural feature of policing, and racial prejudice and discrimination, which are structural features of society, intermingle to provide a framework within which an encounter between a police officer and a black youth is conducted. An explanation of what happens in such a setting has to take account of different structural layers of British society and the ways in which they vie and yield one with the other. At the practical level of policing the streets of urban Britain the police perspective is dominant and, therefore, an alternative view based on care and service, which takes into account black people's perception of the police, as far as this is possible, is trivialised. Certainly, the values of the occupational culture remain in the ascendancy.

A further consequence of the intermingling of structural relations of ethnicity and police rank and file culture for minority ethnic recruitment into the police is that any recruitment drive, policy, initiative or whatever is affected by the tenor of routine policing *and* the routine policing of black and Asian people, with its distinct racial dimensions. Although they have almost inevitably been articulated through police specialist recruiting departments, recruitment initiatives of many different types cannot be sealed and protected from the effects of work undertaken within other organisational sectors, routine patrolling being one. The success of recruitment initiatives, however it is measured, is therefore put at risk by the ways in which routine policing is conducted on the streets by the rank and file.

In my 1984 study of minority ethnic recruitment it was found that 61 per cent of the officers interviewed named prejudice from future colleagues as the factor that might prevent recruitment. Their evidence to support this view was often couched in terms of negative personal experiences of being stopped in the street or of family and friends relating such incidents. Concern about the policing of black people was also evident in the 1988 study. Recruiting caravans were used by two of the research forces for their special local recruitment campaigns and it was found that black youths went to them to make comments about the ways in which officers had dealt with them. Their concern was routine policing not recruitment.

In one of the forces a serious incident following the arrest of some black youths brought a local recruitment campaign to a standstill. A member of the recruiting staff reckoned the effects of this single incident reverberated throughout the force area and for a time damaged all recruitment work among black and Asian groups. The success of the recruitment programme, evaluated both in terms of numbers of applicants and an increased public confidence in the force, was damaged by factors outside of the control of the officers with special responsibility for it. The occupational culture – in all its complexity – was remoulding and maybe virtually negating policies and strategies for minority ethnic recruitment.

Language

Banter, derogatory personal jokes and repartee form a distinct, routine feature of rank and file culture, no matter their subject. Group cohesion, the definition of roles within the work group, the management of danger and stress and the affirmation of the primacy of the rank and file over and against senior officers and 'the public' structure the content of these linguistic exchanges.

Race has been found to be one significant subject within the language of the occupational culture and a subject of jokes and banter. Again, a linkage between wider social structures of race relations and those of the police occupational culture is evident. The articulation of structure and culture, however, is dynamic rather than one-directional. The former does not straightforwardly determine the latter.

Within this context, when during the 1984 study black and Asian officers were asked questions about their experience of police service, concern about prejudice from future colleagues was considerable as they weighed in their minds the possibility of a police career. This was not an inappropriate fear because, during the 1988 project, black and Asian officers frequently described a situation where the subject of race was a daily part of conversation in the police station. Of 30 officers interviewed, 26 said that racialist comments and jokes featured regularly in colleagues' conversation and it was found that they coped with this situation in a variety of ways.

Recruitment initiatives that are implemented within public territory therefore have to reckon with police action within the more private territory of the police station and other locations where conversation is controlled by officers. If potential recruits learn about this setting they are hardly likely to be attracted to the prospect of police employment, unless, as many do, they steel themselves to cope with the experience of racialism. A further twist to this effect of the occupational culture is the possibility, presently being researched, that those officers who, for one reason or another, are not willing or able to work within this setting resign. Constabularies that have conscientiously developed recruiting policies are therefore faced with the situation of simultaneously opening the front door of the organisation to recruits and the back door to resigners. There may then come a day when the path between entry into and exit from police employment is linked. Black and Asian people will prefer to bypass rather than take a direct route into police employment.

Consciousness of Race

Positive police recruitment policies to attract black and Asian people can have a further effect on race relations within the police workforce. For example, in the researched force where an innovative access course was introduced, the recruiting officer received many telephone calls from colleagues who complained that recruiting standards were being dropped to let 'ethnics' in. His counter was to visit virtually all police divisions in his force to tackle the issue head-on. He even offered an opportunity for critics to sit the police educational test to see if they could pass it. Black and Asian officers serving in this force, who had been recruited through routine procedures, also objected to the access course because they were concerned that it reduced standards and introduced two, different methods of entry into police employment. Consciousness of race was raised amongst officers by attempts to ameliorate some of the inequalities that stimulated the development of recruitment initiatives.

Recruiting campaigns targeted on black and Asian people therefore raise for senior officers the issue of the management of a multiracial police workforce. They raise the need for policies of positive action encompassing the difficult but necessary reform of language and action that is racially prejudicial and discriminatory and the need for an appreciation by lower ranked supervisory staff that race is a subject to be addressed when appraising and managing black and Asian officers during their routine work. There is a risk of establishing a process of diminishing returns where recruitment strategies aggravate and harden attitudes of racial prejudice amongst the workforce. Black and Asian serving officers then become increasingly sceptical and perhaps hostile to any recruiting strategies that go beyond the routine because they do not want attention drawn to their ethnic status.

Care, defined as an appreciation of the constraints that limit opportunities for alternative courses of action – taking the view of another, is as relevant to the development and implementation of policies for the police workforce and for the recruitment and retention of black and Asian officers as much as it is for the related ways in which black and Asian people are policed on the streets. The occupational culture, its core at least, tends to retain control in the ascendancy and to sustain banter and jokes as neutral rather than racially offensive. Wider structures of inequality are thereby reconstructed and perpetuated within and beyond the organisational boundaries of the police.

Change

In a recent review of an edited collection of papers about research on the police the occupational culture was described as the 'Berlin Wall of policing' (Savage, 1991). Over more than fifteen years researchers have time and again discovered, elaborated and, as one but by no means the only purpose of research, raised the importance of the occupational culture as an issue for police reform. The goal of cultural change often seems impossible. Prompted by the recent recruitment and retention of black and Asian officers, however, some uncomfortable clues about a way forward may have come to the surface. These originate from black and Asian officers' views about the ways in which they are treated by police colleagues, not white officers' views about how they are or should be regarded. In 1991 PC Singh of Nottinghamshire Constabulary took his chief constable to an industrial tribunal claiming unfair treatment and won his case. During the hearing it became clear that senior officers thought the racialist joking and banter prevalent in their force was all but part and parcel of the conditions of employment for all officers, irrespective of race. Singh's case was a rejection of that view and the successful outcome of his case a refutation of it. Other cases, particularly in the Metropolitan Police, have raised similar issues.

Taking a cue from these and other cases the Metropolitan Police has initiated its own programme of reform through the closest possible involvement of black and Asian officers in the formulation of policy. All black and Asian officers serving in the force have participated in one of a number of seminars where their experience of police employment was discussed. A control group of white officers was similarly engaged in separate discussions and the results of both groups were compared and contrasted in an official report by representatives of the black and Asian officers. A number of working parties, on discipline, culture, and so on were then established with a membership of black, white and Asian officers. Each group had a time-limited objective to produce proposals for change.

One effect of the seminars has been to change the perception of black and Asian officers that they are a small and ineffective group within their force. A network of contacts has been established which, given determination and a framework of policy and management open to change, will create a pressure group of officers who inform and, to a much greater extent than in the past, control recruitment and retention policies. A consciousness of ethnicity has been raised and affirmed amongst the Met's officers.

An alternative, heightened consciousness of race and ethnicity within the police may be dawning. Cases brought by black American police officers against their chief officers and subsequent groupings of black officers forming their own police associations led to significant changes in recruitment patterns and conditions of service (Leinen, 1984). A similar process of change may be in its infancy in Britain. If this is an impetus that has found its day we could see some interesting turbulence within the occupational culture and, indeed, among senior officers who have to manage its effects.

Occupational cultures 'live' because they are perpetuated by those who structure and restructure them within the routines of their work. Within the police the occupational culture depends on a perverse minimum of consensus amongst officers. Black and Asian officers may now challenge that consensus and so further heighten the racial elements of the occupational culture. This could lead to significant change. By taking greater control of their situation black and Asian officers may enhance care and service within police policy. And the unintended consequences of this change await our discovery.

Bibliography

Berger, P. and Luckmann, T. (1966) *The Social Construction of Reality* (London: Allen Lane).

Bittner, E. (1967) 'The Police on Skid-row: A Study of Peace-keeping', *American Sociological Review,* 32, 5, 699–715.

Chatterton, M. (1979) 'The Supervision of Patrol Work under the Fixed Points System' in S. Holdaway (ed.) *The British Police* (London: Edward Arnold) pp. 83–101.

Chatterton, M. (1989) 'Focused Policing' in R. Morgan and D. J. Smith (eds) *Coming to Terms with Policing* (London: Routledge) pp. 64–81.

Ferguson, A. (1767) *An Essay on the History of Civil Society* (London: Printed for A. Millar and T. Cadell).

Fielding, N. (1988) *Joining Forces: Police Training, Socialisation and Occupational Competence* (London: Routledge).

Gaskell, G. and Smith, P. (1981) 'Alienated Black Youth: An Investigation of Conventional Wisdom Explanations', *New Community,* 9/2, 182–91.

Hanmer, J. (1989) *Women Policing and Male Violence* (London: Routledge).

Holdaway, S. (ed.) (1979) *The British Police* (London: Edward Arnold).

Holdaway, S. (1983) *Inside the British Police: A Force at Work* (Oxford: Blackwell).

Holdaway, S. (1989) 'Discovering Structure: Studies of the British Police Occupational Culture' in M. Weatheritt (ed.) *Police Research: Some Future Prospects* (Aldershot: Gower) pp. 55–76.

Holdaway, S. (1991) *Recruiting a Multi-Racial Police Force* (London: HMSO).

Home Office (1982) *Report of a Study Group: Recruitment into the Police Service of Members of the Ethnic Minorities* (London: Home Office).

James, D. (1979) 'Police–Black Relations: The Professional Solution' in S. Holdaway (ed.) *The British Police* (London: Edward Arnold) pp. 62–82.

Kemp, C., Norris, C. and Fielding, N. (1992) *Negotiating Nothing: Police Decision-Making in Disputes* (Aldershot: Avebury).

Leinen, S. (1984) *Black Police: White Society* (New York: New York Press).

Manning, P. K. (1988) *Symbolic Communication: Signifying Calls and the Police Response* (London: MIT Press).

Manning, P. K. (1980) *The Narcs Game: Organisational And Informational Limits To Drug Law Enforcement* (Cambridge, Mass.: MIT Press).

McConville, M., Sanders, A. and Leng, R. (1991) *Case for the Prosecution: Police Suspects and the Construction of Criminality* (London: Routledge).

Metropolitan Police (1992) *Plus Briefing* (London: Metropolitan Police).

Reiner, R. (1992) *Chief Constables* (Oxford: Oxford University Press).

Research Services (1990) *Customer Satisfaction Survey* (London: Research Services Ltd.).

Savage, S. (1991) 'Review of Mollie Weatheritt, Police Research: Some Future Prospects', *The British Journal of Criminology*, 31, 4, Autumn, 440–2.

Scarman, The Rt. Hon. The Lord (1981) *The Brixton Disorders, 10–12 April, 1981: Report of an Inquiry by the Rt. Hon. The Lord Scarman, OBE* (London: HMSO).

Smith, D. and Gray, J. (1985) *Police and People in London* (Aldershot: Gower).

Wilson, D., Holdaway, S. and Spencer, C. (1984) 'Black Police in the United Kingdom', *Policing*, 1, 1, 20–30.

4

The Police and Black People: The Training Response*
Robin Oakley

Britain has a relatively long experience of providing training for police officers on race relations. This experience dates back to the 1960s, although it is only during the 1980s that the task has been approached in a systematic way. Several different approaches to providing training on race relations have been attempted, and some appear to be more successful than others. After sketching the background, this chapter will outline the development of police training on race relations in Britain, and then describe some of the main courses and programmes that have been used. The chapter concludes with an overall appraisal of the progress that has been made, especially with regard to the balance between care and control aspects of policing, and sets out some key considerations for the way forward.

*This chapter is an updated version of an article entitled 'Police Training on Ethnic Relations in Britain', which originally appeared in *Police Studies*, Vol. 13, No. 2, Summer 1990, pp. 47–56. Copyright © 1990 by Anderson Publishing Co.
Published by Anderson Publishing Co., Cincinnati.

Background

Britain, it is now commonplace to remark, has over the post-war period become increasingly a multiracial, multicultural society. This change has posed a major challenge to all service-providing agencies in Britain. The position of the police in this situation has been in many respects the same as that of any other service-providing agency. All agencies have faced the requirement of adapting their service provision to the new circumstances: of understanding different cultural backgrounds, of responding to ethnically diverse needs, and of eliminating elements of ethnocentrism and racism in the policy and practice of the agency. There has also been the challenge in the employment sphere: of ensuring equal opportunities, and of recruiting officers from the black and minority ethnic communities so that staffing reflects the composition of society as a whole (see also Chapter 3 in this volume by Simon Holdaway).

However, in the case of the police there is an additional dimension due to the fact that they are not just a service agency but also the principal agency of control. In their role as law enforcement agency, the police have tended to come into specific conflict with sections of the black community, and in particular with black youth, on a number of issues. The main complaint has been one of 'over-policing' of black people.

Major concerns in the black community have been about the discriminatory use of police powers of 'stop and search' and arrest (in both of which research generally confirms that black people are disproportionately represented), and instances of verbal abuse and physical harassment of black people on the street or in their homes. There have also been concerns about the 'saturation policing' of black areas (for example, as in Brixton prior to the 1981 disturbances), and about over-heavy policing of black social institutions, such as clubs and cafés, and especially the Notting Hill Carnival. Alongside the general complaint of 'over-policing', there have also been complaints of *under-policing* in several respects, most notably with the allegations of inadequate police response to racial violence and attacks (Reiner, 1985 and 1989; Institute of Race Relations, 1987; Gordon, 1990). As early as the 1950s in some areas, conflict between the police and black people has been manifest in a variety of ways, culminating in the disturbances in Brixton and other parts of Britain in 1981, and the further disturbances on Broadwater Farm and elsewhere in 1985 (Scarman, 1981; Benyon, 1984 and 1986; Gifford, 1986).

This then has been the scenario that policy makers and police managers have faced as they have come under increasing pressure over time to address the issues of what has come to be termed the 'community and race relations' (CRR) aspect of policing. Clearly, training forms only one part of the potential organisational response to such issues. However, a remarkable degree of reliance has been placed on training as the means of resolving such issues, at least up until the last few years when broader, organisationally-based strategies have begun to be introduced to achieve the desired change. The chapter will shortly describe how this training response has developed, and how the limitations of a primarily training-led approach have become increasingly exposed.

The Organisation of Police Training

To understand the training response that has taken place, it is first necessary to understand how police training operates generally. There are 43 territorial police forces in England and Wales, ranging in size from London's Metropolitan Police with over 27,000 police officers, down to the small 'county' and largely rural forces with less than one thousand officers. Each of these police forces has its own training school or department. Much of the compulsory training police officers receive, however, is designed centrally, and much of this is delivered at regional centres rather than in individual force training schools. Probationer training, for example, is designed centrally at the Central Planning and Training Unit (CPTU) at Harrogate in Yorkshire, as are the recently introduced courses for new Sergeants and Inspectors. Initial probationer training is delivered regionally (at District Training Centres), but subsequent phases following street experience are delivered in-force. Individual police forces for their part may also run specialist courses which they offer to other forces regionally or nationally. The Metropolitan Police is an exception to all of this since it conducts its training independently, based at the Peel Centre at

Hendon in north London. Senior officer training for the whole
country is conducted at the Police Staff College at Bramshill,
near Basingstoke in Hampshire.

Almost all training within this system is carried out by police
officers. The only major exception is senior officer training at
Bramshill, where police and civilian staff work in tandem.
Postings to training are normally for two to three years only,
with the result that there is a constant turnover of staff in every
training establishment. Compared with operational work, training is seen as a low status activity within the police despite
the very large amount of resources which are devoted to it,
with some 8 to 12 per cent of officers estimated to be involved
in training at any one time. For many years there had been
little change or development in the style of British police training, which strongly relied on didactic teaching methods intended to ensure detailed knowledge of the law. Other learning
for effective occupational performance was expected to take
place subsequently on the job, through a combination of experience and example. During the 1980s, significant changes
took place in the methodology of police training, led by the
CPTU (Southgate, 1988). This now emphasises student-centred
learning, with the trainer shifting more into the role of facilit-
ator, monitor and guide. These changes are still in the process
of implementation and adjustment within the system. The emphasis on experiential as against academic-based learning still
persists though, especially in probationer training, with recruits
first out on the street – albeit under supervision – after some
13–14 weeks (20 weeks in London's Metropolitan Police). Within this complex structure, initiatives on training in community
and race relations (and related topics) have been occurring at
several levels as well as changing over time. What follows is an
attempt to show firstly how these initiatives have developed,
and secondly the precise form some of them have taken.

The Development of Police Training in Community and Race Relations

The earliest response by police forces in Britain to the presence
of immigrant communities was the establishment from the

late 1950s onwards of specialist posts of 'Community Liaison Officer' (CLO) in main areas of settlement. Training for these officers constituted the first instance of specialist police training provision on community and race relations in Britain. Initially in the late 1960s this consisted of an annual training seminar, and then grew into a one-week course and eventually into a four-week form in the early 1990s. (Further details of this and other courses are given in the subsequent section.) All police forces in Britain now have specialist posts of this kind, though they vary in rank and in the degree to which the role is focused on relations with the minority ethnic communities. While such posts clearly serve an important liaison function, this specialist response is sometimes criticised for removing community relations responsibilities from the main body of operational police officers, and thus inadvertently contributing to the very difficulties in police–community relationships it is designed to solve.

Already by the late 1960s calls were being made for training in community and race relations to be extended to operational police officers, and not confined to those with specialist community relations roles. These calls were supported by government reports produced in the early 1970s, which recommended that police officers should be better informed about 'immigrant groups' and have an understanding of the nature of prejudice and its manifestations. At around this time, two specialist courses were introduced for operational managers working in areas of substantial immigrant settlement, both courses being locally-based (in Derbyshire and in West Yorkshire) but national in their coverage and constituency. However, so far as generic force training was concerned, it remained at the discretion of training managers in individual police forces as to whether any action was taken on the recommendations of these early reports. Where a response took place, it usually consisted of one or two lessons inserted into an existing course, with a largely factual content delivered either by a police CLO or by one of the local minority community leaders. An evaluation study of probationer training at the end of the 1970s showed that this approach had very limited effect on both knowledge and attitudes, and any positive effect was quickly countered by peer group influence and experience of police work on the street (Southgate, 1982).

1981 and the Scarman Report

The disturbances in multiracial, inner city areas in many parts of Britain in 1981 caused major public concern about the state of police–community relations in British cities. The report prepared by Lord Scarman, *The Brixton Disorders* (Scarman, 1981), analysed the causes of the disturbances and made a wide range of recommendations on policing, most of which have by now been adopted in some form by police forces and government. The root cause of the disturbances, in Scarman's view, was the breakdown in trust and communication between police and local communities, a breakdown that was especially marked in multiracial, inner city areas. His main recommendations were not only for improved management of public order, but also for better consultation and communication with local communities, and for improved selection, training and disciplining of officers, particularly so far as racial attitudes were concerned. The Scarman Report therefore was a landmark not merely because it translated public protest into proposals for reform, but because it attempted to provide a comprehensive framework for tackling the problem.

The Police Training Council Report

So far as training was concerned, the impetus was carried forward through the national Police Training Council (PTC), which set up a Working Party to review the current state of police community and race relations training, and to make detailed recommendations. It was significant that the Working Party included not only police officers and government officials, but also prominent members of the black and minority communities. It was also significant that the Working Party differed somewhat from Scarman in its analysis of the problem. Whereas Scarman wrote that the problem of 'racial attitudes' was confined to a small number of individual police officers – the 'rotten apples' who let the others down – the PTC Working Party acknowledged that racism was part of the fabric of society generally, and that prejudice must therefore be expected to pervade the police force just as any other public institution. This was less a statement about the attitudes of individual police officers, and more about the *culture* of the society and the organisation, and about the subtle and unintended ways in which *institutional* discrimination might occur.

The report of the PTC Working Party, entitled *Community and Race Relations Training for the Police,* was published in 1983, and still remains the key policy document in Britain on the subject, both because of its comprehensiveness and because of the continued relevance of its analysis and recommendations. The main recommendations of the report can be summarised as follows. First, *all* police officers should receive community and race relations training, and this should be provided regularly and in a developmental manner throughout their careers. Second, the training should be practical, in that it should provide *skills* as well as awareness and information, and it should be *relevant* to the role of the officer and to the local context in which he or she works. Third, the training should be conducted mainly by specially selected and trained police officers (though with substantial lay involvement also), and should be well *integrated* with other subjects in the curriculum. Fourth, while 'race relations' should receive specific attention, it should be approached in the context of training for 'good community relations' generally, so that ethnic minorities do not become stereotyped in a negative way. All these recommendations presented fresh challenges to police training in Britain, since (as noted above) previous CRR training typically involved short isolated inputs by specialists or outside speakers, consisting of information which was often of little immediate relevance or practical help to officers in their work.

Racism Awareness Training

Two special initiatives were proposed by the Working Party. The first was that a 'pilot' course should be set up to assess the potential of American-style 'racism awareness training' in British police forces. Such training, originating in the 'encounter group' movement during the 1960s, and popularly codified in the book *White Awareness: Handbook for Anti-Racism Training* (Katz, 1978; see also Luthra and Oakley, 1990), employs a somewhat confrontational style to elicit and review personal attitudes and feelings on the subject of 'race'. Four pilot courses were run, but were not on the whole well received by the police participants. The evaluation report concluded that while it was important for police officers to be able to acknowledge the existence of racism in themselves and others, the overtly confrontational approach was unlikely to be effective in the policing context. It also emphasised the need for highly skilled and sensitive trainers to conduct awareness training, as well as careful briefing and demonstrable relevance of such training to performance on the job (Southgate, 1984).

Independent Training Support Units

The second initiative recommended by the PTC Report was the setting up of an independent training support unit which was duly established by the Home Office as the 'Centre for the Study of Community and Race Relations' at Brunel University in west London. The role of the centre was to train police trainers in the appropriate knowledge, awareness and skills, and to provide practical assistance to police training schools in designing and implementing the required change in their curricula. Use of the centre's facilities, however, was at the discretion of individual forces, and for a combination of reasons (focusing on police dispositions, the centre's staffing and style, and a lack of central government direction), the support unit did not succeed in securing an effective working relationship with police organisations in Britain as a whole. As a result, despite a number of significant initiatives and specific achievements, the original support unit closed after five years in 1988, without appearing to have made any major impact upon the police training system. (See Oakley, 1989, for a fuller account of this and other aspects of the development of police community and race relations training.)

In recognition that much development work in this area of police training still needed to be done, the Home Office established a replacement 'Specialist Support Unit' in mid-1989, placing this under contract with an independent training and consultancy company specialising in the field of equal opportunities. This company, Equalities Associates, set up a residential training centre at Turvey in Bedfordshire, which is the base for a freshly designed six-week course aimed at police training staff, and for other training support and consultancy work with police forces nationally. The approach is modelled on equivalent programmes used by the American military at the Equal Opportunity Management Institute (EOMI) at Patrick Air Force Base in Florida (Peppard, 1984; Shaw *et al.*, 1987). Particular emphasis is placed on working strategically with police forces at the organisational level as well as that of the individual, and the objective is to target skills and behaviour, and not just knowledge or attitudes alone.

During its first three years, the Specialist Support Unit has developed a programme of work that enables it to act as the driving force for change in police training on community and race relations and on equal opportunities. Its new six-week 'training the trainers' course has produced a cadre of well over a hundred skilled trainers nationally, who become the vehicle for training their fellow-trainers and for delivering a four-phase specialist training programme in all police forces. The implementation of this training programme, and the integration of CRR and EO issues into generic training, is secured through strategic planning with force training management and through close co-operation with the two bodies responsible for training at national level – the Central Planning and Training Unit at Harrogate, and the Police Staff College at Bramshill. Following a successful interim evaluation of its operation, the Specialist Support Unit is aiming to complete this basic programme of work within the remaining two years of its five-year contract. A key issue remains whether there will continue to be a need for an independent training support unit of this kind subsequently.

Current Police Training Programmes on Community and Race Relations

Some of the current British police training initiatives on ethnic relations and related topics are described below. Many of the programmes referred to are free-standing courses on the subject. It is important to appreciate that, as noted above, current thinking emphasises the need to *integrate* the dimension of ethnic relations into police training generally, so that it is both seen and learned simply as part of the social context in which normal policing in a multi-ethnic society is carried out. Clearly, there remains a role for specialist courses or focused inputs, but a balance and indeed integration between these two approaches needs to be created that is appropriate to the particular circumstances.

National Community Liaison Officers' Course

As already noted, this course originated in the late 1960s, and has grown from being an annual seminar into a national four-week residential course run two or three times a year. It is held at the Derbyshire Constabulary's training school at Ripley. It is designed to equip newly appointed Community Liaison Officers from all parts of Britain with the knowledge and skills appropriate to their role. The course makes use of a variety of learning methods, including lectures by visiting experts, group exercises, outside visits, and syndicate group discussions. The subject matter includes minority ethnic groups and ethnic relations, but ranges far more widely than this, reflecting the very broad scope of the CLO's role, which includes not merely other groups in the community but also inter-agency co-operation and public relations.

Holly Royde Seminar for Senior Police Officers

A week-long seminar for senior police officers on the subject of community and race relations is held annually at the Holly Royde Conference Centre in Manchester. The seminar is run jointly by the Home Office and Manchester University. During the 1970s the seminar took a multi-agency form, involving senior prison and probation officers also. Since the early 1980s, a seminar has been held specifically for police officers with senior command responsibilities. Its aim is to allow them to examine and address their local policing priorities and practice with a greater awareness of the multiracial context in which they operate. The style of the seminar has moved progressively from lectures by experts to participative learning, and most recently to emphasising organisational development in the form of strategic planning and the management of change.

Current practice is to have two participants from each police force represented, who work together to develop an action plan to address a local operational policing issue with equal opportunity or community and race relations implications, and who will continue to work together subsequently to implement their plan. Experienced facilitators from police and community relations backgrounds work closely with participants throughout the week's programme.

National Specialist Race Relations Course

This course, which is run by Derbyshire Constabulary but for a national constituency, is the surviving one of a pair of specialist courses that were introduced in the 1970s; the West Yorkshire course having been discontinued. The course is designed for operational managers of mixed rank, though mainly at inspector level, who are working in multi-ethnic areas. Until recently, it employed a traditional format, consisting mainly of lectures by visiting speakers. In 1988 this traditional methodology was replaced by a new course design based upon experiential learning methods. The objectives now go well beyond simply acquiring knowledge, and are concerned more to promote understanding and self-awareness in officers, together with the commitment and skills to tackle racism in the various forms and contexts in which it may arise. The week's programme is organised around a field investigation of a minority community in Derby. Group exercises designed to enhance self-awareness are also used. The course is run jointly by experienced police trainers and a lecturer from the local college of education, and is currently held six times a year.

Courses at the Police Staff College, Bramshill

The Police Staff College at Bramshill has had civilian academic members of staff who have contributed inputs on community and race relations to its courses for 'command band' officers since the 1960s. Since 1982 the college has run a two-week specialist course for senior officers on the subject of 'Police and Ethnic Minorities'. The course was originally designed for divisional and subdivisional commanders and their deputies, and has been held approximately six times a year. About half the sessions are devoted to talks from outside speakers, and the remainder provide for group discussion, exercises, and a day-visit to a multiracial police area nearby. Although originally intended primarily for officers of superintendent or chief super-intendent rank, the majority of participants recently have been chief inspectors or below. The course has recently been subject to review, and has been retitled 'Police and Visible Minorities'. It now includes provision for post-course projects, with a re-convention phase after six months. In 1989 a one week specialist course on 'Equal Opportunities' was also introduced. This course is primarily concerned with the implementation of equal opportunities in the sphere of employment, and covers gender and other dimensions of inequality as well as ethnicity and race. The main target group is both police and civilian heads of personnel departments.

Specialist Courses for Police Trainers

The establishment of a specialist support unit for the develop-ment of community relations training for the police has already been described above, initially at Brunel University and sub-sequently at the replacement centre set up by Equalities Asso-ciates at Turvey in Bedfordshire. A principal objective in each case was to design and deliver a course for police training staff from throughout the country, which would equip them to develop curricula in their own forces, and provide appropriate knowledge and skills to deliver CRR training in the classroom.

The initial specialist support unit established at Brunel Univer-sity in 1983, set up a six-week course that consisted of a basic five-week component followed by a one-week follow-up com-ponent some 4 to 6 months later. This design was to allow graduates to return to their forces to initiate development, and then review this and move their work into a second stage. The course was broadly educational in its approach, and sought to develop participants' understanding of CRR issues within a framework of developing professionalism and reflective prac-tice generally. A major feature of the course was a two-week community placement, during which officers were attached to a statutory or voluntary organisation in the local area. The staff of eight included two seconded police officers, as well as academics and others with a variety of professional and community experience.

The limited success of this original support unit probably had less to do with its course curriculum than with the wider organisational context in which it sought to flourish. However, many of the participants found the academic environment to be unfamiliar and remote, and the course was not perceived to equip participants with the practical skills which they sought. To some extent this was a product of a conflict of expectations, since the centre took the view that curriculum development was the necessary preliminary task, whereas participants were looking for immediate 'tools for the job'. Even where participants indicated a positive learning experience, many felt insufficiently empowered by their organisation to achieve results.

The replacement 'Specialist Support Unit' established by Equalities Associates near Bedford has successfully overcome the difficulties previously encountered. Closer strategic links with police forces, and a more practical and skills-oriented curriculum, are key features of the overall project design. The course curriculum itself is based upon that used for race and equal opportunity training in the American military, but has been anglicised and in other ways adapted to meet the requirements of police training with regard primarily to service delivery. The integral six-week residential course employs a building-block concept, moving from general study of 'individual and group behaviour', through 'cross-cultural knowledge' and 'aspects of discrimination', to direct applications in the field of police community and race relations training. The multiracial staff team is supported by a wide range of outside contributors, mostly from the black and minority ethnic communities. A central feature of the course is that participants spend a weekend placement with an Asian or Afro-Caribbean family, and this has proved a major learning experience for most officers who may previously have had little or no close personal contact with members of these communities. Eleven such courses have been run during the first three years of the project, producing more than 130 specialist-trained police trainers.

This course forms part of a wider programme of work, in which course 'graduates' become the agents of change in their own organisations. Follow-up surveys conducted as part of the unit's own evaluation programme have shown that the level of management support is a major influence on whether 'graduates' can operate effectively. To assist the development process, the unit is now introducing a shorter, two-week course for training managers, aimed at ensuring they have appropriate understanding and skills to support the training development work that is required.

Central Planning and Training Unit (CPTU) Courses

The CPTU is responsible for the design and parts of the delivery of much of the basic training within the British police service. Within recent years, probationer training and initial training for sergeants and inspectors have all been subject to review and radical redesign. No specialist courses are provided since the philosophy of CPTU has been to integrate the community relations dimension into the mainstream curriculum. In the case of probationer training, the new student-centred approach is focused around detailed case studies of incidents, each of which is given some kind of community setting. In the absence of a formal lesson structure, it depends largely on the skill and commitment of trainers as to how adequately the community and race relations dimension will be addressed. A more explicitly structured model of the integrated approach is provided by the new national inspectors' course. Here the basic concept is to prepare officers for the role of the inspector in the community. The social context of the inspector's role is a theme which pervades the six-week course curriculum, and both the equal opportunities and race relations aspects are addressed in specifically focused sessions.

Individual Force Training Programmes

Alongside the national training programmes mentioned above, there has also been activity at individual force level. Until recently, the extent to which individual police forces have responded to the recommendations of the 1983 Police Training Council Report has been uneven. The programme of the current Specialist Support Unit is now stimulating a more consistent and effective response in force training. Some individual police forces, however, stand out for progressing CRR training in their own areas. Mention might particularly be made of the West Yorkshire Police, who were one of the earliest to move towards implementing the main recommendations of the 1983 PTC Report. Amongst other things, they have co-operated closely with outside trainers based in the local community – notably the Northern Race Training Unit – and have created a developmental sequence of CRR training inputs for inclusion in training programmes for officers at successive rank levels. West Yorkshire have also carried out force-wide training for all officers on dealing with racial attacks, in support of a well-developed strategy for effective response to such incidents. Northumbria Police also stand out for having had a well-publicised race relations policy for many years, supported by a specialist race relations unit and a civilian race relations training adviser. More recently, Leicestershire Constabulary have introduced a comprehensive programme of initiatives aimed at ensuring racial equality both in employment and service delivery, including systematic ethnic monitoring and a range of supporting training initiatives including family placements for all police probationers based on the model pioneered by the Specialist Support Unit.

The Metropolitan Police

The Metropolitan Police stand apart from most of what has been written since they conduct most of their training independently. The 'Met' in fact have a long history of including the social and community dimension in their training, dating back well into the 1970s. A more direct focus on 'race relations' tends to date from the early 1980s, when the programme of 'Human Awareness Training' (HAT) was introduced. This covered the three distinct areas of self-awareness, community awareness and interpersonal skills, with the main emphasis in community awareness falling on the race and cultural dimensions. Known since 1985 as 'Policing Skills Training', this programme is one of the few in Britain to have been subject to formal evaluation (Bull and Horncastle, 1983 and 1986). Although the interpersonal skills and personal awareness components received a very positive evaluation, that for community awareness judged it to be weak and relatively ineffective.

Since the late 1980s, efforts have been made to enhance the effectiveness of this aspect of recruit training. The 'Policing Skills' component has been integrated into the wider 20-week recruit training curriculum in a new design in which CRR and EO issues are 'threaded' into a wide range of subjects but also addressed directly in a series of 'focused' sessions covering issues such as racism and minority ethnic communities. This design is supported by specialist training for all trainers, and by the production of a comprehensive student handbook providing basic information on the full range of relevant topics in the field of community and race relations and equal opportunities. Another significant innovation is the 'Reciprocal Training Scheme', which brings members of many different community groups into the training school for role-plays and discussions with new recruits on matters of community concern.

Other training programmes in the Met have also sought to target or incorporate the CRR and EO dimension. A full review of this aspect of training in the Met was prepared by an external consultant in 1988, and a strategy document drawn up by the senior EO postholder within the training system. Since 1986, the Met has declared itself committed to an equal opportunity policy, and has established a small unit designed to take these issues forward. For operational officers generally, a Professional Development Programme was introduced, which incorporated EO and CRR elements as an integral part of 'professionalism' and career development training. At the organisational level, these training initiatives also receive support from the training arm of the Met's 'Plus Programme', launched in 1989 to promote the concept of 'service to the public' throughout the force, and from the equal opportunity training courses for managers run by the Met's own specialist Equal Opportunities Unit. In these respects the Met has played a pioneering role in introducing police training initiatives in this field in Britain.

Appraisal and the Way Forward

Although a decade has passed since Lord Scarman published his recommendations on police community and race relations training and the Police Training Council set out a blueprint for development work in this field, it has only been in the last few years that systematic progress has begun to be made at the national level. Despite the enterprise of some individual police forces and training establishments, the failure of the original Specialist Support Centre to impact on the overall training system has meant that much development work still remains to be done.

As the current driving force for change in the system, there-' fore, the replacement Specialist Support Unit's role is to build on its initial achievements, and to continue to stimulate and support the current impetus towards developing CRR training in the British police service and further implementing the recommendations of the PTC Report. Relations between the police and black communities still remain difficult in many areas, and the perceptions of overzealous and discriminatory policing persist. Although considerable effort has been made by police forces in some areas to recruit more black and ethnic minority officers, the rate of increase in recruitment continues to be slow, and far below the level representative of the minority ethnic population (Oakley, 1988; Holdaway, 1991). Even when the proportion of minority officers does increase, it will not of itself necessarily lead to an improvement in police–community relations (Leinen, 1984). There is no question, therefore, that the British police will need to continue to address community and race relations issues in training throughout the 1990s and beyond.

To achieve the necessary change, three key elements are necessary. The first is the need to adopt a *strategic* approach, aimed at achieving self-sustaining change in the training system as a whole, rather than fostering local and often short-lived initiatives. The second is, in the long run, to achieve the *integration* of community and race relations issues into the mainstream of the curriculum, by threading them throughout the whole training programme rather than confining them to specialist courses or inputs alone. The third is to ensure that *community involvement*, and especially involvement of members of black and minority ethnic communities, is a central feature of police training programmes, both as a means to learning for police officers and as a means to influence by the community over what that learning should be.

Perhaps the major lesson learned from the experience so far, however, is that to rely on training initiatives alone to achieve change is insufficient. If training on community and race relations is to be effective in achieving its goals, these goals must have the full support of management, and must form a clear and strategic policy commitment of the organisation. The rationale for training on these issues then becomes positive and unquestionable, since it is a straightforward one of promoting and implementing policy and professionalism in the force. The initiatives of the Dutch Government's 'Positive Action Plan: Police and Ethnic Minorities' have been conceived and executed very much from this point of view (Oakley, 1990).

The policy context for undertaking this task in Britain is now much more favourable than it was in the early 1980s. In the first place, the Home Office in late 1989 issued a policy circular to all chief constables of the 43 forces requiring them to formulate and implement 'equal opportunity policies' designed to ensure fair employment practice within their force (Home Office, 1989). Although this circular strictly applies only to employment, it has served to establish a more positive ethos with regard to equal opportunity issues within the police service generally. All police forces in England and Wales now possess formal written equal opportunity policies, and the effectiveness with which they are being implemented is currently a priority concern of HM Inspectorate of Constabulary.

The second policy initiative has been a response to the publication of the *Operational Policing Review*, a comprehensive national enquiry conducted within the police service, which included a survey of public perceptions and expectations (Joint Consultative Committee, 1990). This showed a declining level of public confidence generally in the police, and lower levels among minority ethnic groups – especially among those who have had direct contact with the police. It also revealed a substantial mismatch between public expectations of the police, and police officers' own perceptions of priorities in the policing role. Whereas the dominant police conception has been of the technically efficient expert in the field of law enforcement and crime control, the public 'have a very strong preference for the caring community style of policing rather than the firm law enforcer' (JCC, 1990, p. 8). The report concluded that what was required was not the abandonment but the restoration of the concept of 'traditional policing' that had been eroded by recent drives for greater efficiency. In effect, this was a call for a more appropriate balance between the elements of care and control in how this traditional role is carried out.

The policy response to this review has taken the form of a *Strategic Policy Document* issued by the Association of Chief Police Officers (ACPO), with the subtitle 'Setting the Standards for Policing: Meeting Community Expectations' (ACPO, 1990). Centred around a 'Statement of Common Purpose and Values', the policy document sets out a conception of policing generally as a form of public service, within which the law enforcement and service roles are no longer opposed. In this Statement of Common Purpose, alongside crime control and the mainten-ance of public order may also be found the following goals: to protect, help and reassure the community; to be compassion-ate, courteous and patient; and to reduce the fears of the public. The need to ensure that appropriate and sensitive service is provided to vulnerable minorities and to victims of racial or domestic violence is also stressed. Care and control elements are therefore combined in an integral conception of policing as a form of service to the community in general. This view in turn transforms the status within policing of 'community relations', which moves from a peripheral concern to being central to the policing role.

This new feature of the policy context undoubtedly provides support for the kinds of training initiatives in the field of community and race relations that have been described above. Moreover, the ACPO document itself identifies direct training implications of the new strategic policy, though it appears to see the need as one of stressing *commitment* among officers to ser-vice goals rather than for more fundamental change in the nature of police training as such.

It is arguable, however, that if the concept of service is to lie at the centre of the policing role, then issues of 'care' and their relationship to 'control' need also to become far more central to police training, and to be firmly contextualised within a sound intellectual understanding of communities and 'police–community relations'. In these circumstances mere exhortation or an 'add-on' approach is unlikely to prove an adequate training response to support the implementation of the new policy. Instead, it will be necessary to rethink the appropriateness of current police training – and especially police probationer training – as a foundation for a professional 'public service' orientation in the modern world. The new training strategy should build on the experience of the various post-Scarman initiatives, preserving yet also expanding beyond their predominantly race-specific focus, a focus which reflects the fact that it was in the relations between the police and black people that the more general crisis of police–community relations first became nationally apparent. Thus, the new training strategy will need to address the full range of diversity within Britain's communities, and the conflicts of interest that may arise amongst them over how policing as a public service is to be carried out.

The implication of the *Strategic Policy Document*, therefore, is that understanding the nature of the communities which police serve should be one of the most fundamental objectives of both initial and subsequent police training. Given the current tendency for policing responsibilities to be devolved from senior management to local policing teams, the need for junior officers to receive training which is more strongly grounded in professionally-relevant social science knowledge becomes increasingly important. Although over the period since the publication of the Scarman Report the care aspect of policing has gained increased attention in specialist and mainstream training programmes, police training as a whole has yet to achieve a full and balanced integration of both the care and control elements of the policing role. A formal review of this aspect of police training, including a comparison with other public service agencies, would therefore seem appropriate if the implications of the *Strategic Policy Document* are to be fully taken on board by the police service during the 1990s.

Bibliography

Association of Chief Police Officers (1990) *Strategic Policy Document. Setting the Standards for Policing: Meeting Community Expectations* (London: ACPO).

Benyon, J. (1986) *A Tale of Failure: Race and Policing*, Policy Paper in Ethnic Relations, No. 3 (Coventry: Centre for Research in Ethnic Relations, University of Warwick).

Benyon, J. (ed.) (1984) *Scarman and After: Essays Reflecting on Lord Scarman's Report, the Riots and their Aftermath* (Oxford: Pergamon).

Bull, R. and Horncastle, P. (1983) *An Evaluation of the Metropolitan Police Recruit Training in Human Awareness: Interim Report* (London: Police Foundation).

Bull, R. and Horncastle, P. (1986) *Metropolitan Police Recruit Training in Human Awareness: An Independent Evaluation* (London: Police Foundation).

Lord Gifford (Chair) (1986) *Report of the Independent Inquiry into Disturbances of October 1985 at the Broadwater Farm Estate* (London: Karia Press).

Gordon, P. (1990) *Racial Violence and Harassment* (London: Runnymede Trust).

Holdaway, S. (1991) *Recruiting a Multi-Racial Police Force* (London: HMSO).

Home Office (1989) *Equal Opportunities Policies in the Police Service*, Home Office Circular No. 87/1989 (London: Home Office).

Institute of Race Relations (1987) *Policing against Black People* (London: IRR).

Joint Consultative Committee (JCC) (1990) *Operational Policing Review* (Surbiton: Police Federation).

Jones, S. and Joss, R. (1985) 'Do Police Officers Survive their Training?', *Policing*, 1, 206–25.

Katz, J. (1978) *White Awareness: Handbook for Anti-Racism Training* (Oklahoma: Oklahoma University Press).

Leinen, S. (1984) *Black Police, White Society* (New York: New York University Press).

Luthra, M. and Oakley, R. (1990) *Combating Racism through Training: A Review of Approaches to Race Training in Organisations*, Policy Paper in Ethnic Relations, No. 22 (Coventry: Centre for Research in Ethnic Relations, University of Warwick).

Oakley, R. (1988) *Employment in Police Forces: A Survey of Equal Opportunities* (London: Commission for Racial Equality).

Oakley, R. (1989) 'Community and Race Relations for the Police: A Review of Developments', *New Community*, 16, 61–79.

Oakley, R. (1990) *Policing and Racial Equality in the Netherlands* (London: Police Foundation).

Peppard, N. (1984) 'Race Relations Training: The Patrick Experiment', *New Community*, 9, 312–16.

Police Training Council (1983) *Community and Race Relations Training for the Police* (London: Home Office).

Reiner, R. (1985) 'The Police and Race Relations' in J. Baxter and L. Koffman (eds) *Police: The Constitution and the Community* (Abingdon: Professional Books) pp. 149–87.

Reiner, R. (1989) 'Race and Criminal Justice', *New Community*, 16, 5–21.

Scarman, The Rt. Hon., The Lord (1981) *The Brixton Disorders, 10–12 April 1981: Report of an Inquiry by the Rt. Hon. The Lord Scarman, OBE* (London: HMSO).

Shaw, J. W., Nordlie, P. G. and Shapiro, R. M. (eds) (1987) *Strategies for Improving Race Relations* (Manchester: Manchester University Press).

Southgate, P. (1982) *Police Probationer Training in Race Relations* (London: Home Office).

Southgate, P. (1984) *Racism Awareness Training for the Police* (London: Home Office).

Southgate, P. (ed.) (1988) *New Directions in Police Training* (London: Home Office).

5

Recent Developments in Community Policing

Trevor Bennett

Introduction

In the last year or two there has been a quiet revolution in British policing. This has been a result, in part, of a policy of chief police officers to realign operational policing to contemporary needs. This has involved a deliberate attempt to shift the policing paradigm from a narrow conception of police enforcement to a broader conception of police service. The main vehicle for this change has been the influential *Strategic Policy Document* published by the Association of Chief Police Officers (ACPO) and the development within this document of the idea of 'quality of service' (ACPO, 1990).

The implications of these changes are potentially wide-ranging. It seems likely that they will lead to a revision of the nature of the police role and a broadening of policing functions. This is already happening to a limited extent in the form of police involvement in tackling fear of crime and minor public order issues and the development of partnerships between the police and communities and the involvement of professional agencies.

These changes in Britain are reflective of a general reassessment of operational policing which can be found in a number of countries throughout the world. It can also be seen that contemporary debate about policing reform contains common themes such as the development of community crime prevention strategies, an increase in the number of foot patrols, the development of localised command structures, and the creation of systems of local accountability. It has been argued that these changes taken together represent what in effect is a worldwide trend towards community policing (Trojanowicz and Bucqueroux, 1990).

It is too early to say whether the more recent changes in policing philosophy in Britain, as articulated in the *Strategic Policy Document* (ACPO, 1990) and expressed in the structural and operational changes being made in some police force areas, represent community policing. One reason for hesitancy in applying the concept to the system of policing in this country is the awareness that it has already been applied to earlier and quite different policing styles. It has been argued that the 'golden age' of policing before the introduction of motor vehicles and hand-held radios was the original form of community policing (Weatheritt, 1983); we were encouraged to believe that Unit Beat Policing which superseded the fixed-points system of foot patrols was a more modern version of community policing (Weatheritt, 1983); John Alderson as chief constable of Devon and Cornwall told us that he had devised and implemented community policing in his police force area (Alderson, 1978); and now developments in the use of foot patrols and local command structures are identified as elements of community policing (Skolnick and Bayley, 1987).

The main task of the chapter is to consider the theory and practice of community policing and to place these in the context of a debate about the care and control functions of the police. The discussion will focus in particular on recent attempts to implement community policing in practice and to identify some of the issues and some of the problems involved in this process. It will be argued that some of the practical problems associated with implementation offer a visible expression of the conflicts that arise in attempting to 'bolt-on' a caring function to a policing system organised around a dominant paradigm of enforcement and control.

Policing in Britain

Policing in Britain over the last few years has changed both in terms of the dominant policing philosophy and policing practice.

Changing Policing Philosophy

The recent moves to change policing philosophy are in part a result of planned actions taken by the police to change the character of policing in this country. The main outward sign of these developments within the police service was the publication of two important reports.

The first of these, the *Operational Policing Review* (Joint Consultative Committee, 1990), presented the results of a police survey conducted by representatives of the three police staff associations into the current state of policing. The main proposition contained in the report was that drives for greater efficiency within the police service had led to an erosion of service-style policing. This concern was outlined in the terms of reference of the report which, amongst other things, declared that, 'the philosophy of economy, efficiency, and effectiveness is forcing police managers to concentrate their resources upon the quantifiable aspects of police work to the exclusion of the traditional service role of British policing' (Joint Consultative Committee, 1990, p. 27). It was argued in the report that simplistic quantitative measures such as crime rates, detection rates, and traffic law enforcement returns do not reflect the many tasks performed by the police service on behalf of the community. The report noted that in order to maintain traditional policing functions it was necessary to develop new measures of police performance, which reflected the qualitative dimensions of policing and public satisfaction with the police service (see also Walker in this volume).

The second document, the *Strategic Policy Document* (ACPO, 1990), considered the findings of the *Operational Policing Review* and made recommendations. The document reported that public dissatisfaction with the police stemmed largely from inappropriate and outdated policing styles and poor service delivery. The report noted that insufficient effort had gone into monitoring service delivery and assessing the quality with which the service was delivered to the public. The report made a number of recommendations including one to devise a statement of common purpose and values for the police service nationally. It suggested that such a statement should refer to the duties of the police, '. . . to protect, help and reassure the community', to be '. . . compassionate, courteous and patient', and to 'strive to reduce the fears of the public'. The report recommended that attention should be paid to the wishes of individual communities and steps should be taken to ensure that police action reflected public concern and priorities.

Changing Policing Practice

Over the last decade there is some evidence to show that British police forces have been moving towards a more community-oriented style of policing. Some of these changes predate the current debate about quality of service and customer satisfaction and emerged instead out of the review of policing that followed the Brixton and other riots of 1981 and the publication of the Scarman Report (Home Office, 1981). During this period there was an expansion in the number of police community liaison departments and the number of officers allocated to community liaison duties (Phillips and Cochrane, 1988). The period was also marked by the introduction of police consultative committees (Morgan, 1986) and the implementation of the system of lay visitors to police stations (Kemp and Morgan, 1990). There has also been an increase in the number of innovations in patrol strategies such as the Chelmsley Wood split force patrol programme (Butler and Tharme, 1983) and the Metropolitan Police and West Midlands contact patrols programmes (Bennett, 1989).

Surprisingly, there is little evidence available on changes in the use of community constables over the last decade. The only published data that can shed light on this are the results of a survey conducted in the Metropolitan Police District in 1982 by the Policy Studies Institute (Smith, 1983) and a more recent national survey which included a study of the Metropolitan Police District in 1990 (Bennett and Lupton, 1990 and 1992a). The results of the 1982 survey showed that 5 per cent of all officers up to the rank of inspector, and about 10 per cent of all home beat and relief constables combined, were allocated to home beat duties. The results of the 1990 survey showed that approximately 13 per cent of all home beat and relief constables combined were allocated to these duties.

The 1990 national survey also showed more recent innovations in the use of patrol strategies and tactics. The report showed that over a quarter of all forces (13 of the 39 respond-ing) operated some form of geographic or sector policing (Ben-nett and Lupton, 1990). A similar number of forces also operated one or more estates policing programmes involving the allocation of a small team of officers to particular residential areas on a semi-permanent basis. There was also evidence that a number of forces had implemented public contact strategies such as police surgeries and police shops, while other forces had experimented with specialist patrol teams such as dedicated teams and problem-oriented patrols.

The Broader Context

The preceding discussion has identified various ways in which policing theory and practice in Britain over the last few years has become more community-oriented. The issue of whether these developments comprise community policing has not yet been discussed. In this section it is hoped to place these devel-opments in a broader context of international discussion about the theory and practice of community policing. In so doing, it is hoped to identify some of the problems inherent in community policing and in attempts to move towards a more service-style approach to policing.

It is perhaps surprising that despite the large number of attempts to define community policing there is as yet no stand-ard or accepted form of definition. One approach to the prob-lem adopted in the literature is to identify programmes which are proactive and which in some way might benefit the com-munity. Using this approach, Ekblom (1986) identified com-munity constables, community liaison officers, crime analysis, youth programmes, schools liaison, police shops, community surveys, inter-agency approaches and police consultative com-mittees as comprising community policing, and Weatheritt (1986) added to this list neighbourhood watch and local crime prevention. A second approach found in the literature is to identify policing programmes which are considered examples of community policing and to search for themes among them which might identify its essence. This approach has been adopted by Skolnick and Bayley (1987) who reviewed a large number of programmes in a number of countries around the world. They argued that there are four programme elements which can be found repeatedly within schemes referred to as community policing: community crime prevention, foot patrol, systems of accountability of the police to the public and decentralised command. A third approach is to identify the key concepts of community policing as found in the academic literature. Using this technique Trojanowicz and Bucqueroux (1990) identified non-crime problem solving, police–public partnerships, accountability and power sharing.

The main confusion surrounding discussions about community policing seems to lie in the distinction between theory and practice. It seems that a great deal of the confusion can be avoided by defining community policing as a policing philosophy rather than policing practice or a particular kind of programme. This approach has been argued quite convincingly by Trojanowicz and Bucqueroux (1990) who make a distinction between philosophy, strategy, and tactic.

Community policing is viewed fundamentally as a philosophy of policing which has fairly simple and fairly general principles which, according to Trojanowicz and Bucqueroux (1990), include the notion that police officers and private citizens should work together to help solve community problems. The definitions of the words strategy and tactic are based on their original military use. Strategies are described as plans for organising manpower before contact has been made with the enemy (or public) and tactics are described as plans for utilising manpower once contact has been made.

This approach is also favoured by Skolnick and Bayley (1987) who make the valuable point that not every innovation which in any way involves the police and the community can be called community policing as it would empty the phrase of any meaning. They argue that it is not the programme *per se* that qualifies for community policing but the theory behind the introduction of the programme. For example, foot patrols implemented purely for economic reasons would not qualify as community policing while foot patrols implemented to enhance community contact would qualify.

This conceptualisation is both a help and a hindrance to further discussion. The argument that community policing is fundamentally a policing philosophy is intellectually satisfying. It presumes that almost any operational policing strategy or tactic could comprise community policing as long as it was guided by a community policing philosophy. It also presumes that almost any operational policing strategy or tactic that involves the police and the public might not be an example of community policing if it were implemented for reasons unrelated to community involvement or needs.

The concept is a hindrance in that it undermines any attempt to identify community policing programmes in practice, which virtually halts any discussion on the practical value of community policing. This problem cannot wholly be resolved. Nevertheless, it is possible to proceed a little further by identifying (in much the same way as was done by Skolnick and Bayley, 1987) models of policing practice which are commonly regarded as reflective of a community policing philosophy. It would have to be accepted that some practical applications of these models might not be motivated by a community policing philosophy. Nevertheless, it would be estimated that in the majority of cases they would be inspired by a desire to provide a better police service for the community or to involve the community in the decision making or practice of policing.

The development of models of community policing in practice enables a variety of programme types to be grouped under a common heading. A review of the literature specifically on community policing and more generally on community-oriented policing strategies reveals at least six strong models of community policing in practice: (1) area-based policing; (2) multi-agency partnerships; (3) community crime prevention; (4) police–public contact strategies; (5) area-based foot patrols; and (6) community involvement and consultation.

Area-based policing is a phrase used here to describe the deployment of decentralised policing units with independent command. This method of organising local policing is referred to under a variety of names including: neighbourhood policing, geographic policing, sector policing, zonal policing, and team policing. The key characteristics of these programmes are that a small team of officers including supervisors and managers is allocated to a local area in order to provide a full police service for that area. The principal assumption underlying the approach is that the small team will be able to get to know the local community and the area and will be able to respond effectively to the needs of that area.

Multi-agency partnerships have been encouraged by the Home Office (Home Office, 1990) and have been recommended in the more recent Standing Committee on Crime Prevention Report, the Morgan Report (Home Office, 1991), as a vehicle for promoting crime prevention. The partnerships can comprise any combination of agencies although the research evidence suggests (discussed later) that representatives of the police are almost invariably included on the steering committees or project groups of these partnerships. The motivation for the partnership can derive from the police themselves who aim to tackle local problems with the help of other agencies or, more recently, as a result of centrally organised initiatives such as the '5 Towns' or 'Safer Cities' programmes.

Community crime prevention is also a relatively recent form of police collaboration with the community as a means of preventing crime. The most widespread version of community crime prevention in Britain at the moment is neighbourhood watch. The programme is based on the principle that the police and the community can work together to prevent crime and to tackle local problems. The main mechanism for achieving this is for the public to look out for and report to the police anything suspicious that they see in their areas. In some areas neighbourhood watch schemes are operated by the community largely in isolation from the police while in others the police play a major role in the general running of the schemes.

Police–public contact strategies comprise programmes designed to bring the police and the public into face-to-face contact. One of the most common means of achieving this is foot patrols, although the term is more typically applied to more substantial efforts to make contact with the public. These programmes include police shops and police storefronts and to a lesser extent, but fairly common in Britain, police surgeries. They also include contact patrols which aim specifically to encourage police officers to speak to residents by knocking on doors and making proactive approaches on the streets.

Area-based foot patrols is a phrase used here to refer to dedicated community constables and preventive foot patrols allocated to small areas. The aims of community constable and more general foot patrols are poorly specified in the literature and include a broad range of functions including public contact, public reassurance, deterrence, prevention, and intelligence gathering. The central characteristic of community constables is that they are allocated on a semi-permanent basis to a relatively small area and are encouraged to get to know that area and the people living and working in it.

The final model of community policing is referred to here as community involvement and consultation. In practice, this category refers to the formal arrangements implemented in this and other countries to enable the police to consult representatives of local communities about policing matters. It is also extended to refer to the lay visitors scheme and formal arrangements for members of the public to monitor and comment on the quality of policing in their area.

The preceding two sections of this chapter have attempted to identify the conceptual and practical context of community policing. The remaining sections aim to take a more critical stance and consider what happens when attempts are made to implement community policing. In particular, attention will be paid to some of the practical conflicts which arise when attempts are made to expand the police role to include caring and service-style functions.

Empirical Evaluations of Community Policing

There are few published evaluations of programmes called community policing. However, there is a larger body of research evidence available on the kinds of policing programmes identified above as the most common practical applications of a community policing philosophy. The aim of this section is to examine evaluations of the main operational forms of community policing and to determine the benefits and drawbacks of these forms of policing in practice. The review of the literature will be confined to a small number of selected evaluations, chosen on the grounds of relevance to the current debate, and comments about them will be limited to the main issues of interest to the discussion.

Area-Based Policing

One of the most comprehensive investigations of area-based policing in England was conducted by Irving *et al.* (1989) for the Police Foundation in relation to the pilot schemes of the neighbourhood policing programme in Notting Hill in London.

The report showed no change in public attitudes towards the police or the area in which they lived and no change in victimisation rates, apart from an increase in multiple victimisations. The authors argued that the absence of positive outcome findings was a result of programme implementation failure. Geographic responsibility was resisted by the relief officers on the grounds that it undermined reactive cover and manning levels, while home beat officers resisted it on the grounds that allocating proactive tasks to relief officers undermined and confused their position. There was also resistance among the relief officers to changing the roster system to match availability of officers to area workload which was seen as undermining the traditional shift system. The implementation of graded response was widely criticised by the officers and was eventually abandoned and the computerised management information system failed to be operated in a way that could provide useful results. The report concluded that the programme failed to overcome the issue of police conservatism and self-interest of the various policing groups and the strong inertia to change and desire to maintain the status quo among front line police officers and junior managers.

Another study of area-based policing in England found that key elements of the programme were not implemented because of resistance by lower ranking officers (Chatterton, 1991). Chatterton reported that changes in the collection and use of information from a largely manual system to a computerised system threatened the ability of lower ranking officers to control information about their own behaviour. As a result various resistance tactics were adopted including the use of generalised rather than specific descriptions of their activities in written reports, the frequent challenge that 'local knowledge' was a more effective source of information, general opposition to increased paperwork, the submission of reports that were too brief to have any practical use, and frequent complaints of the inaccuracy of the computerised system.

Research on team policing in the United States has offered similar conclusions. Experiments with team policing in New York City, Dayton and Holyoke each resulted in some form of implementation failure. In New York City the programme was reported as being so weak that there was little discernible difference between the new programme and what police officers were doing before. In Dayton and Holyoke internal departmental disputes and low officer morale gradually undermined the programme's changes (Gay *et al.*, 1977). The Cincinnati team policing experiment produced early positive results with officers reported as enjoying the broadened scope of their jobs. Eventually, however, the central police commanders began to reclaim power that had been delegated to team leaders and the programme was disbanded (Schwartz and Clarren, 1977). A review of the literature on team policing in the United States concluded that many of the team policing experiments failed because forces were reluctant or unable to invest the considerable time in training team supervisors and little attempt was made to modify the organisational culture to accept team policing within the time period of the programme (Eck and Spelman, 1987).

Multi-Agency Partnerships

One of the most comprehensive studies of multi-agency partnerships is a retrospective evaluation of the '5 Towns crime prevention initiative' (Liddle and Bottoms, 1991). The research found that tensions often developed between representatives of the professional agencies at the project committee level, the bodies responsible for implementing particular crime prevention projects, which hindered their effective operation. The main sources of tensions reported were differences in the seniority levels of committee members within their respective agencies, dissatisfaction arising from unequal workloads and levels of commitment of individual committee members, the alienation of some members as a result of backstage work by key members of the committee, and clashes between the work of the committee and other agency work. The potential seriousness of these problems was reflected in the conclusion drawn by the authors who recommended that multi-agency co-operation would be more effective if it were limited to the managerial level and if crime prevention at the operational level were restricted to individual agencies.

A study of multi-agency partnerships in three areas in London and one in a northern town also reported tensions between agencies and noted that the agencies did not always work together on an equal basis. They believed that the police often became the lead agency in defining goals and designing initiatives which undermined the authority and the spirit of the other agencies (Sampson *et al.*, 1988).

A fairly detailed account of one multi-agency programme involving the police and other agencies in Exeter provides a graphic example of the conflicts and misunderstandings that can arise when professional agencies work together (Moore and Brown, 1981). A joint action group comprising representatives of the church, the council, local agencies, and the police was formed in Exeter to tackle the problems of crime by young people in the area of a large housing estate. Various problems arose once the agencies attempted to work together. It was reported that one policeman avoided the meetings because he said that he found it difficult to mix with social workers. A social worker said that she found difficulty in discussing community problems with the police when they were in uniform. Many of the professionals in the group felt that their traditional independence and authority was being threatened. Some statutory agency workers saw the new police role encroaching on the territories of other agencies.

Community Crime Prevention

It is widely regarded that neighbourhood watch is the major community crime prevention programme currently operating in this country. The results of the detailed study of two neighbourhood watch schemes in London raised a number of points associated with programme implementation and effectiveness (Bennett, 1990). The programmes had no impact on victimisation and there was no change in reporting rates of victimisations to the police and no change in police clear up rates. There were some positive findings recorded in public attitudes including one finding of a reduction in fear of property crime.

However, this was offset by no change in fear of personal crime and a reduction in the frequency of sightings of local police officers.

The research concluded that the lack of programme impact was a result, at least in part, of programme failure and a weak programme design which limited the level of public involvement in it. Apart from attending the launch meeting and perhaps displaying a neighbourhood watch sticker in their windows local residents took little further active part in the scheme. The police found it difficult to service the increasing number of neighbourhood watch schemes in their area and few additional personnel or other resources were made available to conduct this task. Little encouragement was given to the public, beyond the initial launch meeting, to participate in policing their area and few residents said that they looked out for anything suspicious or reported it to the police.

Research in the United States has also shown limited impact of neighbourhood or block watch schemes on crime and fear of crime. A recent review of the literature reported that most of the best evaluations of neighbourhood watch show very few changes in social interaction, surveillance, stranger recognition, crime reporting, home protection behaviour and attitudes towards the police (Rosenbaum, 1988). The reviewer concluded that organising and sustaining community interest in crime prevention activities is difficult and should not be underestimated.

Police–Public Contact

The research on vehicle and foot patrols has generally produced negative results concerning their potential effectiveness in reducing crime. The frequently cited evaluation of the Kansas City Preventive Patrol Experiments showed that increasing the number of cars allocated to particular beats had little effect on crime rates or reporting rates and there was no effect on respondents' attitudes towards the police or in their fear of crime (Kelling *et al.*, 1974). Similar findings were published from the evaluation of the Newark Foot Patrol experiment which showed little impact of the programme on crime or crime reporting (Pate *et al.*, 1986).

A more recent evaluation of contact patrols in Britain showed that some benefits might be gained from increasing police–public contact. The study of a programme hosted by the Metropolitan Police and West Midlands Police encouraged police officers to knock on doors and to make proactive attempts to speak to residents. The evaluation showed that the programme had little effect on crime or reporting rates (Bennett, 1991). Nevertheless, the results did show a substantial improvement in public satisfaction with police performance during the period of the experiment.

Other studies of foot patrols have also shown that these programmes sometimes can affect public attitudes and fear of crime. The results of an evaluation of a foot patrol experiment in Newark, New Jersey showed that residents exposed to an increase in the number of foot patrol officers in their area became less fearful over the experimental period (Pate, 1986). A similar study of the impact of increased foot patrol in Flint, Michigan found that survey respondents reported that they felt safer during the programme than they did before (Trojanowicz, 1986).

Area-Based Foot Patrols

The largest survey of community constables in Britain was conducted by Bennett and Lupton as part of a national survey of community-oriented policing (Bennett and Lupton, 1990). The research showed that the use of community constables was widespread and that all forces allocated at least some officers to these duties. Nevertheless, there were a number of other findings which suggested that the community constable scheme was not operating as effectively as might be hoped. The proportion of officers allocated to community constable duties was quite low; less than 20 per cent of operational constables (Bennett and Lupton, 1990). Community constables reported that they were withdrawn from their duties to conduct other duties about 20 per cent of their working time. The research also showed that community constables spent on average in excess of one-third of the duty time inside the station and in some forces this rose to more than 50 per cent. Less than 10 per cent of their total duty time was spent on community contacts or preventive or other proactive work (Bennett and Lupton, 1990 and 1992b).

Similar findings have emerged from other studies. An earlier study conducted in England and Wales showed that officers were withdrawn from community constable duties about one-fifth of their working time (Brown and Iles, 1985). The remainder of the time was spent largely on general duties inside the station. Less than 14 per cent of duty time was spent on community involvement. A study in Sweden found that community police officers spent about half their time inside the police station and when outside the station spent only about 12 per cent of their time on foot patrols (Knutsson, 1991).

Community Involvement and Consultation

The major research on police consultative committees (PCCs) in England and Wales has been conducted by Morgan (1986). Morgan looked in detail at PCCs in nine subdivisions covering five police forces and found that PCC members were disproportionately male, middle class, middle aged, and were active members of the community. Few PCC members had adversarial experience of the police nor did they have much contact with people who did have. Members were generally pro-police in their attitudes when they joined. Most PCCs made some efforts to get young people and ethnic minority representatives to join and attend meetings but this generally met with little success. PCC members were fairly ignorant of day-to-day policing methods and procedures and their meetings tended to be dominated by the police and police accounts which tended to stress the rising incidence of serious crime and the paucity of police resources. Overall police priorities or use of resources were rarely questioned and PCC members tended to become sympathetic towards rather than critical of the police.

Theoretical Evaluations of Community Policing

The aim of this final section is to examine what academics and other commentators have said about community policing and to relate these observations to the issue of care and control. The section refers not only to statements directed at theoretical formulations of community policing – of which there are few – but also insights, hunches, and speculations which are based more on ideas rather than empirical fact. The review is selective with the general aim of raising issues relevant to the interest of the current chapter.

In one of his strongest attacks on community policing Bayley lists a large number of problems which he believes weakens the value of the approach (Bayley, 1988). His criticisms cover a wide field of concerns. Community policing, he argues, is based on the notion that the police can only succeed in tackling crime and public disorder with the assistance of the community. However, so far there is no convincing evidence that community policing strategies are any more effective than traditional ones. He is concerned that focusing the attention of the police on the development of close relations with the public will undermine the determination of the police to take strong enforcement action when it is needed. What will happen, he asks, when community police officers are called upon to quell a riot? Community policing provides the police with new objectives such as tackling fear of crime and improving public confidence which are less demanding than the objective of reducing and detecting crime. These new objectives are worthwhile pursuits but are they what the police should be doing? He also notes that community policing might encourage unequal enforcement of the law. If police operations are determined by community wishes, there is a danger that policing will reflect the interests of those groups who can obtain the ear of the police. There is also the problem in a heterogeneous society of deciding whose interests and values the police will aim to uphold. Short (1983) has written about the danger that community policing might place the police in a position to make political decisions about the organisation and lifestyle of a community. She was concerned about the style of policing implemented in Devon and Cornwall in the late 1970s which involved the police in contesting decisions relating to social policies and urban planning.

A different kind of criticism of community policing is offered by Waddington who argues that there are clear dangers in attempting to expand the role of the police beyond its legitimate law enforcement functions (Waddington, 1984). The police were introduced in their modern form to contain the growing violence that accompanied urbanisation. They retain today the same essential role as the sole possessors of the legitimate use of force. Waddington argues that it is important that the police exercise this function with impartiality and are not asked to refrain from enforcing the law in one area while encouraged to enforce the law in another. He believes that the police should spend their time becoming more professional in conducting their enforcement function effectively and fairly rather than being distracted by what he sees as the futile task of creating social harmony.

Conclusion

The specific historical development of the police in Britain and in many other countries has resulted in a modern police system which is primarily and fundamentally organised around the effective provision of control. One important consequence of this is the tendency for more innovative caring functions, such as community policing, to be 'bolted-on' or 'transplanted on' to the existing and traditional control system. This can generate a conflict between the policing system and the policing paradigm. It is perhaps as a result of the tensions created by the traditional philosophical differences between the care and control functions of the police, and as a result of the fact that the control function provides the dominant paradigm that some of the operational difficulties involved in implementing community policing have emerged. Some examples of the problems which can arise during the 'transplantation' process are noted below.

First, the empirical research evidence suggests that there is often resistance among lower ranking officers to efforts to implement policing programmes which are in some way different to traditional enforcement policing methods. There is also some evidence that the further away from the enforcement model of policing the greater the resistance. Recent attempts in UK constabularies to implement area-based policing, which can comprise a radical departure from traditional policing methods, have experienced considerable difficulty in obtaining the acceptance of front line officers. Anecdotal evidence from sources other than those referred to above indicate that inertia and resistance of front line officers to alter policing styles is presenting a formidable obstacle to attempts to reform. Schemes such as police–public contact programmes and the introduction of additional foot or vehicle patrols, which are less radical in their approach, appear to experience less resistance from lower ranks.

Many of the reasons for resistance to change among the lower ranks can be traced to the police subculture (Holdaway, 1983, 1989, and in this volume; Chatterton, 1989). Goldstein (1990), for example, noted that police subculture is a product of a wide range of factors associated with the essential nature of the police job, including the threat of physical danger, hostility from the public, the vulnerability of officers to allegations of wrongdoing, unreasonable demands and conflicting expectations, and the pressures each day to get the job done. He argues that for any change in policing style to succeed it must reduce rather than increase the tensions of practical policing which generate and sustain the subculture.

Second, there is evidence of a lack of knowledge among senior officers about the practical realities of the more innovative programmes and the problems that they are likely to face. It is likely that the more innovative the programme, and the further the programme from traditional enforcement policing, the less information that there will be for senior managers to draw upon. It is possible that at the time of the force-wide launch of neighbourhood watch by the Metropolitan Police Commissioner the main model of the programme was contained in the report of the scheme operating in Seattle in the United States (Bennett, 1990). It would be interesting to speculate on how many senior officers in this country had ever seen neighbourhood watch in practice before they implemented it in their police force areas. There appear to be similar problems of knowledge about the practical realities of area-based and team policing which is almost certainly providing a hindrance to programme development among some forces.

Third, there is almost certainly an implementation problem associated with management and planning. It is likely that police managers are less experienced in implementing *community-*

oriented policing programmes than law enforcement programmes and as a result fail to provide the appropriate machinery for effective implementation. This problem is currently of nation-wide concern and has been taken on board by Her Majesty's Inspectorate of Constabulary (HMIC), which is currently involved with the Home Office in developing qualitative perform-ance indicators. The development of community policing pro-grammes will require further changes to management processes including the development of appropriate police training, methods of performance review, effective, relevant, and useful management information, and management styles including, perhaps, greater involvement of the junior ranks in manage-ment decisions.

In addition to these problems, which are in various ways linked to conflicts between police paradigm and police practice, there are further problems associated with implementation that can be explained more in terms of the philosophies and prac-tices of other agencies.

First, there appear to be problems associated with developing partnerships between the police and the community. The re-search on police–community consultation arrangements shows that, for a number of reasons, the community do not provide an effective input into policing even when given the opportunity to do so. The research on neighbourhood watch also shows that the public are reluctant or unable to make much of an impact in policing their areas or in helping the police to do it for them. Similar evidence can be found on the effectiveness of police surgeries which tend to be poorly supported by the public. It is possible that some of the apparent reluctance of the public to become more fully involved in policing is a product of the nature of the arrangements that are currently being made. There is some evidence from the research on contact patrols that it is easier to get the police to go to the public than to get the public to go to the police (Bennett, 1989).

Second, there appear to be fundamental problems associated with developing partnerships between the police and other agencies. It would be expected that further expansion of the police role and further developments in community-oriented approaches to policing would almost inevitably lead to greater involvement of the police with other agencies. The research is clear and almost unanimous in its conclusions that multi-agency collaboration, as it is currently conceived, is limited in its effectiveness. One solution proposed in the literature is to limit multi-agency collaboration to the planning stage and managerial level of contact. Most practical work could then be conducted by independent agencies working within an agreed planning framework. Another solution is to recognise the problems associated with multi-agency partnerships and take steps to tackle these problems directly.

The results of published research and discussion on the theory and practice of community policing have identified some key issues which have substantial implications for policing practice. It is important that the evidence contained in this literature is thoroughly considered by those responsible for policing policy before more radical changes are attempted. In particular, attention should be given to the appropriateness and the consequences of broadening the police role. It must be considered whether such a move will either add to enforcement or undermine enforcement by eroding the organisational structure and police culture that supports it. Particular attention should also be paid to practical considerations of the way in which the care functions of the police can be integrated into an existing or revised policing paradigm. A mismatch between paradigm and practice will inevitably lead to tension and conflict, which should be addressed before rather than after attempts to reform the police are made.

Bibliography

Association of Chief Police Officers (1990) *Strategic Policy Document. Setting the Standards for Policing: Meeting Community Expectations* (London: ACPO).

Alderson, J. (1978) *Communal Policing* (Exeter: Devon and Cornwall Constabulary).

Bayley, D. H. (1988) 'Community Policing: A Report From The Devil's Advocate' in J. R. Greene and S. D. Mastrofski (eds) *Community Policing: Rhetoric or Reality* (New York: Praeger) pp. 225–37.

Bennett, T. H. (1989) *Contact Patrols in Birmingham and London: An Evaluation of a Fear Reducing Strategy*, Report to the Home Office (Cambridge: Institute of Criminology).

Bennett, T. H. (1990) *Evaluating Neighbourhood Watch* (Aldershot: Gower).

Bennett, T. H. (1991) 'The Effectiveness of a Police-Initiated Fear Reducing Strategy', *British Journal of Criminology*, 31, 1, 1–14.

Bennett, T. H. and Lupton, R. (1990) *National Review of Community-Oriented Patrols: Report*, Report to the Home Office Research and Planning Unit (Cambridge: Institute of Criminology).

Bennett, T. H. and Lupton, R. (1992a) 'A Survey of the Allocation and Use of Community Constables in England and Wales', *British Journal of Criminology*, 32, 2, 167–82.

Bennett, T. H. and Lupton, R. (1992b) 'A National Activity Survey of Police Work', *The Howard Journal of Criminal Justice*, 31, 3, 200–23.

Brown, D. and Iles, S. (1985) *Community Constables: A Study of a Policing Initiative*, Home Office Research and Planning Unit Paper No. 30 (London: HMSO).

Butler, A. J. P. and Tharme, K. (1983) *Chelmsley Wood Policing Experiment: Evaluation Report* (Birmingham: West Midlands Police).

Chatterton, M. (1989) 'Managing Paperwork' in M. Weatheritt (ed.) *Police Research: Some Future Prospects* (Aldershot: Avebury) pp. 107–36.

Chatterton, M. (1991) 'Organisational Constraints in the Use of Information and Information Technology in Problem-focused Area Policing', Paper presented at the British Criminology Conference held in York, June.

Eck, J. E. and Spelman, W. (1987) *Problem Solving: Problem-Oriented Policing in Newport News* (Washington, D.C.: Police Executive Research Forum).

Ekblom, P. (1986) 'Community Policing: Obstacles and Issues' in P. Willmott (ed.) *The Debate about Community* (London: Policy Studies Institute) pp. 16–30.

Gay, W. G., Day, T. H. and Woodward, J. P. (1977) *Neighborhood Team Policing: Phase One Report* (Washington, D.C.: Government Printing Office).

Goldstein, H. (1990) *Problem-Oriented Policing* (London: McGraw-Hill).

Holdaway, S. (1983) *Inside the British Police: A Force at Work* (Oxford: Blackwell).

Holdaway, S. (1989) 'Discovering Structure. Studies Of The British Police Occupational Culture' in M. Weatheritt (ed.) *Police Research: Some Future Prospects* (Aldershot: Avebury) pp. 55–75.

Home Office (1981) *The Brixton Disorders, 10–12 April 1981: Report of an Enquiry by the Rt. Hon. The Lord Scarman, OBE*, Cmnd 8427 (London: HMSO).

Home Office (1990) *Partnership in Crime Prevention* (London: Home Office).

Home Office (1991) *Safer Communities: The Local Delivery of Crime Prevention Through the Partnership Approach* (Morgan Report) (London: Standing Conference on Crime Prevention).

Irving, B., Bird, C., Hibberd, M. and Willmore, J. (1989) *Neighbourhood Policing: The Natural History of a Policing Experiment* (London: The Police Foundation).

Joint Consultative Committee (1990) *Operational Policing Review* (Surbiton: Police Federation).

Kelling, G. L., Pate, T., Dieckman, D. and Brown, C. E. (1974) *The Kansas City Preventive Patrol Experiment: A Technical Report* (Washington, D.C.:, Police Foundation).

Kemp, C. and Morgan, R. (1990) *Lay Visitors to Police Stations*, Report to the Home Office (Bristol: Bristol Centre for Criminal Justice).

Knutsson, J. (1991) 'Community-oriented Policing: The Swedish Experiences', Paper presented at a conference in Dublin, Ireland.

Liddle, A. M. and Bottoms, A. (1991) *Implementing Circular 8/84: A Retrospective Assessment Of The Five Towns Crime Prevention Initiative*, Report to the Home Office (Cambridge: Institute of Criminology).

Moore, C. and Brown, J. (1981) *Community Versus Crime* (Dorchester: Bedford Square Press).

Morgan, R. (1986) 'Policing by Consent: Legitimating the Doctrine', in D. J. Smith and R. Morgan (eds) *Coming to Terms with Policing* (London: Routledge) pp. 217–34.

Pate, A. M. (1986) 'Experimenting with Foot Patrol: The Newark Experience' in D. P. Rosenbaum (ed.) *Community Crime Prevention: Does It Work?* (London: Sage) pp. 137–56.

Pate, A. M., Wycoff, M. A., Skogan, W. G. and Sherman, L. W. (1986) *Reducing Fear of Crime in Houston and Newark* (Washington, D.C.: Police Foundation).

Phillips, S. V. and Cochrane, R. (1988) *The Role and Function of Police Community Liaison Officers*, Home Office Research and Planning Unit Paper No.51 (London: Home Office).

Rosenbaum, D. P. (1986) *Community Crime Prevention: Does It Work?* (London: Sage).

Rosenbaum, D. P. (1988) 'Community Crime Prevention: A Review and Synthesis of the Literature', *Justice Quarterly*, 5, 323–95.

Sampson, A., Stubbs, P., Smith, D., Pearson, G. and Blagg, H. (1988) 'Crime, Localities and the Multi-Agency Approach', *British Journal of Criminology*, 28, 478–93.

Schwartz, A. L. and Clarren, S. N. (1977) *The Cincinnati Team Policing Experiment: A Summary Report* (Washington D.C.: Police Foundation).

Short, C. (1983) 'Community Policing: Beyond Slogans' in T. H. Bennett (ed.) *The Future of Policing* (Cambridge: Institute of Criminology) pp. 67–81.

Skolnick, J. H. and Bayley, D. H. (1987) 'Theme and Variation in Community Policing' in N. Morris and M. Tonry (eds) *Crime and Justice* (Washington D.C.: National Institute of Justice) pp. 1–37.

Smith, D. J. (1983) *Police and People in London: A Survey of Police Officers* (London: Policy Studies Institute).

Trojanowicz, R. (1986) 'Evaluating a Neighborhood Foot Patrol Program: The Flint, Michigan Project' in D. P. Rosenbaum (ed.) *Community Crime Prevention: Does It Work?* (London: Sage) pp. 157–78.

Trojanowicz, R. and Bucqueroux, B. (1990) *Community Policing: A Contemporary Perspective* (Cincinnati: Anderson Publishing Co.).

Waddington, P. A. J. (1984) 'Community Policing: A Sceptical Appraisal' in P. Norton (ed.) *Law and Order and British Politics* (Aldershot: Gower) pp. 84–99.

Weatheritt, M. (1983) 'Community Policing: Does It Work and How Do We Know?' in T. H. Bennett (ed.) *The Future of Policing*, Cropwood Conference Series No.15 (Cambridge: Institute of Criminology) pp. 127–42.

Weatheritt, M. (1986) *Innovations in Policing* (London: Croom Helm/Police Foundation).

6

Domestic Violence and Sexual Assault
Susan S. M. Edwards

Introduction

Nowhere is the dual function of police as 'carers' of victims and 'controllers' of offenders more apparent than in areas of police work where the police are charged both with the investigation of crime and apprehension of the suspect in securing the best possible evidence and in providing support necessary to the future protection and wellbeing of victims. Violence against women, and sexual assault perpetrated by male intimates are two areas of police work where these dual functions of care and control meet, sometimes in a manner complementary, whilst at other times they co-exist in conflict.

This chapter principally examines the approach of the police, but as the police operate as a part of a justice process, consideration is also given to prosecutors and sentencers. In addition, it raises some of the ideological dilemmas facing these agencies in the criminal justice system in pursuit of the twin goals of protecting victims of domestic violence and rape and the prosecution of offenders at a time when police budgets are under review, and police reorganisation nationally and in metropolitan areas, with the advance of sector policing, is underway.

Caring for Victims

Care for the complainant/victim by police in the course of routine police work has been traditionally derided by many officers who see it as social work and not the proper function of police. Yet, whatever the privately held and institutionally espoused attitudes, in responding to calls from the public much of routine 'reactive' police work has compelled officers to take on just this 'social work' or service function. Punch and Naylor (1973) in an analysis of calls made to the police in three Essex towns found that between 49 and 73 per cent of calls made to police were service calls, the largest category being domestic occurrences. Other research confirms these empirical findings (see, for example, Ekblom and Heal, 1985) and also demonstrates that service to the complainant/victim varies considerably dependent on the crime alleged. Police managers, notably John Alderson, ex-Chief Constable of Devon and Cornwall, has argued over the years for a positive recognition of the service function. As Reiner notes (1985, p. 110): 'A perennial chestnut of debate about the police role has been whether the police are best considered as a force, with the primary function of enforcing the criminal law, or as a service, providing a balm for a sea of troubles'. Despite the manpower hours devoted to the caring role, organisational intransigence and individual attitudes continue to reinforce the already deeply ingrained belief that attending 'domestics' and dealing with rape between intimates are family problems and not the proper function of police (Graef, 1990, pp. 156–61). This view has been held both by police managers and by rank and file officers who, as Maguire and Corbett (1987) found, felt it their job to deal with offenders and not victims. Police officers have neither been encouraged, nor properly trained to respond positively or professionally to demands for assistance from the public that do not conform to the stereotypical crime-fighting role of police. Moreover, officers have not been educated to perceive domestic violence, abuse, and rape as part of a crime prevention role which emerged in respect of what was considered to be public crimes in the 1980s.

Domestic violence, rape and sexual assault perpetrated by known males has traditionally been regarded as a private arena not requiring public intervention but rather dispute resolution and mediation by non-police agencies. In this private arena it is both parties, including the victim, who are seen to share responsibility for the violent outcome. As for domestic disputes, Reiner (1985, p. 95) noted that where the police found 'the husband and wife going hammer and tongs, you have got to separate them, calm them down before you go. And you are not doing a policeman's job, you are doing a socialist's [sic]' (see also Edwards, 1989; Bourlet, 1990). It was just this police perception of domestic incidents which, in 1983, resulted in John Dellow (Assistant Chief Constable of the Metropolitan Police) making one of the most damaging remarks regarding police handling of domestic disputes. At a time when some police policy makers were trying to restore public confidence in police ability to deal with these offences, he was reported in *The Times* as saying that domestic disputes might best be dealt with by civilians. By 1983, the police were discussing with the Home Office proposals to hand over some police duties to civilians. Given the police culture and the criticisms of police in the handling of domestic violence, such proposals were neither seen as evidence of further professionalisation nor as recognition that the police were poorly trained, but rather as a ploy to dump the troublesome 'domestic'. Domestic violence and sexual assault between known parties is immensely problematic for police, time consuming, unresolvable and with no clear finality. Such incidents require continuous call backs and delicate handling. Moreover the technical gathering of evidence and corroboration takes place at a time when the principal witnesses are still associated with the offender and often in fear of reprisal. With cases of rape the police frequently expect the allegation to be false, to be withdrawn somewhile later or dropped due to lack of evidence. Since the police role is investigatory and prosecutorial (McConville, Sanders and Leng, 1991) and since performance indicators depend on successful investigation and ultimately prosecution, support for the victim, even though quintessential in the gathering of the best possible evidence, has not been seen as a central part of the police function.

Controlling the Offender

Whilst police are said to be prosecutorially-minded, it is the case that prosecutions are reserved for the more aggravated of cases. This has arisen not solely as a result of police scepticism about the credibility of such allegations but also the whole way in which the trial focuses on the issue of consent. Even in the Glasgow rape case in 1982 where the victim was hideously attacked, sustaining many razor blade cuts to the face and body, much was made of the fact that she had been drinking heavily. The complainant was not fit to undergo the trial and the case was dropped against the three youths and a decision to offer no evidence tendered. This led to Scotland's first private prosecution for fifty years (reported in Chambers and Millar, 1986, p. 5; Blair, 1985, p. 9). Frequently the police have not pursued charges, arguing that to charge a suspect is a waste of time as victims rarely wish to proceed beyond making the initial complaint. Whilst there is some evidence for charge dropping by the victim (Edwards, 1989), victim withdrawal has facilitated and provided further legitimation for what already exists, namely police reluctance to pursue cases vigorously. It has largely been this feature of case mortality – the withdrawal of charges by a complainant – which has resulted in less scrutiny. The police response has been influenced by the insuperable difficulties these offences generate in determining successful performance indicators, that is clear-ups. Whatever is done for victims in these areas would not be reflected in existing performance indicators that are based more on the early 1980s ethos of high clear-up rates rather than on the ethos of the 1990s where the focus shifted to include quality of service to victims and a broader concept of professionalism, which embraces a greater willingness to assist victims and a growing scepticism over the importance of clear-ups.

In the case of rape, Blair's research in the UK revealed that allegations of rape made to the police where officers decided the evidence was insufficient were then written off and classified as a 'no crime'. The 'no crime' classification is legitimately used to classify the allegation that is recorded in error and is subsequently discovered to have no foundation. A good example of the 'no crime' is where a complainant reports an item missing as stolen and where police record a theft. Where the missing item is subsequently discovered the original crime sheet detailing a theft must now be reclassified to reflect the original error. It is here that the 'no crime' is issued. Research over the years has discovered the classification 'no crime' to be routinely used to erase from records those incidents which police recognise as having happened but where detection and/ or prosecution is impossible. The result is a massive distortion in recorded incidents whereby only those cases with a good prognosis of being prosecuted are likely to be recorded. Blair argues that the number of rapes 'no crimed' is considerable and suggests that many rapes are disposed of as 'no crimes' rather than as undetected crimes; the obvious advantage to the police is that they have no impact on the clear-up rate. Any fall in the clear-up rate resulting from rape cases being recorded and then remaining unsolved would be an anathema to supervisory detectives (Blair, 1985, p. 80). Additionally, Blair argues that police officers hold the attitude that a large number of rape allegations are false and that such attitudes influence the investigation of the crime as well as recording practices. Again, for the Metropolitan Police, such findings on the use of the 'no crime' are echoed by Smith's work on rape in the London boroughs of Islington and Lambeth during 1984–6. Of the reported rapes made during this period, 52 per cent were subsequently recorded as a crime and therefore a notifiable offence included in the criminal statistics. Forty eight per cent were not recorded, although the proportion of reported rapes 'no crimed' over the years fell from 61 per cent in 1984, to 44 per cent in 1985 and further to 38 per cent in 1986 (Smith, 1989, pp. 23–4). In Scotland there are similar indications of the 'no criming' of rape allegations. Chambers and Millar's (1983) seminal study demonstrated the routine use of the 'no crime' as a legitimate means to dispose of problematic cases. Research conducted in provincial police forces further supports the routinised disposal of rapes via the 'no crime' classification (Wright, 1980).

In the area of domestic violence, studies by Edwards conducted during the years 1984–6, 1988, and 1989–90 found a staggeringly high proportion of cases subsequently 'no crimed'. A study of two London boroughs in 1984–6 revealed a 'no crime' rate as high as 80–90 per cent. A later follow-up study in 1988 of the same boroughs revealed a significant decline in the use of 'no crime' to 65 per cent (Edwards, 1991, p. 151). A further follow-up of one of these two boroughs for 1990 (Holloway) and an additional borough (Streatham) revealed a further decline in the use of the 'no crime'. Holloway, in September and October 1989, recorded 46 per cent of cases as 'no crimed' (Buchan and Edwards, 1991, Table 12). Streatham, with its new cautioning policy, recorded for the year 1989, 33 per cent of incidents as 'no crimed', compared with 67 per cent for the months of September and October in 1988. Service delivery to victims of domestic violence from the attendance of first officer at the scene to the subsequent investigation has been traditionally poor. That is to say, the police have offered little support to the victim, and have not controlled the offender through prosecution or formal sanction. Where police have provided care, officers have done so without adequate training and frequently exposed the victim to greater harm and danger. Krishna Sharma died on 8 March 1984, found hanged in her house following eight years of domestic violence. The night before her death she phoned Southall police. Dr John Burton halted the inquest so that inquiries could be made to see if there was anywhere she could have been referred to for advice. The police had referred her to the Citizens Advice Bureau but, unbeknown to the officer giving that advice, the CAB had actually been closed for many years (cited in Edwards, 1992, p. 256).

Facelift for Policing: Care and Control

The Victim Centred Approach

By the mid-1980s in both the areas of rape and domestic violence police managers were pressing for a new approach to the handling of such offences. The new caring model of policing was facilitated as part of the agenda to secure the best possible evidence in these and other cases, and as part of a growing concern for the ongoing and future safety, welfare and wellbeing of victims. It was further developed as part of other broader police agendas, including crime prevention, safer cities initiatives, community policing, and the multi-agency partnership. In police resource terms, of course, a domestic offence not dealt with in the early stages was likely to mean a repeat offence and possibly a more serious offence, potentially homicide.

Research and statistical analysis, which demonstrated that a fifth of all homicides were committed on female spouses, together with an awareness that domestic violence was an ongoing repeat offence with a certainty of violent escalation also assisted in shaping the police response in the years to come. By the mid-1980s there was a new approach to the investigation and handling of domestic violence and rape allegations. Part of this victim-centred approach also involved victim support since the police were also recognising that the victim was a forgotten part of the criminal justice system. By the late 1980s victim support referrals as part of this wider agenda were well-established. Police referrals to Victim Support Schemes numbered some 137,000 in 1990 (Report of the Commissioner of Police of the Metropolis, 1990, p. 10).

Changes in Policing Practice: Rape

Service Delivery

Police have, over the years, changed their approach at both the point of service delivery, investigation, prosecution and recording practice to the handling of victims of rape. This has followed pressure and mounting public awareness from other non-police organisations including the work of the Women's National Commission (1985) and the guidance issued to police in the Home Office Circular on *Violence Against Women*, published in 1986, which endorsed the main recommendations in the Women's National Commission Report. Since the mid-1980s provincial and metropolitan forces have developed victim examination suites (Hanmer, 1989). In the Metropolitan Police District there are already ten of these suites with an eleventh scheduled. The suites are intended to create a safe and relaxed atmosphere for the victim; they comprise small living rooms with coffee-making facilities and a medical examination room, all of which are located within a police station. However, a separate entrance means that the victim does not have to pass through the police station itself to gain entry to the suite.

Using this new approach officers involved in the investigation of rape must undergo a course in sexual offences investigation training (SOIT). Each SOIT course is for a period of four weeks with the addition of two extra days for officers involved in the investigation of male rape. Officers are trained in the Metropolitan Police District (hereafter MPD) in each of its eight divisions, one division having 246 trained officers. The course covers treatment and sympathetic handling of victims, statement taking, multi-agency referral, and rape trauma. In giving support to victims a 'chaperon system' is in operation whereby continued support is provided to the victim from the beginning of the investigation through to the conclusion of the court case. Victims are kept informed of the progress of the case through the criminal justice system and are referred to a Sexually Transmitted Diseases clinic as a priority patient. The investigation is supervised by an officer of detective inspector rank or above. The 'chaperon' is present with the victim during the court case to provide support.

Recording

The generic use of the 'no crime' classification for disposing of cases has been consistently challenged since the publication of the Home Office Circular of 1986 in which all forces were encouraged to use this classification only in exceptional circumstances. In the MPD a special policy (operative from 4 November 1990) applies to the recording of rape and serious sexual offences. The latter is defined as 'rape and buggery, together with indecent assault involving oral sex, use of instruments, exercise of violence including attempt in each instance, and any other circumstances deemed to be especially serious by the investigator'. It is only in cases where the victim admits the allegation to be false, or if there is special evidence that corroborates such an allegation to be false that the 'no crime' is used. This decision to 'no crime', unlike in earlier years, is now made by the area detective chief superintendent, and the victim is required to make a written statement to this effect. It may be that some victims, fearful of reprisals, are dropping charges and subsequently claiming them to be false. Evidence from Smith, however, indicated '. . . that it is still the classic stereotype of rape which is more likely to be officially recorded as a crime' (1989, p. 26). When it comes to the recording of rape allegations the police are still using the 'no crime'. Despite the fact that this classification should be reserved for false accusations and accompanied by the complainant's written statement to that effect, there is some indication that the 'no crime' classification is still being used inappropriately.

Table 6.1 *Notifiable Offences of Rape recorded by the Police in England and Wales*

Year	No of Offences	% Change
1977	1,015	
1978	1,243	+22
1979	1,170	−6
1980	1,225	+5
1981	1,068	−13
1982	1,336	+25
1983	1,334	—
1984	1,433	+7
1985	1,842	+29
1986	2,288	+24
1987	2,471	+8
1988	2,855	+16
1989	3,305	+16
1990	3,391	+3

Source: *Criminal Statistics, England and Wales 1990*, reproduced with the permission of the Controller of Her Majesty's Stationery Office.

Nevertheless, improvements in the recording of rape have been made, the result of which is reflected both in national and MPD statistics for notifiable offences of recorded rape. Table 6.1 shows the increase over the years in notifiable offences of rape recorded by police for England and Wales. Since 1977 an increase in the number of offences recorded can be observed. Indeed, the percentage increase in 1990 over 1980 is 177 per cent. Either we are rapidly becoming a more violent society, more women are reporting rape or there has been a change in police preparedness to record such allegations. In the MPD the rise in recorded rape has been especially significant. In 1980, 269 rapes were recorded, and in 1984, 365. Following Blair's work in 1986 this figure had risen to 824, and by 1991, 1,142 offences of rape were recorded. During the years 1984–7, 4.0 offences of rape per 100,000 population were recorded by the police nationally. In the MPD the rate was 8.6 per 100,000 population, followed by Bedfordshire (5.0), West Yorkshire (4.9) and the West Midlands (4.9). These variations in rape rates are reflective of changes in police policy regarding the recording of such offences rather than indicative of a real rise in the commission of the offence (Home Office Statistical Bulletin, 1989, p. 3).

Prosecuting Rape

Despite improvements in policing at both the level of care for victims and the control of the offender through prosecution, difficulties are encountered by the victim at the prosecution and trial stage. These additional difficulties result in women's reluctance to prosecute. Moreover, whilst rape victims are compellable witnesses, the Crown Prosecution Service (hereafter CPS) rarely if ever compels a rape victim to give evidence. The Law Commission in its final report, *Rape Within Marriage* (1992a), raised the issue of compellability and stressed that wives in sexual offences should be compellable (see also Law Commission Working Paper, 1990).

Research has shown that three-quarters of all reported rapes are committed by persons known to the victim (Smith, 1989). A survey of 1,007 married women in the United Kingdom found that 96 per cent of them thought that rape in marriage should be made a crime and that one in seven women had had sexual intercourse with her husband without her consent (cited in Law Commission, 1992a). Despite recent significant improvements in policing and recording of rape, the proportion of rape allegations which are subsequently prosecuted remains low. In 1984, 653 offences were proceeded with, constituting 46 per cent of reported rapes; in 1986, 925 rapes were proceeded with, a total of 40 per cent of all recorded rapes; in 1987 this rose to 42 per cent of reported rapes, totalling 1,046 male suspects proceeded against. In 1987, 491 suspects were committed for trial and remanded, whilst 374 suspects were committed for trial and released on bail, 45 proceedings were discontinued in the magistrates court and 127 proceedings were discharged under the Magistrates Courts Act 1980 section 6 (Home Office Statistical Bulletin, 1989). Whilst improvements have been made in the police handling of cases, the trial remains as daunting as ever notwithstanding the provision in the Sexual Offences Amendment Act of 1976, which abolished in principle the cross-examination of the complainant as to past moral character. The Criminal Law Revision Committee in its final report, *Sexual Offences*, published in 1984 supported the cross-examination of the complainant in rape trials.

> ... it seems that some people, and in particular some women's organisations, think that these statutory provisions are proving ineffective for the protection of complainants because many judges, so it is alleged, grant leave to cross examine about a complainant's previous experience upon being asked to do so. Critics do not seem to appreciate that a complainant's previous sexual experience may be relevant to the issue of consent. (Criminal Law Revision Committee, 1984, p. 25, para.2.87)

Changes are still required in the court treatment of victims. Victims are without legal assistance, the geography of the court and lack of facilities for victims increase their ordeal, and once the trial judge rules that cross-examination as to moral character is permissible there are no restraints imposed. Whilst the Bar Council Rules of 1965 state that cross-examination must be within certain limits, what these limits are and how far judges are encouraged to consider them remains unknown. There is no penalty clause, for example, for insult or annoyance to the complainant/victim and, although unnecessary cross-examination is to be reflected in the taxation cost of the case, it is not known whether judges actually attempt to control prolonged and unnecessary cross-examination in this way. Numerous observations from rape trials demonstrate the continuing appalling treatment of rape victims by the defence (Lees, 1989). Moreover, where the past moral character of the complainant is deemed to be of relevance, cross-examination by the defence proceeds as it has always done. Leading questions cannot be asked by prosecution but can be asked by the defence. The corroboration warning, although now abolished for the unsworn evidence of children (Criminal Justice Act 1988, section 34(1)), remains intact in cases involving adult rape. Moreover, continuing education programmes for judges are as ever urgently required. In 1983 an Old Bailey judge commenting on the man who had intercourse with a friend's seven-year-old daughter said that it was 'one of the kind of accidents that could almost happen to anyone'. In May 1985 a magistrate remarked that the rape of a prostitute was 'an odd thing – it is like a contradiction in terms'. Judge Kenneth Cooke placed on probation a 61-year-old man convicted of indecent assault on a four-year-old girl. In giving him probation he said: 'I am going to give you a friend and a shoulder to cry on'. More recently in 1993, a trial judge imposed a three year supervision order on a 15-year-old boy for rape on a schoolgirl and ordered him to pay £500 compensation to the girl so that she could have a good holiday and forget all about it (*New Law Journal*, 1993, p. 189).

Home Office research shows that in 1984–5, for cases of rape involving not guilty pleas, 70 per cent of defendants were convicted and 30 per cent acquitted. Moreover, sentences have often been lenient, certainly before the introduction of the *Billam* guidelines. Lord Lane, in *Billam* 1986, notes that 'the nastiness of rape cases has certainly increased and what would 10 years ago have been considered incredible perversions have now become commonplace'. These sentencing guidelines are far more specific than those suggested in *Roberts* (1, *All England Law Reports*, 1982) and proceed from the assumption that rape should involve a custodial sentence in all but the most exceptional cases. Sentencing guidelines were set at five years for rape by an adult pleading not guilty with no mitigating circumstances. Home Office figures for 1984 show that rapists in the pre-Billam period were given overly lenient sentences. Eighteen per cent of convicted rapists were jailed for between four years and five years and only 8 per cent for five years and over. In 1987, just over 80 per cent were given sentences of five years and over compared with 45 per cent pre-Billam in 1985; 74 per cent of offenders convicted of rape had at least one previous conviction for a standard offence. Thirty-one per cent had between one and five previous convictions and over a quarter had more than 10 previous convictions (Home Office Statistical Bulletin, 1989, p. 4). The Criminal Justice Act 1991 section 1 emphasises the importance of passing a custodial sentence where the offence is of a violent or sexual nature, since only such a sentence would be deemed adequate to protect the public from serious harm. This provision may result in achieving more realistic and appropriate sentences in rape cases (see also Zedner, 1992, pp. 275–6). The courts, however, are still finding their way round the Criminal Justice Act 1991. In *Robinson* (*Criminal Law Review*, 1993, p. 143), the appellant was convicted of attempted rape on a 90-year-old woman in her home in the course of a burglary. The appellant was sixteen at the time of his trial and the appeal court upheld the sentence of eight years imposed.

Changes in Policing Domestic Violence

Service Delivery

Since the Home Office Circular of 1986, police forces have been encouraged to review their handling of domestic violence. The Metropolitan Police since 1987 have established domestic violence units with dedicated, trained officers at most stations across the MPD. The unit idea was pioneered in north London in 1987. By 1993 there were 62 domestic violence units in the 'Met' staffed by some 120 domestic violence officers. The units give support to victims, refer victims to local agencies, provide a chaperon for the victim for subsequent prosecution, keep the victim informed of the progress of the case including details about when the offender is leaving custody, conduct follow-up visits and are involved in the collation and monitoring of domestic violence allegations in the police division.

Recording

Following the Home Office Circular and instructions issued by chief constables to their own forces, police recording practices for allegations of domestic violence have improved substantially and the dramatic increase in offences recorded for violence against the person for England and Wales reflects this. All cases of violence against the person have increased from 97,246 in 1980 to 184,655 in 1990, an increase of 89 per cent. Threat or conspiracy to murder has increased from 528 in 1980 to 4,162 in 1990, an increase of 688 per cent and assault occasioning actual bodily harm has increased from 90,654 in 1980 to 169,764 – an increase of 87 per cent, whilst grievous bodily harm has increased from 4,390 in 1980 to 8,920 in 1990, an increase of 103 per cent. As for common assault, in 1980, 557 offences were proceeded with. In 1988, section 39 of the Criminal Justice Act provided for a new offence of common assault and battery triable in the magistrates court only. By 1990, over four thousand such offences were recorded and proceeded with in the magistrates court. The increase in recorded violence against the person is reflective of the preparedness of the police to record cases of domestic violence.

The Metropolitan Police responded to the Home Office Circular by issuing their own instructions to officers, emphasising the need to support victims, to improve service delivery and recording practices. In the MPD alone in 1985, 20,242 offences of violence against the person were recorded; in 1986, 20,308; in 1987, 22,625; in 1988, 27,004; in 1989, 32,255; in 1990, 35,521 and in 1991, 37,854, a 67 per cent increase over 1987. There are, however, still a handful of stations without a domestic violence unit, including Southall. In the MPD in 1991 reported cases of domestic violence rose by 46 per cent over 1990; and reports of domestic violence have risen from 860 in 1987 to 8,510 in 1991 (see also Edwards and Halpern, 1991).

Since 1987 police in the MPD have been continually trying to improve service delivery and the recording of domestic violence. Developments have centred on training of domestic violence unit officers and on improving the response of the first officer at the scene. Giving instruction to the first officer at the scene emphasises the two main objectives of the guidance; namely, 'to meet the needs of victims' and 'to initiate an investigation which will provide the best chance of apprehending the offender'.

Prosecuting Domestic Violence

The control of offenders by police is reflected in arrest and formal sanctions. A central aspect of the control of the suspect in domestic violence and rape is the use of arrest, arguably the most powerful means of police control. The Metropolitan Police Crime Desk Manual states: 'the response of the first officer at the scene is most important in ensuring that the victim is protected and that the offender is dealt with in a firm and positive way; to protect the victim, to investigate fully the offences, to offer compassionate and practical support, to fully report the allegation and to record the investigation; to apprehend the offender and to have the person arrested'. Police orders in most forces following the Home Office Circular remind officers of their powers of arrest in domestic violence.

Despite an increased willingness to arrest, it is still the case that too few cases proceed to a prosecution. The reluctance of victims to give evidence and uncertainty over how to enforce compellability continue to influence the prosecution process. In *Renshaw* (reported in Edwards, 1989) a woman was sentenced to seven days for contempt of court when she refused to give evidence against the man alleged to have assaulted her. A further instance of this erroneous enforcement of compellability was reported in the *Daily Mail* for 31 March 1989, when a Nottingham magistrate fined a woman £300 for refusing to give evidence. The Police and Criminal Evidence Act section 80 (3)(a) renders spouses compellable where 'the offence charged involves an assault on, or injury or threat of injury to, the husband or wife of a person who was at the material time under the age of sixteen'. This statutory provision reverses the House of Lords decision in *Hoskyn* v. *Metropolitan Police Commissioner* (*All England Law Reports*, 1978, p. 136). Improvements are indicated, however, in the desire to protect victims through the use of court remand. Of a sample of suspects charged and proceeded against at Streatham, south London, 75 per cent were kept in custody, 25 per cent were bailed to appear in court. Yet, it still appears to be the case that those convicted do not receive appropriate sentences. In a study of sentencing conducted by Edwards, Armstrong and Brady (reported in Buchan and Edwards, 1991), of all the offenders who were sentenced at court where results were known, one offender was convicted of unlawful wounding and received a one year sentence of imprisonment, one offender was convicted of assault occasioning actual bodily harm and received a sentence of 10 weeks' imprisonment.

The decision to charge, to caution, or to take no further action is a matter for both the investigating officer and custody officer.

Following a Home Office Circular on cautioning issued in 1985, which held the view that 'delay in the entry of a young person into the formal criminal justice system may help to prevent his entry into that system altogether', a later circular in 1990 endorsed cautioning as an option for the adult offender. By 1989, Streatham had introduced a cautioning policy to deal with the domestic violence offender. The aim was to influence police discretion at each stage of the process, for example, arrest, custody and caution, to encourage a positive approach by the police and to provide a better service to victims. Officers were encouraged to arrest and in cases of very minor assault a deferred decision to prosecute was made and the 'suspect' released on bail for a period of two months. The purpose here was to allow for monitoring of his behaviour, through police keeping in contact with the victim. Fingerprints are taken from the suspect and he is detained for a period of time. During his release on police bail the investigating officer makes further enquiries. If the suspect reoffends then he is charged with the first and the subsequent offence. Out of a total of 204 arrests, 66 cases (32 per cent) were considered appropriate for caution and the decision was deferred for a two-month period and the suspects released on bail. After this period in 44 of the 66 cases (67 per cent) adult cautions were administered. Four offenders (6 per cent) were charged, and in a further 7 cases (11 per cent) no further action was taken. In the remaining 11 cases (17 per cent) the offenders failed to appear to answer bail. The impact of the cautioning policy was dramatically to increase the number of arrests, crimed cases and prosecutions overall, and thus to heighten awareness of domestic violence. The fears that cautioning may 'net widen' were not borne out during the period of research evaluation.

Conclusion

Policing practice in both the areas of rape and domestic violence has changed and improved very much as a result of public awareness and pressure. Victims are often caught up in the conflicting efforts of the police both to care for them and to control offenders by bringing offenders to trial, at which the victim is expected to give evidence and to support the prosecution.

The desire to care and to respond to the victim's apparent needs and wishes has to some extent resulted in the mediation bandwagon steaming ahead. Mediation is being promoted widely by the Lord Chancellor and the Law Society, and was considered by the Law Commission in its paper *Domestic Violence and Occupation of the Matrimonial Home* (1992b). In England and Wales, Alternative Dispute Resolution (ADR) is being promoted in separation, divorce and neighbourhood disputes and also in commercial and civil disputes. The Lord Chancellor, Lord Mackay, has said: 'I do see the potential for methods of dispute resolution other than formal recourse to the courts'. The Law Society in its report *Alternative Dispute Resolution* (July 1991) suggests that: 'Mediators can assist parties by establishing a safe and constructive environment' and that 'Mediation agreement is on a "without prejudice" basis'. To ensure that something constructive rather than destructive comes out of any mediation process, all organisations involved in mediation, such as family conciliation and Victim Support, need to draw up clear guidelines as to when mediation is appropriate and to ensure the personal safety of both parties and mediators. As Hilton (1991) points out, mediation assumes that both parties come to the process with equal power and control. In domestic violence this is not the case and mediation can only serve to increase women's powerlessness. The Home Office Circular of 1990 on domestic violence warns police of the dangers of seeking conciliation between assailant and victim: 'police officers should rarely attempt conciliation if the victim has been, or claims to have been, violently assaulted'. Hilton suggests that mediation is in many ways a response to the reorganisation of the court structure and the overcrowded and underfunded court system. She goes on to argue that mediation services can be seen as an attempt to return wife assault to the private sphere.

This effort to empower the victim through placing choice in her hands has led to much confusion over the nature of that choice. Some prosecutors and courts have accepted victim statements and pleas made by victims on behalf of aggressors, resulting in a more lenient treatment of the offender. The quality of choice must be in question where victims are fearful of partners (for further discussion, see National Association of Victim Support Schemes, *Report on Domestic Violence*, 1992). Astounding as it may seem, courts have frequently taken pleas by victims into account, although such pleas are unlikely to be made of free volition. In *Krause* (*Criminal Appeal Reports: (Sentencing)*, 1989, p. 361), where the male cohabitee raped, buggered and assaulted the victim, the court took into account (at the appeal against sentence) love letters she wrote to him whilst he was in prison (see also *Stapleton* in *Criminal Appeal Reports: (Sentencing)*, 1989, p. 364). In *Crane* 1991 (not reported) where Lord Justice Bingham said it was not for victims to determine sentences, he also said that the trial judge did not hear her plea for leniency and now it could be properly taken into account. Similarly, in the case of *Carr* (not reported) who put a pillow over his wife's head and tried to strangle her, a charge of attempted murder was ordered to lie on the file. Justice Judge, taking the wife's plea into consideration, said: 'your wife has written begging me not to send you to prison'. Again in *Woulahan* (Court of Appeal, 11.10.89, unreported) where a husband had kicked his wife in the head and face, Justice Tucker said she was a wonderfully forgiving wife and in this case the court felt able to suspend the sentence of six months' imprisonment previously imposed. In trying to care for victims and empower women, and at the same time control the sexual and violent offender, the police are faced with the difficulty of encouraging victims to prosecute and of enforcing the criminal law. The latter must be pursued, in my view, regardless of the apparent wishes of the victim.

The report of the New South Wales Task Force on Domestic Violence (1981, p. 55) succinctly identifies the dilemma: 'The placing of a choice in the hands of the woman herself is almost an act of legal cruelty, and it imposes upon her a tremendous burden which complainants in other cases do not face ... It leads directly to the intimidation of the woman. The husband knows, or will be told by his friends, that the wife does not have to give evidence. The temptation for him to "heavy" her, either directly or indirectly, is very often not resisted.'

This dilemma is one which lies at the heart of the police role of care and control.

Bibliography

Blair, I. (1985) *Investigating Rape: A New Approach for Police* (Beckenham: Croom Helm, and the Police Foundation).

Bourlet, A. (1990) *Police Intervention in Marital Violence* (Milton Keynes: Open University Press).

Brownlee, I. (1990) 'Compellability and Contempt in Domestic Violence Cases', *Journal of Social Welfare Law*, 2, 107–15.

Buchan, I. and Edwards, S. (1991) *Adult Cautioning for Domestic Violence*, Police Requirement Support Unit, Science and Technology Group (London: Home Office).

Chambers, G. and Millar, A. (1983) *Investigating Sexual Assault*, Scottish Office Central Research Unit (Edinburgh: HMSO).

Chambers, G. and Millar, A. (1986) *Prosecuting Sexual Assault*, Scottish Office Central Research Unit (Edinburgh: HMSO).

Criminal Law Revision Committee (1984) *Sexual Offences*, Cmnd 9213 (London: HMSO).

Criminal Statistics, England and Wales (London: HMSO).

Edwards, S. (1989) *Policing 'Domestic' Violence* (London: Sage).

Edwards, S. (1991) 'Policing Domestic Violence' in Abbot, A. and Wallace, C. (eds) *Gender Power and Sexuality* (London: Macmillan) pp. 113–56.

Edwards, S. (1992) 'Perspectives on Race and Gender' in S. Casale and E. Stockdale (eds) *Criminal Justice Under Stress* (London: Blackstone Press) pp. 246–64.

Edwards, S. and Halpern, A. (1991) 'Protecting Victims of Domestic Violence – Time for Radical Revision', *Journal of Social Welfare and Family Law*, April–June, 94–109.

Ekblom, P. and Heal, K. (1985) 'Police Response To Calls From The Public' in K. Heal, R. Tarling, and J. Burrows, (eds) *Policing Today*, Home Office Research and Planning Unit (London: HMSO) pp. 65–78.

Graef, R. (1990) *Talking Blues* (London: Fontana).

Hanmer, J. (1989) 'Women and Policing in Britain' in J. Hanmer, J. Radford and E. Stanko (eds) *Women, Policing and Male Violence* (London: Routledge) pp. 90–124.

Hilton, N. Z. (1991) 'Mediating Wife Assault: Battered Women and the "New Family"', *Canadian Journal of Family Law*, 9, 29–53.

Home Office Circular No. 14 (1985) *Cautioning* (London: Home Office).

Home Office Circular No. 69 (1986) *Violence Against Women* (London: Home Office).

Home Office Circular No. 59 (1990) *Cautioning* (London: Home Office).

Home Office Statistical Bulletin (1989) *Statistics On Offences Of Rape 1977–1987*, Issue 4/89.

Law Commission (1990) *Rape within Marriage*, No. 116 (London: HMSO).

Law Commission (1992a) *Rape within Marriage*, No. 205 (London: HMSO).

Law Commission (1992b) *Domestic Violence and Occupation of the Matrimonial Home*, No. 207 (London: HMSO).

Lees, S. (1989) 'Blaming the Victim', *New Statesman and Society*, 1, December, 14–15.

Lloyd, C. and Walmesley, R. (1989) *Changes in Rape Offences and Sentencing*, Home Office Research Study, No. 105 (London: HMSO).

Maguire, M. and Corbett, C. (1987) *The Effects Of Crime And The Work Of Victims Support Schemes* (Aldershot: Gower).

McConville, M., Sanders, A. and Leng, R. (1991) *The Case for the Prosecution* (London: Routledge).

Punch, M. and Naylor, T. (1973) 'The Police: A Social Service', *New Society*, 24.

Report of the Commissioner of Police of the Metropolis, abridged (London, 1990).

Report of the National Association of Victim Support Schemes (1992) 13 July.

Report of New South Wales Task Force on Domestic Violence, Women's Co-ordination Unit (Sydney, 1981).

Report of the Women's National Commission (1985) *Violence against Women* (London: WNC, Cabinet Office) December.

Reiner, R. (1985) *The Politics of the Police* (Brighton: Harvester).

Smith, L. (1989) *Concerns about Rape*, Home Office Research Study, No. 106 (London: HMSO).

Wright, R. (1980) 'Rape and Physical Violence' in D. J. West (ed.) *Sex Offenders in the Criminal Justice System*, Cropwood Conference Series No. 12 (Cambridge: University of Cambridge, Institute of Criminology) pp. 100–13.

Zedner, L. (1992) 'Sexual Offences' in E. Stockdale and S. Casale (eds) *Criminal Justice Under Stress* (London: Blackstone) pp. 265–85.

7

Police Encounters with the Mentally Ill: The Role of the Crisis Intervention Service

Mike Stephens

Introduction

With the advent of new drug regimes in the 1950s more and more mentally ill patients found themselves being discharged from long-term incarceration in hospital. In 1961 this policy of deinstitutionalisation became official when Enoch Powell, the then Minister of Health, suggested that the majority of long-stay mental hospitals should be closed. As a result, the number of patients housed in long-stay hospitals in England and Wales fell from about 150,000 in the mid-1950s to 60,000 by the beginning of 1992. In March 1992, it was reported that 60 of the remaining 90 psychiatric hospitals were planned for closure over the next five years. The policy of deinstitutionalisation clearly has further mileage. Indeed, the 'twinning' of deinstitutionalisation with the development of community care initiatives has, in large part, served to justify the closure of psychiatric hospitals and the discharge of their patients.

However, neither the policy of deinstitutionalisation nor that of community care of the mentally ill has been free from controversy and trenchant criticism. For some years critics, such as the National Schizophrenia Fellowship, have accused the government of allowing mental hospital closures to occur at a faster rate than community care facilities can cope with the number of patients who have already been discharged. The Fellowship has spoken of seriously mentally ill people being 'tossed out into the street with little or no follow-up, back-up or proper provision' (*The Independent*, November 29, 1988, p. 3). Moreover, at least six of the 60 psychiatric hospitals due to close in the next five years have admitted that they have been forced to put back their closure dates because of a lack of adequate community-based facilities for the care of the mentally ill. While in the period 1981–91, 22,000 beds were closed in long-stay mental hospitals, only 4,500 new beds were created in the community to replace them. Moreover, of the 28,500 patients discharged from psychiatric hospitals between 1979 and 1986, less than one in 10 had the chance of a place in a day-centre for the mentally ill. These statistics fuel even more the criticism that community-based facilities for the mentally ill have not been expanded at a rate to match the closure of mental hospitals.

What happens to patients discharged from mental hospitals? A new system of community care, organised by the local authorities, came into being in April 1993. It is designed, following many of the recommendations of the Griffiths Report, to provide a well-planned system of monitoring, treatment, and support for those leaving institutional care. Given the rate at which deinstitutionalisation has taken place, and the existing poor provision of community care facilities, the local authorities and the other various agencies involved have a massive series of problems to overcome if they are to make a reality of an efficient and humane system of community care. In the interim, the answer to the question 'what happens to those discharged from hospital?' must include the statement that far too many end up with little or no support at all; that some gravitate towards a different kind of institutionalisation within the prison system; and that others when not a part of the 'revolving door' syndrome become homeless. Various surveys have put the number of homeless people who have a history of mental illness or who have recently been discharged from psychiatric hospitals at between 20 and 40 per cent. The extra £8m committed by the government in January 1992 to help mentally ill people sleeping rough in London has been widely criticised by charities in the field as too little. In the massive policy and resources shortfall between the realities of deinstitutionalisation and the rhetoric of community care, there is more than ample scope for discharged patients, often without proper support in the community, to come to the attention of the police.

Police Use of Section 136 Mental Health Act 1983

The police operate not only as a law enforcement organisation but also as a 24-hour emergency agency in which many of their various activities are devoted to what has been called 'the secret social service'. With the advent of both increased de-institutionalisation and inadequate community care facilities, a growing number of discharged mental patients have become displaced, disoriented, or homeless. Without proper community-based treatment for such individuals in the form of hostel accommodation, day-care facilities, and social services support, the behaviour of a growing number becomes more unstable. Florid or bizarre behaviour, exhibited in a public place – most frequently the streets of our towns and cities – brings these ex-mental hospital patients to the attention of the police. One typical mode of intervention by the police in such circumstances is the use of section 136 of the Mental Health Act 1983, which allows a constable to remove a person to a place of safety in that person's own interests or to protect other people, if the police officer, having found that person in a place to which the public have access, believes him or her to be suffering from a mental disorder. The purpose of this procedure is to allow for the psychiatric assessment of the person detained under section 136.

When individuals are subject to police attention under section 136 there is the potential both for a controlling and a caring outcome. However, in the absence of proper psychiatric services to support the police, the potential caring function – as a further manifestation of a system of community-based treatment – is being left largely unfulfilled. One reason for this is the large variation in the levels of police use of section 136 throughout the country (Thomas, 1986, pp. 28–9), and the tendency of many police officers not to see this kind of service as constituting 'real' police work. Teplin's research in America and the work of Murphy (1986, p. 7) confirm a view prevalent among many British officers that '"handling mentals" was not regarded as a good pinch and was largely unrewarded by the [police] department' (Teplin 1984, p. 165). Officers in the UK frequently complain that dealing with such disturbed individuals can be extremely time-consuming and that they are too frequently unable to arrange for the swift attendance of a social worker at the police station to help with the case. The antipathy felt between the police and the social work profession in relation to this issue was summed up by the Police Superintendents Association, which argued:

> There is a tendency that 'on call' social workers having a particular speciality are loath to respond to emergency calls if this is not in their field. This is evident with regard to mentally disturbed people and a tremendous amount of police time is wasted in dealing with these people because the social worker either doesn't know how to deal with these situations, often has to be persuaded to respond, and frequently takes a long time to get to the station. (Thomas, 1986, p. 30)

For its part the social work profession has been concerned in the past about the police being initially responsible under the provisions of section 136 for identifying someone as mentally disordered. It was suggested (Thomas, 1986, p. 27) that the lack of relevant training might lead to mistaken determinations of mental illness. Ironically, there is evidence to suggest (Kelleher and Copeland, 1972, p. 220) that the police are as good as general practitioners in recognising those who are in need of psychiatric treatment.

Given the fragile nature of working relations between street-level police officers and front line social workers, there is an obvious danger that the best interests of mentally disturbed individuals who come to the attention of the police are not being met. One method of ensuring that the caring function takes precedence in the manner in which the police handle mentally disturbed individuals is to put in place a psychiatric crisis intervention service. Although community care facilities for the mentally ill in America have also attracted much criticism, a model for a crisis intervention service does exist in Madison, Wisconsin, USA.

Mental Health Crises and the Madison Police Department

The process of deinstitutionalisation has happened in America at an even faster pace than in the UK and, arguably in many large USA cities, such as New York, the community-based facilities to support discharged mental patients are largely unable to cope with the demands placed on them. Consequently,

> law enforcement has been burdened with inappropriate responsibilities for the mentally disabled. The virtual absence of community mental health emergency services has left the police agencies, by default, to answer the urgent and routine needs of the mentally ill. Their response to date has not always been exemplary, but, in fact, they have not received any significant guidance from the mental health profession on how to manage the mentally ill. Rather, police agencies have found themselves under attack for their handling of the mentally disabled. Local media, mental health professionals and judiciaries have stated that the police have failed in their attempts to manage these encounters and often exacerbate rather than mollify the problem. (Murphy, 1986, p. i)

As a result of the lack of sufficient support from community-based services, the needs of many newly discharged mental patients in the USA were not being met. Throughout the 1960s and 1970s a growing number of these individuals, forced to exist without proper care and support, simply could not cope with the normal processes of social interaction; a failing that frequently brought them to the attention of the police. Faced with a street-level encounter with such an individual a police officer can move the person on, perhaps to a less public place, or the officer can try to have the person hospitalised. Arguably neither option is satisfactory and the latter can be extremely time-consuming for police officers who frequently have to tour various hospitals in the locality seeking an emergency admission. The final option, arrest and subsequent incarceration in a prison, is the worst one of all.

With the level and standard of community care in the USA generally poor and subject to wide geographical variation, many police forces came increasingly under great strain to deal with the problem of the mentally ill, so much of whose lives were played out on the city streets. While the general picture is a disappointing one, there are, however, some cities that pursue what might be termed good practice and Madison may be considered as one of these. In the 1970s a vigorous hospital closure programme gave rise to increasing numbers of former mental patients gravitating towards the city of Madison, in part attracted by the city's relatively liberal welfare policies (Finn and Sullivan, 1987, p. 80).

Located in Dane County, Madison has a population of 170,000 and is policed by the Madison Police Department (MPD). Both the MPD and the Dane County Mental Health Center (DCMHC), also located in Madison, noticed the increasing number of so-called 'street crazies' who were exhibiting bizarre behaviour in the city centre area. The police were receiving a growing number of calls from shop owners wanting these ex-mental hospital patients removed from the area. In addition, there was spreading resentment among patrol officers that they were having to handle these incidents without much support from other agencies. The MPD chief of police was not prepared, however, simply to 'solve' this problem by incarcerating the ex-patients in jail or by finding hospitals to accept them on a short-term basis. For its part, the DCMHC realised that it was largely failing to provide any support or treatment for these individuals and, accordingly, it wished to capitalise on the MPD's initial contact with them through the development of a crisis intervention programme.

In May 1975, funded by the DCMHC but jointly planned with the MPD, the Crisis Intervention Service (CIS) was set up. CIS is a 24-hour service, able to respond to any call for assistance within Dane County from a police officer (or anyone else) who has encountered a mentally disturbed person who is exhibiting behaviour of a bizarre or unacceptable nature or who is in great emotional turmoil. The scheme caters mainly for suicide attempts and threats, family crises, psychotic individuals, and potential involuntary hospitalisations. The response from CIS can involve either advice given over the telephone or radio to a police officer, or on-scene attendance. The MPD's Social Services Co-ordinator maintains close contact with CIS and other mental health agencies and takes responsibility for ironing out any day-to-day problems experienced by police officers in their dealings with CIS. The appointment of the Social Services Co-ordinator, a serving police officer, was part of the process within the MPD to adopt a more community-oriented style of policing (Couper and Lobitz, 1991, pp. 15–16), and to adopt policies designed to address specific problems (Goldstein, 1990, p. 52). Behind the operation of CIS is the following rationale:

> Police agencies have traditionally provided the primary and generally the only 24-hour mobile emergency service available in the community. Although the police are best known for their crime management responsibilities, the fact is that over 80% of their time is spent in non-crime-related activities ... Such involvement puts the officer in a *key case-finder role*. (Cesnik, Pierce and Puls, 1977, p. 211. Italics added)

Punch also refers to the case-finding or gatekeeping role of the police, frequently performed before other welfare services intervene, and argues that 'the police turn out when a crisis is happening and represent a visible, available, and well known agency which, more than any other mental health institution, has mobility and authority in situations where violence is often an element' (Punch, 1979, p. 107). Although the police were seen as crucial gatekeepers or case-finders, the scheme still had to ensure the co-operation of patrol officers if it were to be successful. Senior personnel within the MPD and the DCMHC recognised that the CIS would have to respond, in the first instance, to the perceived needs of patrol officers if the programme were to capitalise effectively on the police case-finding role (Cesnik, Pierce and Puls, 1977, p. 212).

Accordingly, CIS was not to be confined to a traditional mental health role (Cesnik and Stevenson, 1979, p. 38), but was to be available 24-hours-a-day and be prepared to attend swiftly at the scene of any crisis following a police referral. With minor problems patrol officers would normally place the disturbed person in the custody of family or friends. If an officer is not comfortable with that option, the officer can consult with CIS and receive advice about the most appropriate disposition. When the police request the on-scene attendance of CIS personnel the mental health professionals would then take the major responsibility for the handling of the disturbed individual and would immediately begin an appropriate treatment plan. Arrest is reserved for those who have committed serious crimes (Finn and Sullivan, 1987, pp. 81–2). Co-ordinated planning by the MPD and the DCMHC has allowed the mental health professionals to familiarise themselves with the operational concerns and needs of patrol officers and to develop a scheme designed not only to address those concerns, but also to address the therapeutic needs of disturbed individuals.

When CIS became fully operational, following a period in which CIS personnel received police training in how to intervene in potentially life-threatening scenarios and accompanied patrol officers on 'ride-alongs' to become more familiar with the work of the police, the scheme soon built up a reputation for prompt response to police referrals. Out of 150 referrals per month, over a third came from MPD officers (Pierce and Cesnik, 1978, p. 3). Typically, when CIS personnel respond to a call the police give them what information they have about the individual and the circumstances in which he or she came to the attention of the patrol officers. The police then leave the person in the care of CIS whose fieldworkers begin a psychiatric evaluation of the individual in order to develop a treatment plan. There is no automatic assumption that hospitalisation need be a part of that plan; indeed, the philosophy of CIS is to ensure whenever possible that people are treated in the community. The goal here is to capitalise on the crisis itself, which has brought on the kind of behaviour that has led to initial police involvement, and to use the crisis in a therapeutic manner. It is not uncommon, therefore, for CIS mental health professionals to return the disturbed individual to his or her home and to collect friends and relatives there in order to explore the meaning of the crisis. The idea is to create a milieu in which the new client of CIS can 'live through the crisis and benefit from it ... Crucial in making such interventions meaningful is the promise of intensive involvement by staff members throughout the crisis period' (Cesnik and Stevenson, 1979, p. 38).

If necessary, CIS personnel have the option of referring the client to outpatients' clinics and to other community-based mental health facilities and services. In short, CIS is one part of a *co-ordinated network of such services,* which exists in Madison and in Dane County. Thus, while CIS focuses on handling patients in crisis, the fact that it can refer clients to other services means that fewer individuals are likely to manifest themselves again as 'street crazies'.

After each referral the appropriate patrol officers are given feedback about the outcome of the referral and the nature of the client's treatment plan and progress. In this way, should there be any subsequent contact between police officers and the disturbed individual, the officers will be able to react appropriately. Furthermore, the feedback information serves as a recognition that the officers of the MPD are providing a worthwhile service to the community as well as to the mentally disturbed individuals they encounter.

Thus, the major way in which the CIS maintains good operational relations with the MPD's patrol officers is through the quick response to referrals and the immediate management and treatment of clients. However, in-service training programmes also provide another mechanism through which to improve relations. CIS personnel train patrol officers in emergency mental health principles and techniques, which allow officers to recognise mental disturbance more expertly and, thereby, improve referral practices. Moreover, police officers in plain clothes have also accompanied CIS staff on emergency call-out so that officers might gain first-hand knowledge about the techniques employed by CIS. Through such a process officers begin to understand that community-based treatment is an effective alternative to hospitalisation and they become more willing to refer cases to CIS (Pierce and Cesnik, 1978, p. 10). By meeting the need of patrol officers for a swift response to situations that many police personnel find 'messy' and not 'real' police work and, by maintaining a highly professional stance, which involved keeping the police informed about the programme and its methods, the scheme resulted in 'a relatively stable and cooperative working relationship between the crisis service and law enforcement agencies' (Cesnik, Pierce and Puls, 1977, p. 215).

Police Practice in the UK

In Britain section 136 of the Mental Health Act 1983 provides the police with a form of social control whereby those individuals suspected of being mentally disordered may be removed from a public place to what is termed a place of safety in order to carry out an assessment of that person's condition or to make arrangements for that person's treatment. The place of safety is frequently a police station, particularly outside London. Given the powers involved in section 136 to deprive a person of his or her liberty, the increasing frequency with which the police encounter the mentally disordered as a direct result of the inadequacy of community care facilities, and the obvious special needs of people detained under section 136, it is not surprising that police procedures have come under ever more detailed scrutiny. One issue to examine immediately is whether the police can judge effectively who is suffering from mental disorder.

The competence of police officers to recognise mental disorder has been noted for some time (Kelleher and Copeland, 1972) and the study by Rogers and Faulkner (1987, p. 32) found that 90.5 per cent of people referred under section 136 by the police were subsequently diagnosed by assessing psychiatrists as suffering from some form of mental disorder. However, while doubts about the ability of the police, in general, to recognise appropriate individuals for referral under section 136 may have been eradicated, there have been other concerns about the role of the police. Criticisms have been expressed about the regional variations in the use of section 136 by the police, the over-representation of black people, and the tendency of detention under this section too often leading to hospitalisation.

Although the Department of Health collates statistics on the number of people admitted to hospitals under section 136 – with a heavy concentration of admissions in the four Thames Regional Health Authorities – these figures tell us very little about police use of this section. There are different local arrangements; and where use of section 136 does not result in hospitalisation, it is not always recorded in official statistics (Rogers and Faulkner, 1987, p. 8). However, while we cannot be sure about the true level of use of section 136, nevertheless the official figures do give rise to concern.

For instance, in their study of police use of section 136 in London, Rogers and Faulkner (1987, p. 19) found that the black population was 'over-represented in comparison with its proportion in the general population . . .' A follow-up study by Bean *et al.* (1991, pp. 25–6) also found a very high proportion of people of Afro-Caribbean origin in its sample of those detained by the police under section 136. While Rogers and Faulkner (1987, p. 39) admit that the majority of both black and white people detained under section 136 and subsequently assessed by psychiatrists were, in fact, diagnosed as being mentally ill, the suspicion of racial discrimination on the part of the police still persists and has been echoed in a number of studies (Mercer, 1984; Black Health Workers and Patients Group, 1983).

The over-representation of black people in the section 136 statistics may be due to a number of explanations, such as the possible tendency for black people to express disordered behaviour more visibly and strongly and, therefore, to stand a higher chance of coming to the attention of the police (Hitch and Clegg, 1980). Reiner (1985) suggests that since section 136 cases are largely initiated by the public, the high proportion of black people among them may be due to 'transmitted discrimination', in which the police act as receivers and transmitters of wider public discrimination. Given the complexities of this issue, Bean *et al.* were unable to make a conclusive statement about the nature and extent of any police discrimination in section 136 procedures.

> While the study did not demonstrate overt racist behaviour on the part of the police, the disproportionate number of people of Afro-Caribbean origin was clear and may well represent covert racism in the operation of the provision. A number of officers made unprovoked remarks which suggested racial stereotyping of mentally disordered people. (Bean *et al.*, 1991, p. 150)

A major criticism of the section 136 procedure, especially where the police take a person suspected of being mentally disordered directly to a mental hospital as the place of safety, is that it leads to over-frequent hospitalisation with little or no exploration of alternatives – a tendency that a crisis intervention scheme would eradicate. Rogers and Faulkner (1987, p. 36) found that:

> The hospital dealt with police referrals in a routine manner, using section 136 as a means of short term compulsory admission. The very low numbers of discharges and other immediate disposals suggest that admission under section 136 is done as a matter of course irrespective of diagnosis. The overwhelming majority, 89.9% of the 129 patients who were admitted under section 136, were generally detained for three days.

In the hospital where Rogers and Faulkner (1987, p. 43) conducted their research, all the people detained under section 136 were kept for three days in a locked ward, and 70 per cent of them received medication during this period. Given that some of these individuals may have accepted treatment simply because they were detained, and that there is still considerable stigma attached to incarceration, not to mention the fact that all of them were removed from their social networks and possible alternative forms of care, the use of section 136 in this manner runs counter to the ethos of the community care philosophy. It might be argued that detention and assessment in a police station, as a designated place of safety, is a better alternative than taking disordered people directly to a mental hospital, particularly where the hospital tends to treat section 136 as a short-term admission order rather than as an assessment order. However, many police stations are either too busy or too ill-equipped to handle mentally disturbed individuals for any length of time; a deficiency that only serves to highlight the benefits that a crisis intervention scheme could bestow on both the police and the mentally ill. Not the least of these benefits would be the ability of such a scheme to carry out assessments at its own premises and to arrange for suitable community-based forms of treatment and support.

Care and Control: The Policy Overlap

Crisis intervention programmes are rare in the UK; of the four in the country the 24-hour-a-day emergency service in Coventry closed at the end of 1992. The decision to end the scheme was partly motivated by financial reasons and partly by the limited nature of its operations. The crisis intervention scheme in Coventry had never been fully interdisciplinary and, lacking the direct involvement of psychiatrists, had been unable to take on as clients those with a formal diagnosis of mental illness. It was intended that some of the resources saved as a result of the closure of the scheme would be devoted to more generic community-based services for the mentally ill, a part of whose remit will be to offer emergency services when appropriate.

However, notwithstanding this new strategy, at the very time when the system for caring for the mentally ill is switching with increasing speed to a community-based service, we are failing to provide effective responses to the needs of the mentally ill. Without crisis intervention programmes an increasing burden will fall on the police, but the policy lessons of the CIS in Madison are clearly available should the UK wish to create such schemes.

No matter what consultation and joint planning may have taken place among the senior personnel of the agencies involved in the development of a crisis intervention programme, the co-operation and trust of junior police officers is vital to the success of any such scheme. It is this latter group who act as the vital case-finders and it is essential, therefore, that the needs of patrol officers are properly identified if this case-finding role is to be exploited effectively. One such need is for information, for all police officers are wary and suspicious of matters they cannot predict and, thus, fear they cannot properly control. Accordingly, patrol officers should be carefully informed about the programme's goals and methods of working, so that police personnel are clear both about the responsibilities that the crisis intervention workers are prepared to take on and about their own role in relation to the disposal of mentally disturbed individuals.

The other major need of the police is that the crisis intervention programme be a credible one. In particular, this means not only that the programme's mental health specialists act in a highly professional manner, but also that the service should be a 24-hour facility, able to respond swiftly to any calls from patrol officers anywhere within the programme's catchment area. Where a crisis intervention programme can consistently deliver a rapid and highly professional response to police calls, the levels of suspicion and hostility that have too often charac- terised relations between the police and welfare organisations begin to decrease. This process may be accelerated, and indeed even result in the establishment of more constructive relations, where regular in-service training schemes are developed, which allow the police, social workers, and other mental health professionals to gain a better understanding of their respective roles and their *common* interests.

It is clear that the success of a crisis intervention programme depends heavily on the quality and extent of inter-agency co-ordination and co-operation. In the past, the police have frequently been criticised for dominating multi-agency forums and using them for their own ends to gather information and to enhance their methods of social control over selected and per- ceived 'troublesome' populations (Baldwin and Kinsey, 1982, pp. 59–103). One must acknowledge that such a risk exists in order to ensure that any crisis intervention programme oper- ates ultimately for the benefit of mentally disturbed individuals. Thus, in Madison, although the CIS took account of police needs and interests, it was specifically developed to improve on the procedures for handling mental health emergencies. Had the crisis intervention programme in Madison aspired to be no more than a ferry service – relieving the police of their former responsibilities to drive the mentally ill from one hospital to another in search of an emergency admission – the scheme would certainly have operated only in the interests of the MPD. However, the CIS went far beyond such limited horizons and became a part of a network of services for the varying needs of the mentally ill. In order to capitalise on the police's case- finding role, CIS personnel responded swiftly to referrals. In this way, the programme did satisfy an important police need. How- ever, when the referral had been made and the CIS personnel had assumed responsibility for the case, it was the needs of the disturbed individual that were paramount. Police interests no longer figured in the disposition of the case; what mattered here was the wellbeing of the individual and the principles of crisis intervention through which to attempt to secure that wellbeing. The police played no part in decisions relating to treatment, nor in those relating to the kind of community-based facility to which an individual might be referred.

There is, then, a continuity of interests between the police and mental health agencies in the case-finding and case-referral stages of public events involving bizarre and florid behaviour exhibited by the mentally disturbed. The police's primary interest in social control is in no way undermined by the operation of a crisis intervention programme. Indeed, since an efficient programme relieves the police of many time-consuming duties, it actually allows them to focus more strongly on the preferred crime management aspects of their role. In the handling of most cases involving disturbed individuals, there is an overlap between the social control function of the police to 'do' something about people who exhibit such 'strange' behaviour and the caring function of mental health professionals who are seeking to secure appropriate treatment and support for their clients. Indeed, there is evidence from Madison that exposure to the operation of an effective and professional crisis intervention programme leads to some police officers taking a more active interest in the handling of the mentally ill and, thus, being able to respond more appropriately when such officers first encounter an on-street incident involving a mentally disturbed person. The regular feedback provided by CIS to patrol officers about the progress and treatment of police-referred individuals also helps to encourage this process.

While not all police officers would willingly acknowledge it, their involvement with the crisis intervention programme in Madison was in itself an overlap of control and care functions. Many officers are uncomfortable with an emphasis on the caring side of police work, preferring instead the harder image of technologically sophisticated professionals dedicated to catching criminals and quelling large-scale public disorder. Yet, in Madison, officers came to acknowledge the worth of the CIS.

The Madison Police Department and the Dane County Mental Health Center have developed, implemented, and maintained a successful program for handling the mentally disordered.

The interaction of the two agencies has enabled the police to improve their management of this population. Officers know how to identify and interact with the mentally disordered and how to seek emergency detentions; they have also become familiar with the mental health center, its philosophies, and referral agencies. The mental health center, for its part, has achieved its goal of being able to identify, locate, and monitor the mentally disordered. Between them, the two agencies have also reduced inappropriate hospitalizations and incarcerations. (Murphy, 1986, p. 88)

Care and control are often emotive words, frequently applied in a stereotypical fashion to 'sum up' the operational activities and philosophies of agencies such as the police and social services. Professionals working in one agency or the other can too easily praise their own activity and philosophy while minimising or even criticising those of another organisation. However, the legal and social context in which the police and social workers operate is too complicated to allow for a simple dichotomy between care and control. In many areas there is a distinct overlap in which the police and other groups of professionals share common interests and seek a common goal. The identification and subsequent treatment of those experiencing an acute episode of emotional turmoil or mentally disturbed behaviour is one such area where the police, social workers, and other mental health professionals can effectively work together in pursuit of shared goals. The lessons from Madison show that this is possible. Care and control can sit side-by-side in appropriate circumstances. The tragedy in Britain is that many of the mentally disturbed who would benefit from this overlap in the form of crisis intervention programmes are being too often abandoned to their fate because there is neither care nor control – unless it be imprisonment. Indeed, all too frequently, there is simply indifference.

Bibliography

Baldwin, R. and Kinsey, R. (1982) *Police Powers and Politics* (London: Quartet).

Bean, P., Bingley, W., Bynoe, I., Faulkner, A., Rassaby, E. and Rogers, A. (1991) *Out of Harm's Way* (London: MIND).

Black Health Workers and Patients Group (1983) 'Psychiatry and the Corporate State', *Race and Class*, 15, 2, 50–63.

Cesnik, B., Pierce, N. and Puls, M. (1977) 'Law Enforcement and Crisis Intervention Services: A Critical Relationship', *Suicide and Life-Threatening Behavior*, 7, 211–15.

Cesnik, B. and Stevenson, K. (1979) 'Operating Emergency Services', *New Directions for Mental Health Services*, 2, 37–43.

Couper, D. and Lobitz, S. (1991) *Quality Policing: The Madison Experience* (Washington, D.C.: Police Executive Research Forum).

Finn, P. and Sullivan, M. (1987) *Police Response to Special Populations* (Washington, D.C.: U.S. Department of Justice, National Institute of Justice, Issues and Practices).

Goldstein, H. (1990) *Problem-Oriented Policing* (New York: McGraw-Hill).

Hitch, P. and Clegg, P. (1980) 'Modes of Referral of Overseas Immigrant and Native-Born First Admissions to Psychiatric Hospital', *Social Science and Medicine*, 14a, 369–74.

Kelleher, M. J. and Copeland, J. R. (1972) 'Compulsory Psychiatric Admission by the Police', *Medicine, Science and the Law*, 12, 3, 220–24.

Mercer, K. (1984) *Black Communities' Experience of Psychiatric Services* (Proceedings of the Transcultural Psychiatry Conference).

Murphy, G. R. (1986) *Special Care. Improving the Police Response to the Mentally Disabled* (Washington, D.C.: Police Executive Research Forum).

Pierce, N. and Cesnik, B. (1978) 'Training Police in Crisis Intervention: The Police Patrol Model', paper presented at the 11th Annual meeting of the American Association of Suicidology, New Orleans, 1–11.

Punch, M. (1979) 'The Secret Social Service' in S. Holdaway (ed.) *The British Police* (London: Edward Arnold) pp. 102–17.

Reiner, R. (1985) *The Politics of the Police* (Brighton: Wheatsheaf).

Rogers, A. and Faulkner, A. (1987) *A Place of Safety* (London: MIND).

Teplin, L. (1984) 'Managing Disorder: Police Handling of the Mentally Ill' in L. Teplin (ed.) *Mental Health and Criminal Justice* (Beverly Hills: Sage Publications) pp. 157–75.

Thomas, T. (1986) *The Police and Social Workers* (Aldershot: Gower).

8

Police and Juvenile Offending
David Thorpe

A Measure of Diversion

The Criminal Statistics for England and Wales in 1987 show that males under 17 years of age who were cautioned by the police averaged 66 per cent of all those cautioned and prosecuted. These national statistics, however, fail to reveal the local variations in police cautioning of juveniles. The lowest cautioning rate occurred in Staffordshire, where the police cautioned only 41 per cent of under 17 year old males and prosecuted 59 per cent. The highest rate belonged to the Northamptonshire Police, which cautioned 86 per cent of those cautioned or prosecuted (Home Office, 1987). This chapter will give an account of the processes whereby the Northamptonshire Police, by the late 1980s, were diverting more than 8 out of 10 apprehended juvenile offenders from the juvenile courts. The specific mechanism developed within that county, for the purposes of increasing levels of diversion for delinquents, was that of the Juvenile Liaison Bureau (JLB). The JLB model of service was introduced as an experimental pilot scheme in two of Northamptonshire's towns – Corby and Wellingborough – in 1980/1. The success of the JLB scheme in those areas was such that the procedures and practices developed there were implemented countywide by the mid-1980s. When the pilot projects were set up in Corby and Wellingborough, members of staff of the Department of Social Administration (now Applied Social

169

Science) at the University of Lancaster were contracted to research the schemes under the direction of the author.

During the 1970s, police cautioning of juvenile offenders became a widespread practice throughout England and Wales. In most jurisdictions, cautions were issued for minor acts of delinquency primarily as an administrative device which only involved other agencies if the police perceived an immediate crisis requiring welfare intervention. Some police authorities however directly involved other agencies with a statutory concern for children at the time cautions were administered. Their aim was not merely to deal with juvenile offenders solely on a procedural level, it was also to provide services to youths wherever it was considered they were needed. In effect, some police forces were redefining their role as gatekeepers to the juvenile criminal justice system into that of responsibility for referral to child welfare agencies. This was the model of practice that the Northamptonshire Police chose to implement, using police officers as part of inter-agency teams providing direct service to juvenile offenders. In that sense, the police were shifting their response to juvenile offending from that of formal administrative processing to that of providers of welfare. It was, in both theory and practice, a shift from control to care by choosing to involve police officers directly in the provision of services to youths.

This role was very much in direct contrast to the way in which police cautioning had developed in the past. The practice by police officers of issuing a formal caution to offenders as an alternative to prosecution had been in evidence for a very long time. In fact Steer (1970) mentions that 'the records of the Metropolitan Police Force show that a form of cautioning was used as early as 1833' (Steer, 1970, p. 54) and that successive Metropolitan Police commissioners encouraged this use of police discretion in respect of *minor* offenders. Minor offenders fell into a whole range of categories. Some of them included encouragements to caution street lottery scheme organisers (in 1833), juveniles 'running alongside omnibuses and turning summersaults' to attract the attention and coins of passengers (in 1858), attempted suicides (in 1916), and women soliciting (in 1958). These cautioning practices arose in part as an administrative convenience. If every offence to which offenders admitted guilt were reported by the police for prosecution, then the courts would very rapidly become clogged with cases. The sheer volume of police time devoted to the prosecution process is quite considerable. Therefore, the use of police cautions in respect of 'non-serious' crime, which serves to reduce the organisational burdens associated with the administration of justice, has always had its attractions.

The administrative rationale for diversion from prosecution forms only a small part of the argument however. Overwhelmingly, the reasons given for the practice of diversion are professional ones; they are very simply a recognition of the potentially negative consequences of subjecting offenders – particularly the young and elderly – to the experience of criminal prosecution in a court of law. Apart from their arbitration functions, criminal courts act primarily as highly symbolic instruments of society in dealing with conflicts between individuals and the state. They are deliberately designed to demonstrate publicly the power and majesty of the state and they act in such a manner as to defame, discredit and stigmatise those classed as wrongdoers. Whatever form of judicial administration different societies adopt, whether it be the 'self-criticism' groups of the Chinese Cultural Revolution, the gatherings of aboriginal elders to administer tribal laws in Australia, or the criminal courts of the western tradition, the mechanism always acts to set an individual *apart* from society. Despite this necessity for public denunciation, it has long been accepted that while the primary aim of boundary maintenance is achieved (the reinforcement of distinctions between right and wrong, the demonstration of the power of the state), such events can serve to reinforce a deviant identity in individuals subject to legal administrations. The maxim 'give a dog a bad name and he'll keep it' has been replaced by the sociological truism 'if a situation is defined as real, then it is real in its consequences'. In the case of the prosecution process, that can become 'if an individual is publicly defined as criminal, then his or her behaviour will become modified. He or she will become a more committed criminal'. Very simply, if prosecution does damage, then it does so by creating behaviour in the offender which is in accordance with the expectations created by the prosecution experience.

Juvenile offenders have long been seen as fit subjects for diversion, for not only are the bulk of their misdemeanours relatively trivial, but also there is a relatively low risk of further offending. Two simple lessons have not escaped the attention of criminal justice system planners. First, the bulk of youngsters who are reported by the police do not offend again. Second, when youngsters reach school leaving age, they are less likely to get into trouble.

In view of these extensively recognised features of delinquency, combined with an awareness of the 'labelling' consequences of prosecution, it is not surprising that moves to divert juvenile offenders from prosecution on a large scale have been under consideration for a long time. The 1960s and 1970s saw growing pressure from central government on the police and youth-serving agencies to increase diversion. Section 5 of the much-maligned 1969 Children and Young Persons Act (CYPA), had it been implemented, would have imposed on the police a whole new range of administrative, legal and professional procedures aimed specifically at avoiding prosecution. These procedures clearly suggested that informal attempts at resolving the issues surrounding an offence would have had to be made before the police could attempt a prosecution.

The range of legally binding measures prescribed in section 5 of the 1969 CYPA would have had the effect of diverting a substantial proportion of delinquents away from the juvenile court, now known as the youth court. The police would no longer have been able to act in isolation in determining juvenile court intake populations. Instead, they would have had to approach other agencies; specifically, local authority social services and education departments to try to resolve the problems of delinquent behaviour informally. Shortly after the 1969 CYPA was passed, a new Conservative government was elected which had opposed the passage of the Bill. Crucial, diversionary sections of the Act were not implemented and succeeding Labour and then Conservative governments refused to implement these sections.

By the early 1970s, however, anticipating that section 5 diversionary procedures might become a reality, several police forces had already begun to appoint officers who specialised in dealing with juvenile offenders. Additionally, despite the absence of legislation, successive governments continued to exhort the police to exercise their discretion in respect of cautioning. The major thrust of these exhortations is perhaps best summarised in paragraph 37 of the 1980 White Paper, *Young Offenders*.

> The government believes that it is by increased consultation and co-ordination of this kind that effective progress is likely to be made in containing and reducing juvenile crime. It does not, however, take the view that this can be best achieved by legislation. Circumstances vary greatly from area to area and statutory requirements for the formation of specific consultative machinery may do as much to harm existing satisfactory local arrangements as to encourage consultation where none exists. The Government therefore intends to continue to do everything possible to encourage inter-agency co-operation at a local level without imposing any centralised formula. (Home Office, 1980, p. 12)

The number of juvenile offenders receiving a caution increased considerably during the 1970s. A number of studies were undertaken to discover the effects of these changes in police practice and they showed that this use of professional discretion had generated a number of unintended consequences. One of the first of these unintended consequences was concerned with the enormous variation in cautioning rates between different police forces in England and Wales, a variation which emerged as a result of different types of local police practice. In 1974, in response to a written question, the House of Commons was presented with statistics by the Home Office showing varying local cautioning rates in 1972. These ranged from a rate of 64.8 per cent (youths cautioned as a percentage of all those cautioned and found guilty) in Devon and Cornwall in the south west of England to only 11 per cent in Teesside in the north east of England. It was clear even at that stage that an apprehended youth's chances of being diverted from the juvenile court appeared to depend more on where he or she lived than on what he or she had done.

The first study of post-1969 CYPA cautioning was published by the Home Office in 1976; it suggested that the new police juvenile bureaux had not only succeeded in increasing the number of juvenile offenders cautioned, but that they had also increased prosecutions as well (Ditchfield, 1976). The implications of the study were that some 'net-widening' was occurring. In 1981, the *British Journal of Criminology* published a paper by Farrington and Bennett which very firmly demonstrated net-widening as a consequence of increased cautioning. They concluded that: 'After the introduction of the cautioning scheme there was a widening of the net of arrested juveniles . . . it is implausible to suggest that there was anything approaching such a marked increase in juvenile offending' (Farrington and Bennett, 1981, p. 128). These UK studies showed that while the cautioning of juvenile offenders was increasing, the prosecution rates were not decreasing at a commensurate rate. 'Net-widening' is an expression which describes a situation where, once a new alternative and less stigmatising procedure becomes available to the police and other juvenile justice agencies, it is not used exclusively for those youths who would otherwise be prosecuted, but becomes instead a method of dealing with youngsters against whom, hitherto, no formal action would have been taken.

The research literature on the effectiveness of juvenile justice reforms is replete with examples of net-widening. Austin and Krisberg, evaluating the research evidence in the United States, described the process thus:

> Criminal justice agencies are in a constant state of change. Laws are passed which change their authority, new theories of social control are promoted and funded, budgets expand or contract. Administrators are forced to decide which activities will be emphasised, terminated, or begun anew. As justice system agencies change, so do the nets. This is not to say that the social control system is shaped exclusively by subordinate organisational factors. Instead, social control and organisational change must also be understood as part of changes in the political and social milieu. Reform strategies that ignore powerful ideological and economic forces will fail or have unintended consequences. (Austin and Krisberg, 1981, p. 69)

After reviewing diversion studies, the authors concluded that: 'placed under the control of a criminal justice system diversion programmes have been transformed into a means for extending the net, making it stronger, creating new nets . . .' (Austin and Krisberg, 1981, p. 71).

In effect, the option to divert from prosecution by means of a caution offered the police a third control option, the two pre-existing options being no further action or prosecution. The new option supplemented formal processing and formalised previously informal organisational practice. Evidence that the use of new discretionary powers by the police had precisely this effect abounds in 1970s cautioning schemes in England and Wales. Even when police–social services liaison schemes were used, little measurable effect was discernible as a consequence of consultation procedures.

By early 1985, the government was able to issue a circular that strongly recommended inter-agency liaison, co-operation by senior officers and referred to the charges of net-widening. Home Office Circular 14/1985 explicitly encouraged senior officers to examine their procedures together.

> However, he (the Home Secretary) wishes chief officers to be aware of his view that the issue of guide-lines should also provide the opportunity for a review of local arrangements, where this has not already been done, to ensure that liaison arrangements with social services departments, the probation service and where appropriate the Education Welfare Service, are such as to encourage the participation of those agencies in decision making. (Home Office, 1985, p. 2)

In the circular, for the first time, the government explicitly invited the police to share their discretionary powers to caution delinquency with other youth-serving agencies and raised the issue of net-widening as a potentially negative effect of the increased use of diversionary measures. Ten years of research and experiment had finally led to very specific government recommendations.

The Northamptonshire Experience

The Juvenile Liaison Bureau experiment in Northamptonshire, beginning in Wellingborough at the end of 1980 and then extending to Corby twelve months later, provided the first examples of such inter-agency co-operation where the police agreed to be directly influenced in their decision-making by other professionals. As models of co-operative work, the North-amptonshire Bureau possessed several unique features. The first was that liaison extended beyond the immediate bound-aries of the police and social services and included the proba-tion service and the education department (both school and youth work sectors). The second was the secondment of per-sonnel from each of these agencies to work as a *team*. The third was the range of services to be supplied by the team (counsel-ling, no action, restitution, welfare) and the fourth was a very specific set of objectives. These objectives were originally agreed by the relevant chief officers who established a study group and later a management group to maintain oversight of the bureau. The objectives of the bureau, articulated by North-amptonshire's Chief Executive, Mr Jeffrey Greenwell, were as follows:

(a) to try and reduce the rising number of offences com-mitted by juveniles; and

(b) to try and find a way out of the rapidly increasing costs of bringing juveniles before the courts with costs incurred by Police, Social Services and Probation; taking children into care or under Supervision Orders; residential placements for children in care; and by breaking the 'escalator' of criminal sophistication produced by institutionalised treatment to keep more children out of the system and reduce the rate of re-offending. (Greenwell, 1984, p. 29)

Judging from the evidence of previous studies, the ambitious aims of the Northamptonshire experiment would not easily be fulfilled. What is of interest here, however, is that for the first time, specific financial issues are raised as potential advantages of diversion, in addition to the more commonly accepted 'so-cial' gains.

The Corby Juvenile Liaison Bureau (JLB) commenced its reform efforts in the local juvenile criminal justice system in November 1981. The bureau team's primary aim was to reduce the numbers of youths entering the juvenile court, thus lowering juvenile court workloads and developing a less stigmatising way of dealing with juvenile delinquents. These reforms were to be achieved by means of intervention in the police decision-making process. Before November 1981, youths reported by the police for crimes and offences were processed internally by the police after some consultation had occurred with relevant local agencies (the social services, education and probation departments). As with much of the rest of the country, this consultation process was very much a 'paper exercise'. The intention was that the observations of other agencies would be of assistance to the police in helping them to decide whether or not a caution was an appropriate way of dealing with individual cases. The response to police notifications was very much a haphazard affair, the bulk of notifications were returned by the social services and probation departments with 'not known by the agency' types of comment. Even when youths were known, social workers and probation officers generally preferred not to make a specific recommendation to the police since they either believed that they were unable to influence police decision-making or they preferred to stand aside from the process.

No detailed information was available on the effectiveness of this process since responses to police notification were so variable and inconsistent. Systematic records of responses did not exist other than in individual police files. Generally speaking, the creation of the JLB in Corby was to a certain extent the direct result of police – and to a lesser degree social services – discontent with this seemingly unreliable, *ad hoc* and haphazard system of consultation. The new JLB system had an immediate effect on the consultation process by virtue of the fact that it constituted a much more reliable and effective method of responding to police reports on juvenile offenders. The intention was that the JLB would provide three important additions to the consultation process. These were: first, routine and systematic investigation of all relevant police notifications; second, the provision of direct services to individual juvenile offenders or where appropriate through other agencies; and third, a firm recommendation to the police in respect of decisions to caution or prosecute.

The Research Findings

The decision-making process within Northamptonshire Police was reconstructed as a flow chart in which information about youths (age, offence type, previous offending histories and previous sentencing/cautioning histories) was linked to formal responses by the agencies which made up the JLB in Corby. This information, on all police-apprehended youths in Corby between 1 January 1980 and 26 June 1983, was placed on computer file and analysed.

For the purposes of recording and analysis, the January 1980 to July 1983 period was split into seven successive six month periods and each designated as a file.

FILE 1   January–June 1980*
FILE 2   July–December 1980*
FILE 3   January–June 1981*
FILE 4   July–December 1981*
FILE 5   January–June 1982
FILE 6   July–December 1982
FILE 7   January–June 1983

(The asterisks denote the period prior to the creation of the JLB)

These files were subject to computerised frequency and cross-tabulation analysis. The results of these analyses (Tables 8.1 to 8.6) refer to numbers of police referrals and *not* to numbers of youths. On many occasions, several referrals were sent to agencies for observations on one individual during a six-month period. The outcome of the consultation process may have then led the police to issue a caution or to prosecute *one* individual on *one* occasion even though this was the result of having issued several referrals. File 1, for example, consists of 365 police referrals, but it does not refer to 365 youths. Some individuals may have been cautioned and then prosecuted during a given six-month file period as a result of two or more referrals being made by the police. Tables 8.7 and 8.8, however, use data collected separately by the Corby JLB. These tables refer to individuals prosecuted and the sentences which they received.

Table 8.1 *Ages and Numbers of Police Referrals*

	% Aged 10–13	% Aged 14–17	Numbers
FILE 1	37	63	365
FILE 2	35	65	209
FILE 3	39	61	210
FILE 4	34	66	239
FILE 5	39	61	367
FILE 6	38	62	205
FILE 7	42	58	396
Average	37.7	62.3	284

Table 8.1 analyses the age structure of police-reported youths. It shows that while there was some fluctuation in that structure, on the whole, approximately just over one-third of reported youths were under the age of 14 years, with less than two-thirds aged between 14 and 17 years. Variations in the numbers of reports during that time are much more marked, especially between Files 6 and 7 (July–December 1982, and January–June 1983). In the former period 205 reports were made and in the latter period this had almost doubled to 396. From this table it can be seen that File 7 was not typical of the 1980–1983 period, with an above-average proportion of reports of younger delinquents and a well-above average total *number* of reports being made.

Table 8.2 *Types of Offences Committed by Youths Referred by the Police*

	'Less Serious' %	'More Serious' %
FILE 1	57	43
FILE 2	59	41
FILE 3	55	45
FILE 4	67	33
FILE 5	72	28
FILE 6	76	24
FILE 7	71	29
Average	65.3	34.7

For the purposes of this analysis, those offences classed as 'Less Serious' include theft, damage and police-defined (public order issues), while 'More Serious' offences refer to the taking and driving away of motor vehicles, burglary, assault, arson and serious assaults including robbery and actual or grievous bodily harm. Generally speaking, the offending patterns shown by reports changed during the 1980–3 period, with crimes and offences becoming on the whole less serious, particularly after the JLB became operational in November 1981.

Given the above-average representation of younger youths referred and the higher incidence of less serious offences committed in the 1982–3 period, it may be argued that a 'net-widening' was occurring insofar as the police had become less reluctant to refer youths because of the existence of the JLB. Table 8.3, a compendium of Tables 8.1 and 8.2, uses the averages of 1980–3 reports to show that the 1982–3 period saw a qualitative and numerical change in youths entering the system.

Table 8.3 *A Comparison of Pre- and Post-Bureau Police Referrals*

	Average % Aged 10–13	Average % 'Less Serious' Offenders	Average Numbers
FILES 1–4	36.25	59.5	255.7
FILES 5–7	39.6	73	322.6

On the whole, youths referred by the police after the JLB began its operations were younger and less delinquent and there were more of them. This phenomenon is closely in accord with comparable British and American studies, which show that when diversionary reforms are introduced into juvenile criminal justice systems, the availability of a new 'formal' disposal is used by the police to extend the net of formal surveillance and control. Another interpretation of this would be that in transforming their role from that of overt, formal controllers to informal carers, police officers, aware of the personal difficulties of apprehended youths, saw referral to the JLB as a means of solving these problems and potentially reducing the likelihood of reoffending. In that sense, once ideologies and practices change from those of coercive control to the provision of welfare, then police activity cannot be regarded as one of problem solving rather than formal processing. Ironically, it may be that since the system is seen not only as being 'softer' but also as one that positively helps, then referral becomes easier. In such conditions of reform, 'net-widening' becomes inevitable since the services are perceived as beneficial as opposed to potentially harmful.

Table 8.4 *Police-Referred Youths Cautioned or Prosecuted*

	NFA	Caution	Prosecute	Totals
FILE 1	9(2%)	117(32%)	239(65%)	365
FILE 2	5(2%)	75(35%)	129(61%)	209
FILE 3	4(1%)	94(44%)	112(53%)	210
FILE 4	8(3%)	100(41%)	131(54%)	239
FILE 5	19(5%)	224(61%)	124(33%)	367
FILE 6	29(14%)	116(56%)	60(29%)	205
FILE 7	26(6%)	244(61%)	126(31%)	396

Table 8.4 gives information which is crucial to answering the question 'did the JLB's efforts produce results?' The answer, with qualifications, was overwhelmingly *yes*. Cautioning rates of reported youths in the two years before the JLB became established averaged 33.5 per cent of all referrals in 1980 and 42.5 per cent of all referrals in 1981. During 1982 and the first half of 1983, these rose to 59.3 per cent, representing an increase of some 21.3 per cent. Presented diagrammatically, it can be seen that despite the increase in reported youths after 1981, there were real reductions in the numbers prosecuted.

Figure 8.1 *Numbers of Referrals Resulting in a Caution or Prosecution*

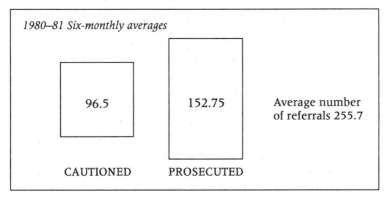

1980–81 Six-monthly averages

96.5 — CAUTIONED

152.75 — PROSECUTED

Average number of referrals 255.7

Figure 8.2 *Numbers of Referrals Resulting in a Caution or Prosecution*

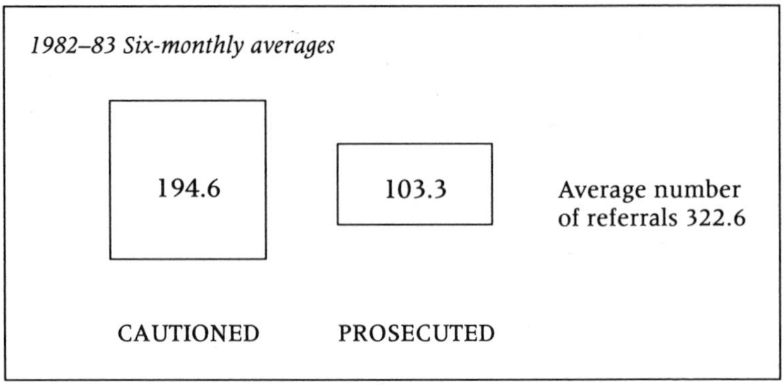

1982–83 Six-monthly averages

194.6   103.3   Average number
                                 of referrals 322.6

CAUTIONED   PROSECUTED

Figures 8.1 and 8.2 show that the JLB had a real impact on police decision-making in Corby. The ratio of cautions to prosecutions went from approximately 2:3 to approximately 2:1.

Table 8.5 *Cautioning Histories of these Referrals which Resulted in a Caution*

No. of previous cautions	0	1	2 or more	Total
FILE 1	107(91%)	6(5%)	0(0%)*	117
FILE 2	72(96%)	0(0%)	0(0%)**	75
FILE 3	86(97%)	3(3%)	0(0%)	89
FILE 4	77(77%)	11(11%)	0(0%)***	100
FILE 5	178(78%)	44(19%)	2(2%)	224
FILE 6	—	—	—****	—
FILE 7	164(67%)	55(23%)	25(10%)	244

*   Cautioning histories of 4 cases not recorded.
**   Cautioning histories of 3 cases not recorded.
***   Cautioning histories of 12 cases not recorded.
****   Cautioning histories of all cases in this file not recorded.

For totals see Table 8.4 'Caution' column.

Table 8.5 shows that the increase in cautioning rates achieved by the JLB's activities arose primarily as a result of administering *second* cautions to youths who had already received a caution. Despite the increased number of younger, less delinquent youths reported by the police from 1982 onwards (Files 5, 6 and 7), the JLB was not seduced into focusing its diversionary efforts on that group. In other studies of cautioning schemes increases in the numbers of youths cautioned rarely led to reductions in the numbers prosecuted. In the case of Corby, however, the numbers prosecuted in 1983 were approximately less than half of what would have been expected without the JLB. Table 8.4, for example, shows us that in Files 1, 2, 3 and 4, 600 out of the 1,023 reports resulted in prosecutions (a rate of 59.7 per cent) compared with 310 out of 968 (a rate of 32 per cent) in Files 5, 6 and 7. Had the JLB not existed, one would have expected 578 prosecutions of reports in Files 5, 6 and 7, 268 more than actually occurred.

It would appear, therefore, that in the first 18 months of its operation, the Corby JLB successfully diverted 268 reports from prosecution, or 89 for every six months' work it performed.

Attention will now be paid to the workings of the JLB during the first six months of 1983 (File 7), the recommendations it made on referred youths and the outcomes in terms of police decisions and JLB services.

Table 8.6 *Corby JLB Recommendations and Police Decisions*

JLB Recommendation	Police Decision Outcome		
	NFA	Caution	Prosecute
Not Applicable	0	1	1
No Recommendation	9	3	6
NFA	8	4	0
Caution	0	100	2
Caution & Bureau Service	0	36	3
Caution & Apology	2	36	0
Caution Contact & Apology	0	20	3
Prosecute	0	0	18
'Not Guilty'	2	0	0
Totals	21	200	33 (254)

Table 8.6 gives some indication of the complexity and specificity of the JLB's work with individual delinquents. Discounting the Not Applicable, No Recommendation, No Further Action, Caution, Prosecute and 'Not Guilty' categories of recommendation, it would appear that the three major new options introduced

by the JLB, midway as they were between a Caution and a Prosecution, represented a total of 98 (46.2 per cent) of the 210 firm recommendations made to the police. These three types of recommendation represented increasingly more intensive involvement with youngsters, ranging from a Caution backed up by a service from the bureau (involvement in an activity, counselling, etc.), through Caution and Apology (carefully structured confrontation with a victim), to a combination of these two services (Caution, Contact and Apology). Sometimes this included compensation to a victim. (For a discussion on these services see Blagg, 1985.)

Out of the 202 recommendations for cautioning made by the JLB (Caution, Caution and various JLB services) shown in Table 8.6, the police responded positively to 192 by issuing a caution; they took No Further Action in 2 cases and Prosecuted in 8 cases. In all 18 cases where the JLB recommended a prosecution, the police took the matter to the juvenile court, and in 6 cases where no specific recommendation was made the police also decided to prosecute. The police take-up rate on JLB recommendations for diversion by means of a caution was therefore 95 per cent. In the 8 cases where there was disagreement on this issue, the Bureau had offered its services to six. This suggests a very high degree of confidence by the police in the JLB's recommendations to proceed by means of a caution.

The Corby Juvenile Court

One of the aims of the JLB experiment was that it should lead to fewer residential and custodial sentences. Evidence abounds on the failure of residential and custodial measures to reform or rehabilitate juvenile offenders. In theory, reduced rates of entry into the juvenile court should have had the knock-on effect of changing sentencing patterns for those youths whose behaviour was so intractable as to merit prosecution.

For the purposes of comparison, File 2 and File 7 were selected to see if evidence existed for changes in sentencing as a result of the JLB's efforts to reform juvenile justice in Corby. Table 8.4 shows that in File 2 (July–December 1980), 209 referrals were issued by the police, 75 (35 per cent) of which resulted in a caution and 129 (61 per cent) of which resulted in a prosecution. In contrast, in File 7 (January–June 1983), 396 referrals were made, 244 (61 per cent) of which resulted in a caution, and 126 (31 per cent) of which resulted in a prosecution.

Despite the fact that the numbers of referrals leading to a prosecution outcome were roughly the same (129 in File 2 and 126 in File 7), 156 youths received main final sentences in the former period and only 70 in the latter period. The reasons for this discrepancy are three-fold. First, some prosecuted youths inevitably bypassed the referral process, especially when they were arrested, charged and very rapidly brought before the court, initially with a police request for a remand in care or custody. Since prosecution was already occurring and the police had to respond urgently to some delinquents, there was little point in consultation because the NFA and Caution options were effectively ruled out. Not all court appearances were preceded by consultation. Second, even when referrals were issued, delays in the prosecution process caused youngsters whose referral was issued in one six-month period, to appear before the court in a subsequent one. Not all the referrals in File 2 would have appeared before the Corby juvenile court before the end of December 1980, and when courts remanded and adjourned cases, the final sentence outcome could be delayed by months. Third, the numbers in Table 8.4 refer to referrals, and not individuals, so as many as three or four referrals may have generated only one individual main final sentence.

Tables 8.7 and 8.8, therefore, which show the main final sentence outcomes of the Corby juvenile court, were not *directly* linked with the referrals or individuals shown in Files 2 and 7. They do, however, represent something of the *climate* created by the old and new juvenile criminal justice systems in Corby and were a reflection of the changes brought about by the existence of the JLB.

Of the 157 juvenile court disposals in this period, 18 per cent were to care or custody – the 13 section 7(7) Care Orders, 13 Detention Centre Orders and 3 referrals to Crown Court. A further 22 per cent, or 35 sentences, were concerned with Supervision Orders, with and without Intermediate Treatment conditions.

Table 8.7 *Corby Juvenile Court, Main Final Sentences, July–December 1980*

Sentence	Nos.	%
Absolute Discharge	2	1
Conditional Discharge	37	23
Deferred Sentence	13	8
Fine	20	13
Attendance Centre Order	21	13
Supervision Order	35	22
Care Order	13	8
Detention Centre Order	13	8
Referred to Crown Court	3	2
Total	157	98

Table 8.8 *Corby Juvenile Court, Main Final Sentences, January–June 1983*

Sentence	Nos.	%
Absolute Discharge	0	0
Conditional Discharge	21	30
Deferred Sentence	4	6
Fine	10	14
Attendance Centre Order	12	17
Supervision Order	17	24
Care Order	3	4
Detention Centre Order	3	4
Referred to Crown Court	0	0
Total	70	99

The picture of post-JLB disposals emerging from the Corby juvenile court was dramatically different from that portrayed in Table 8.7. To begin with, the numbers of youths who received sentence were less than half those of the earlier period. In part, this may be a reflection of the outcome of referral procedures in File 1 (365, with 239 prosecutions), as opposed to those in File 6 (205, with only 60 prosecutions). However, it is the *patterns* of disposals which seem to have changed so markedly, with a halving of the proportion of care and custody sentences – down from 18 per cent of all disposals in July–December 1980 to only 8 per cent of all disposals in January–June 1983. Conditional Discharges appear to have held up, indicating that by early 1983, the extensive use of cautioning did not erode the lower half of the penal tariff and that welfare disposals (the Supervision Orders) continued to retain their place in juvenile justice. On the whole, recommendations and decisions made in response to police referrals and the ensuing juvenile court outcomes suggested that the aims of the Corby JLB were achieved by early 1983. The crude evidence of this limited empirical survey shows that there were significant reductions in prosecutions, and in the use of care and custody for juvenile offenders.

Northamptonshire County Council's decision to establish a multi-professional inter-agency team in order to reform the county's juvenile criminal justice system appears to have brought significant benefits. The Corby JLB, on the basis of the Lancaster research, fulfilled all the objectives set for it. It met the expectations of the chief officers who originally formulated the very specific aims of the Bureau. Juvenile justice in Corby was no longer the product of the machinations of several large bureaucracies, but a carefully graded reaction to youthful mis-behaviour. Caution/Prosecution ratios were substantially altered from 2:3 to 2:1. Juvenile court sentences, which had the ex-pensive and ultimately counterproductive effect of removing youths from the community, were being sharply reduced. The agencies, which made recommendations on delinquent youths and ultimately took responsibility for community reactions to them, did so on an informed basis, and were prepared to recognise the contributions which they made to providing con-structive solutions in respect of problem youngsters.

The research showed, however, that these successes were not achieved without difficulty and in certain respects developments occurred which could have jeopardised the whole operation. The first, most obvious and most easily predictable 'unintended consequence' was the tendency of the police to push in younger and less seriously delinquent youths. The tables in this chapter suggest that this was becoming something of a flood during early 1983. This is not in the least bit surprising since it was the police who experienced the greatest changes in their reactions to delinquency. They had to adjust to a great scrutiny of their work (through the JLB) and also to rapidly taking on board the new options presented by the JLB's existence. The other agencies involved in the juvenile criminal justice system also experienced changes and criticism. For those whose professional identity was closely linked to juvenile court work – social services and probation – this was especially difficult. Nevertheless, a key factor in the success of the JLB experiment appears to have been the 'Corporate Strategy'. Corby JLB members were directly responsible to senior officers in their own agencies and both parties on either side of the managerial divide appeared to have kept their lines of communication open sufficiently to respond creatively and supportively to the conflicts inherent in the situation.

One researcher whose task it was to observe the Bureau team in Corby recognised that it was faced with a range of difficulties both internally and externally. This was the 'melting pot' in which different professional and agency cultures had to be modified in a way which produced outcomes in line with the Bureau objectives. The easiest and most likely outcome of the Bureau's efforts might have been that it would simply have to develop new services, not as an alternative to prosecution, but primarily as an alternative to a caution or no further action. Virtually all existing diversionary studies suggest that this is what one would normally expect. The introduction of new services does not reduce reliance on the old, it tends instead to supplement them. This net-widening phenomenon is more or less the norm, yet it appears to have been avoided in Corby. There is evidence to suggest that the upheavals experienced by JLB members during the first year or so of its existence might in part have been a result of the very fact of its success. Had the JLB concentrated on delivering services to first offenders and oiling the wheels of the system, then net-widening would have occurred and there would have been relatively limited conflict within the team. As it was, the disagreements about *who* should receive JLB services and *what* those services should be reflected a determination to make real inroads into juvenile court prosecution lists. Conflict could have been reduced had this not been the case.

On another level, the research highlighted what is perhaps the fundamental problem confronting all professionals and agencies who are concerned with delinquency. Time and time again, respondents in the study – professionals, victims and offenders – betrayed a confusion about what the juvenile crim-

inal justice system could achieve. One simple social event, superficially described as 'apology and reparation', was interpreted by
onlookers as being punishment, diversion, reform, deterrence
or even welfare. Each participant and onlooker, depending on
his or her perspective, interpreted such events differently.
Clearly, contradictions and inconsistencies abound in the way
in which we think about and respond to juvenile offenders.
However, within the context of the Northamptonshire model,
the police saw their role as providing concrete and practical
solutions to offending which avoided the stigma of prosecution.
In order to do that they had to work in teams whose task was
to provide help and to facilitate the resolution of conflicts.
Caring was not an abstract ideology which somehow handed
help to youths, but practical, human service activities focused
on the immediate crisis experienced by both offenders and
victims. In no sense did the police operations here resemble
what many professionals describe as 'treatment'. Whether they
could be described as 'care' or 'control' becomes irrelevant,
since the act of 'caring' manifestly performs the function of
'controlling'. Diversion on this model serves four purposes.
First, it eliminates the administrative expenses incurred in
prosecution. Second, it avoids stigma. Third, it offers *intervention*; that is to say, delinquency is not ignored. Fourth, it provides
services designed to reduce the likelihood of reoffending.

The advantage of the JLB model of delinquency management
was that these issues arose around concrete human situations,
rather than as abstract organisational ideologies such as those
of so-called 'Justice' or so-called 'Welfare'. The informal nature
of the Bureau's services served to humanise the frequently
impersonal and alienating process of receiving juvenile justice.
In that sense, it represented a very real and important initial step
forward in rendering intelligible and meaningful on a human
level the process whereby the state maintains the boundaries
between certain types of right and wrong. The real success of
the JLB experiment in Corby may not lie so much in its financial and less stigmatising advantages, as much as in the fact that
it made the system credible to all those who chose or who were
forced to participate in it.

Faced with the practicalities of resolving the issues surrounding each individual delinquent act as they related to both

offenders and victims, the police JLB team member proved to be neither more nor less caring or controlling than counterpart team members from the social work, probation, teaching and youth work professions. The police officers who were seconded to the scheme showed themselves every bit as capable of undertaking assessments, formulating intervention plans and seeing them through as the other professionals involved in the JLB team. In both their attitudes to the job and their day-to-day practices, they were indistinguishable – yet they retained a clear 'police officer' identity, which was translated into the view that the work they did within the JLB was a legitimate policing activity. Their notion of policing was indistinguishable from that of caring. This would suggest that once operational instructions relate to the achievement of specific tasks, which are to be performed in specific inter-agency settings, then the context determines the outcome. Since the Northamptonshire scheme was very much a police-inspired enterprise, then its success in a sense was guaranteed.

Bibliography

Austin, J. and Krisberg, B. (1981) 'Wider, Stronger, Different Nets: The Dialectics of Criminal Justice Reform', *Journal of Research in Crime and Delinquency*, 18.

Blagg, H. (1985) 'Reparation and Justice for Juveniles', *British Journal of Criminology*, 25, 267–79.

Ditchfield, J. A. (1976) *Police Cautioning in England and Wales*, Home Office Research Study 37 (London: HMSO).

Farrington, D. P. and Bennett, T. (1981) 'Police Cautioning of Juveniles in London', *British Journal of Criminology*, 21, 110–22.

Greenwell, J. (1984) 'An Historical Perspective and Philosophy' in *Crime Prevention: Diversion – Corporate Action with Juveniles* (Lancaster: University of Lancaster Centre of Youth, Crime & Community).

Home Office (1985) *The Cautioning of Offenders* (London: HMSO).

Home Office (1980) *Young Offenders* Cmnd 8045 (London: HMSO).

Home Office (1987) *Criminal Statistics* (London: HMSO).

Steer, D. (1970) *Police Cautions – A Study in the Exercise of Police Discretion* Oxford University Penal Research Unit, Occasional Paper No. 2 (Oxford: Blackwell).

9

Against the Grain: Co-operation in Child Sexual Abuse Investigations

Nigel G. Fielding and Sue Conroy

Care and control

Like other dichotomies, the distinction between care and control in the work of social agencies is a convenient heuristic which can obscure as much as it illuminates. When law, or probation work, or the investigation of child sexual abuse, are seen as comprising 'particular proportions of consent or coercion along a unilinear dimension between the two polarities' (Hunt, 1981, p. 52), differences are exaggerated, connections are obscured. The complexity of the social world is lost.

The polarization of care and control seems particularly stark in the investigation of child sexual abuse. In the conventional, long-established division of labour, social services were the agency of care, and police the agency of control. The brief of social services was extensive, to put the interests of the child first but also to value the family. The brief of the police was intensive, to identify and prosecute offenders. Over time, then, social services had a long-term involvement with the principal parties to a case. The net would be cast wide, including contacts with health and education agencies. While social services 'enjoyed' an extensive knowledge of the case and would be best placed to perceive the overview, the police role would be confined to the investigations necessary to exert their monopoly on formal social control. Contact with other agencies was confined to making the case. This done, police surrendered any long-term watching brief over victim and family to social services.

In a previous critique of dichotomous distinctions in criminal justice, one of us saw a need to 'look beyond the polar points of the dichotomy to the gradations of practice between' (Fielding, 1984, p. 171). This was written purely as an analytic injunction. But in the case of child sexual abuse significant policy developments have reinforced the message. Following dramatic cases during the 1980s, public awareness and concern greatly increased. One official response was to call for more police and social services co-operation, an approach with which the agencies themselves had been experimenting. From the perspective of our concerns here, the policy afforded a chance to look again at the 'controlling' and 'caring' elements in the work of both agencies and, particularly, to examine the efforts of a 'control' agency to offer 'care', and of a 'caring' agency to get to grips with exerting 'control'.

Police: An Agency of Control?

Whatever the merits of a finer-grained analysis, it must be acknowledged that the overwhelming ethos of the police is that of an agency of social control. True, the early history of the police contradicts this, for order maintenance was prioritised ahead of social control (Fielding, 1991). Society had to be in a state of 'tranquillity' before efforts to control crime could succeed; without this, for instance, public assistance could not be expected. But there is little serious doubt that, in the minds of both public and police, the agency is about crime control. It is obvious that 'social service' does not feature in this discussion, and it is only since the early 1970s that there has been attention to the social service functions the police perform (usually because activity studies show more police time is spent in service work than crime control; see Shapland and Vagg, 1988).

The tensions within the police organisation over its mission are played out in differences of orientation between various functions, different strata of its quasi-military hierarchy, and in differences of motivation between individuals, as this extract from an interview with a recently-promoted inspector suggests. 'There are elements of management, there are elements of supervision. I feel that the balance is important. It's the balance that is lacking in the police service and the guidance given as to what is expected. And often what is expected in written terms in general orders or on the surface is not actually what's expected from you on the underlying feelings of, if you like, the culture of the police service . . . I think it's the culture that's wrong. I think the pressure from underneath, from within the service itself, is something that it tries to maintain with a public front which is a different sort of image . . . It definitely causes me some concern' (Interview, 26 November 1991).

The police perspective is widely seen as hard-bitten, cynical and drawn to rigid in-group and out-group distinctions. There seems little point in documenting such a familiar stereotype, but it is worth noting that some see in the machismo of the occupation a quality very similar to that of criminal offenders. Ryder writes that his years as a psychologist working with teenage offenders convinced him that what chiefly motivated their offending was conformity to values of machismo entrenched in their peer group (Ryder, 1991). We are not in the business of amplifying stereotypes, but if there has to be a bipolar distinction it seems clear which side social scientists, the public and the police themselves would locate police officers. While Ryder argues that machismo is increasingly dysfunctional, he concedes that 'of course it is useful in a warlike society which must defend itself against attack . . . and it is an especially important quality where hand-to-hand conflict and extreme physical hardships need to be endured' (Ryder, 1991, p. 13). To the police, the working world sometimes seems like that. The enduring and dominant image of policing as social control is nowhere more apparent than in the plausibility of these stereotypes despite the evidence that police spend more time in social service than fighting crime.

Social Services: A Caring Agency?

The core function of social services departments (SSDs) is the delivery of social work by people who have been trained that social work is a generic profession. Despite their brief to promote the welfare of citizens in need 'from the cradle to the grave', the argument is that these varying demands will be commonly susceptible to counselling interventions. Workers are expected to appreciate both individual and social causes of disadvantage and deprivation, and to address problems through counselling as much as by providing material resources.

The power of social workers extends beyond decisions to grant or withhold resources, be they financial aid or admission to an old peoples' home. When social workers help to withdraw people who are thought to be mentally ill from the community they wield considerable powers of social control (see also Stephens in this volume). But perhaps the most widely-known and feared power possessed by the agency is the power to 'take your children away'.

To many ordinary people the social services are not a benign agency, but a threatening force of bearded intellectuals and busybodies whose speech and reasoning are incomprehensible and whose decisions are capricious at best. In the terms of another dichotomy, this agency is decidedly on the 'Them' side of 'Them and us'. It is worth mentioning that, in the interviews conducted with parents of child sexual abuse victims in our research, most criticism was reserved for social services, not police. Further, the social work literature includes a subtheme presenting social workers as the 'soft cops' of the state.

Drawing together these threads, we would maintain that, while the place of the two agencies on their accustomed side of the care/control dichotomy is undoubtedly merited, there is much in their work and culture that runs against the grain of the stereotype. There is a further practical point. These are very large agencies. Any large organisation will contain factions as well as enclaves to protect those whose orientation or tasks run against the mainstream.

A final preamble brings us back to child sexual abuse. The sensitivity of any case in which a child is the victim and, within that, the extreme concern where the victimisation is sexual, probably accounts for the willingness of the agencies to change their established practices, even in ways which contradict hallowed ways of working. But, for policy makers, the changes in practice are no longer seen as confined to the special case of child sexual abuse.

Police and Social Services in Child Sexual Abuse Cases

Our introduction suggests that the relationship between police and social services in investigation and case-preparation in child sexual abuse cases has historically been marked by tensions, by virtue of different emphases within the care and control matrix. As Brian Hayes, then Surrey's chief constable, put it:

> enquiries are often commenced by social services in order to establish the facts or extent of such abuse, and then the police are informed and an investigation commences. This system entails duplication, with the victim being interviewed and possibly medically examined by both agencies. The shortcomings of dealing with children in this way were apparent and showed a lack of professionalism, with the agencies appearing more concerned with their own role than the present and future welfare of the child. (Foreword to Conroy, Fielding and Tunstill, 1990)

Child sexual abuse had, then, been of professional concern for some years, but did not prompt widespread public anxiety until the launch of ChildLine, a telephone help-line, in 1986. In 1987, an unprecedented increase in diagnosed cases of child sexual abuse in Cleveland led to a major public inquiry. The inquiry concluded that the reasons for the crisis were complex, but highlighted a 'lack of proper understanding by the main agencies of each others' functions in relation to child sexual abuse; a lack of communication between the agencies; [and] differences of views at middle management level which were not recognised by senior staff' (DHSS, 1988a, p. 243). It urged 'the development of interagency cooperation' (DHSS, 1988a, p. 248).

Both the then-DHSS (1988b) and the Home Office (1988) issued guidelines for professionals, coinciding with the publication of the Inquiry Report. The Home Office circular focused on child sexual abuse, whereas the DHSS guide was concerned with child abuse generally. Both, however, were concerned about agencies working together. The DHSS document's chapter on sexual abuse noted that 'sexual abuse has features which require separate consideration in order to see how existing interagency procedures can be adapted to include it . . . a particularly high level of cooperation between social services departments or the NSPCC and police and doctors is essential during the investigation because of the likely nature of the evidence' (DHSS, 1988b, p. 33). The Home Office circular recognised the welfare of the child as 'the overriding concern of all the professional agencies, who should work together to protect children from abuse and assist in their future safety' (Home Office, 1988, p. 9). Wherever possible, arrangements should be established for police officers and social workers to investigate allegations together.

In the revised edition of *Working Together* (1991a), issued jointly by the Home Office and the Department of Health, sexual abuse is no longer given special consideration from other forms of child abuse, and joint investigation is regarded as applicable wherever a criminal offence is suspected. Similarly, the Home Office circular issued to coincide with the revised *Working Together* does not focus solely on sexual abuse, stating that, 'the general principles which apply to child sexual abuse often apply to cases of physical and emotional abuse' (Home Office, 1991b, p. 6).

Full details of arrangements nationwide were not available before our research, although in 1988 the Social Services Inspectorate published a survey of inter-agency co-operation from the perspective of SSDs in England and Wales (Social Services Inspectorate, 1988). It found that, in autumn 1987, 83 per cent of the 108 local authorities in England and all 8 in Wales said they had already established satisfactory arrangements for co-operation with police on child sexual abuse (CSA) cases, with further joint developments planned. In 31 areas, however, there was no agreed joint consultation policy. In 71 areas the practice of joint investigation had been adopted 'wherever practicable', and a further 26 were considering doing so. But only 22 areas had joint training for joint investigation.

There remain strong reservations about collaboration between agencies. Concern is focused on whether it is possible to achieve collaboration on an equal basis, and, secondly, the effects this might have on the children and families who receive the attention of powerful agencies working together. Blagg and Stubbs (1988, p. 13) suggest that 'inter- and intra-agency relations are bounded by conflict rather more than cooperation, that agencies might, in any case, have very different roles, and that any cosy relationship between them might result in dangerous, unintended and unforeseen consequences'. Furthermore, sceptics maintain that the different agencies start on unequal terms, and police activities may have great impact on social services, without the impact being reciprocated (Thomas, 1988). The suspicion with which police and social workers usually view each other has been widely remarked. For example, Cornick (1988, p. 26) suggests that 'recruitment into both agencies attracts very different people, and their . . . training . . . would seem to create further divisions . . . Police officers are likely to see social workers as wishy-washy, indecisive and intellectual do-gooders, while many social workers . . . will view the police as omnipotent, inflexible and with a rule book mentality'.

Blyth and Milner argue that effective partnership requires a fundamental appraisal of the effects of power differentials on agency workers. Questions of male violence, ownership of expertise and the subordinate position of women and ethnic minorities need to be taken into account. Moreover, 'conflicting views and opinions should be embraced rather than fought over or avoided [because] interchange of ideas not only illuminates debate and aids understanding but prevents the establishment of cosy and collusive relationships; . . .excessive familiarity and interdependence can lead to blurring of roles [and] . . .duplication of functions' (Blyth and Milner, 1990, pp. 209–10).

Waterhouse and Carnie (1990) found that dissatisfactions associated with collaboration included the involvement of several people in decisions, delay in passing information on, competing aims and objectives, and mutual indecision. Satisfaction was influenced by adherence to a shared model of inter-agency practice and emphasis upon informal lines of communication. Three models of practice were indicated: the 'minimalist', where only basic information is exchanged, and through formal channels, with limited discussion; the 'collaborative', featuring free exchange of information on an informal basis, close consultation about progress and collaboration in deciding on and executing case management; and the 'integrated', with joint interviewing, joint investigation and joint appraisal of cases by a specialist multi-disciplinary team operating as a single entity. The existence of such a range of responses suggests some of the problems the agencies face in collaborating. Stevenson (1989) has noted the fragmentation of accountability and authority that may result and identified a need for organisational rewards from co-operation. She also cites the potential for attitudes to class, ethnicity and gender to excite inter-agency conflict about perceptions of what is abuse.

Training is often seen as the solution to these problems. The Cleveland Inquiry Report recommended that 'there is a need for inter-agency training and recognition of the role of other disciplines. For example, police officers and social workers designated to interview children should have joint training in their approach to this task' (DHSS, 1988a, p. 251). *Working Together* (DHSS, 1988b, p. 37) stated that 'staff involved in investigating sexual abuse need training in the task, part of which should be on a multi-disciplinary basis involving police, social workers, health visitors, doctors and local authority lawyers'.

The revised edition of *Working Together* notes that although 'in cases of child abuse both the police and social services have as their foremost objective the welfare of the child, their primary functions, powers and methods of working are different . . . difficulties will be encountered in joint inter-agency investigations but these can be minimised by the selection of specialist staff who undergo appropriate inter-agency training' (Home Office *et al.*, 1991a, p. 17). Investigators and supervisors should 'fully understand the responsibilities of both agencies, the powers available to them and the different standards of proof that exist in relation to criminal and civil proceedings. This will assist to remove some of the tensions that can otherwise exist' (Home Office *et al.*, 1991a, p. 17). Similarly, the Home Office circular cites a 'distinct possibility' of differences over, for example, the length and frequency of interviews with the child or the role to be played in questioning and asserts that 'joint training with members of the social services department and other relevant professionals remains the key to effective inter-agency working' (Home Office, 1991b, p. 3).

The Investigative Process in Child Sexual Abuse

The investigation and diagnosis of a CSA referral is likely to involve a number of professionals and steps, including collation of background information, both about children and their fam-ily, and about the allegation itself; an interview with the child; consideration of whether a medical examination is advisable; an interview with the child's parent(s); an interview with the suspect, if appropriate; and, finally, an interdisciplinary proced-ure for sharing information and making decisions. The precise course of the investigation depends partly on the nature of the referral, including how the abuse came to light (Jones and McQuiston, 1988).

The UK literature generally agrees that there is a role for both police and social workers in interviewing children, but clear guidance on just how joint interviewing should be accom-plished is only now being addressed. Bannister and Print (1989, p. 6) suggest that 'although joint interviews [by police and social worker/therapist] are preferable to the child being inter-viewed more than once, only one person at a time should question the child and the two interviewers must determine who will lead the interview from the outset. However, the child's response to the interviewers must be carefully noted and if the child responds better to one person rather than another then that person should lead the interview'.

The secondary effects of professional interventions should also be taken into account. Although little research has been done on these (Browne and Finkelhor, 1986), attention has been drawn to a number of practices which seem likely to have a negative impact: multiple interviews, insensitively performed medical examinations, removal of the child from home, and repeated court appearances, particularly if accompanied by de-lays and postponements, as they often are (Jones and McQuiston, 1988). There is very little research literature on parents' views about investigation and diagnosis.

The Implementation of a Local Scheme

By the time of the Cleveland controversy, one of the earliest experiments in joint working between police and social services was already underway in Bexley, Kent (Metropolitan Police and Bexley London Borough, 1987). Shortly after this, and galvanised by the events in Cleveland, police and social services started a system of joint investigation in Surrey, which we evaluated (Conroy, Fielding and Tunstill, 1990). The evaluation, which was broadly positive, led to the national survey of investigative arrangements reported below. Linked to the survey was detailed monitoring of the inauguration of joint arrangements in two different areas, one a county scheme for investigating CSA and one a metropolitan scheme for investigating all child abuse referrals. This afforded some insight into the perspectives of police and social workers on their opposite numbers.

We will profile findings from the metropolitan area, consisting of an outer London borough and parts of an adjoining county which were covered by one Metropolitan Police Child Protection Team. The police there had experience varying from three and a half to 25 years' service, and from no child protection experience to extensive involvement. Only two had any previous child protection training, and two had sexual offences training. The social workers varied from a few months to eight years' post-qualification experience. Most had child protection experience and had undergone child protection training, although three (out of 22 interviewed) had limited child protection experience and, of these, two had no child protection training. Four police officers had taken a joint training course and one had taken the trainers' course. Three of the four were positive overall about the course but one felt it a 'waste of time' and 'dangerous', although worthwhile for getting to know social workers and how they operate. The other three also cited this as beneficial, together with input on interviewing techniques. The self-awareness exercises were criticised and officers felt there should have been a better balance between police and social workers on the course.

Nine social workers had taken the joint course and eight were positive, citing the value of meeting their police opposite numbers, discussing roles and dispelling stereotypes, although some felt that interdisciplinary issues were not tackled in sufficient depth. Input on interviewing was again valued.

Four police officers reported limited previous contact with social workers. One had felt 'a bit wary' but others had 'no strong opinions' or said 'I've seen good and bad'. Those who had previously had more contact commented: 'I've got on well with social workers', 'I've had no problem, I realised our aims and assessments were often the same' and felt 'reasonably positive'. The 'wary' officer had been 'pleasantly surprised . . . they're easier to work with than I'd thought', while of the three with no strong opinions, one was 'very happy, very impressed', and the others referred to both good and bad relationships with social workers. The four who had previously felt positive remained so or felt 'very positive now, I have a lot of sympathy as well, they really are society's scapegoats'.

Almost all the social workers reported contact with police prior to the new arrangements, either in child protection or juvenile justice. Six felt 'quite' or 'wholly' positive about their previous contact, eight felt 'mixed' or 'it depends what you make of it . . . Some police officers are easier to work with than others', five had felt 'wary' or 'fairly worried', and three had insufficient local experience to comment. All now felt positive towards the child protection team officers, commenting 'they are much more sensitive', 'I feel I can trust them more', or 'you get a much more consistent approach'. Some stressed that this did not necessarily apply to other police.

Reviewing advantages of joint investigation, five police cited better communication between professionals, three the combining of skills and experience, three the avoidance of repeated interviews and three cited access to more information. Eleven social workers cited the combination of skills, perspective and roles, ten the provision of support and sharing of responsibility, nine mentioned better planning, communication and co-ordination, three said the new system emphasised the seriousness of the matter, three noted the avoidance of repetition for the child and one cited increased information. In sum, there were different emphases but considerable overlap.

Six police reported no disadvantages, but one thought any investigation, however conducted, was damaging to the child.

Two said joint investigation was sometimes slower, with the need to involve a social worker affecting the speed of response to a referral, and one said that families sometimes feel it heavy-handed to involve police. The social workers were more likely to perceive problems, including concern that the police may 'steamroller us and lead us to one side', that 'social workers may be seen as police officers' and that 'we may get into legalese too quickly'. These data from one locality sensitized us to features to explore in the national survey.

A National Survey of Investigative Arrangements

Between June 1989 and February 1990 we conducted a national survey of CSA investigative arrangements by telephone interviews with key staff in social services departments and police forces in England, Scotland and Wales. Some 97 out of 132 SSDs (75 per cent) and 48 of a total of 51 police forces (94 per cent) participated. While 90 per cent of police forces and 85 per cent of SSDs averred that they had adopted a formal joint investigative approach, the distinction between joint and separate is simplistic; an 'investigation' has many components, and each may be executed separately, singly by joint agreement, or jointly. The terms 'separate' and 'joint' should be conceptualised as representing two ends of a continuum.

Allegations of CSA were not necessarily treated as a referral needing joint investigation. They may be categorised as 'suspicion only', or 'vague information', and handled differently. This classification process served to gatekeep entry to the joint investigation system. Some 73 per cent of police forces and 74 per cent of SSDs identified a phase of initially assessing 'received information' before taking investigative action.

A further sign that the agencies' functional integration in investigation was not as great as it may initially seem was that joint investigation of CSA referrals was not automatic in 44 per cent of police forces and 48 per cent of SSDs. This is a sign of the definitional disparity commentators have raised. Most referrals not jointly investigated were *not seen as child sexual abuse*, including incidents not perpetrated by a 'family member', sexual intercourse between young teenagers, and allegations classed as very minor. Further, even when a referral was defined as CSA, one agency might proceed alone if action was urgently needed or opposite numbers were unavailable.

Joint investigation, with its staffing demands and time-consuming nature, was kept for more serious cases. Some 58 per cent of the SSDs occasionally jointly investigated non-sexual abuse referrals, compared with 33 per cent of police forces (25 per cent of forces said they *always* used a joint approach in other child abuse referrals, while 10 per cent of SSDs stated this). This reflects differences in referrals to the respective agencies. Social services' child protection work covers a range of seriousness. But police tend to be involved where a criminal offence is suspected and so have a higher proportion of more serious cases. This distinction is important since, despite official advice, it might not be appropriate or efficient for police to be involved in all the cases social services would label as 'child abuse'. Further, where joint investigation of other child abuse referrals was the norm, influential factors for both agencies concerned the degree of seriousness, so that minor physical abuse, or emotional abuse, would not warrant joint investigation.

A substantial minority of forces (15 per cent) and SSDs (12 per cent) did not notify all suspicions and allegations to the partner agency, again reflecting ideas on the appropriateness of joint investigation. Social services might not notify police of incidents that had taken place long ago (e.g., an adult revealing childhood abuse) since there would be no likelihood of prosecution, whilst the police might not notify sexual assault perpetrated by someone outside the family, or a stranger, or cases constituting unlawful sexual intercourse, if they saw no need for social work input.

Personnel resources pointed up another difference between agencies. Police had a higher requirement for officers to undergo specific training in sexual abuse than social services, with 90 per cent of police forces requiring this against 50 per cent of SSDs. This reflected both the more frequent police practice of designating officers (and hence training them) for sexual abuse cases, and the smaller numbers of police officers designated, which posed fewer problems for secondment to training. Some SSDs lacked resources to ensure workers were trained before participating. Most police forces (88 per cent) designated staff for CSA investigations, compared to under half the SSDs (42 per cent).

The police use of designated staff reflects a structure where operational models are not generally client-based (e.g. elderly people) and hence there is a need specifically to nominate and train officers to undertake investigations. In SSDs whose operational model is service-based (rather than generic), staff will already be specialised by client group. Organisational differences also marked whether CSA referrals were always dealt with by designated staff, in those agencies that did designate. While lack of availability due to shift systems or shortage of designated workers was an important cause, in some police forces serious incidents required the participation of senior officers. In SSDs, cases already allocated to a social worker were often dealt with by that worker, although there would be support by the designated person; in some SSDs the designated person had a consultative role and only dealt personally with the most difficult cases.

Some 20 per cent of designated workers in each agency still retained general duties and in the police this included keeping officers in general operational work. However, the majority of both agencies had designated staff who retained general child protection duties. In a number of police forces, designated officers were also used in victim support. Few forces or SSDs used designated officers solely for CSA work.

Provision of training for supervisors in both investigative and supervisory skills related to CSA was patchy. Some respondents reported that this led to problems with investigators being effectively supported, as well as with hierarchical relationships. In previous research (Conroy *et al.*, 1990) line managers also expressed disquiet at their staff having more skills than they possessed as a result of joint investigative training. The national data revealed that police line managers were often investigators too, and so a high proportion (32 per cent) had the same training as those they supervised, or the same training plus CSA management training (19 per cent). However, if officers above the line manager did not sufficiently understand the approach to CSA investigation, there could be pressures on designated officers and their line managers to act more 'traditionally' in the pace of investigations, the collection of evidence and the pursuit of prosecutions.

All the police categorised the interview with the alleged offender as always or usually a sole activity. But 17 per cent of SSDs did not concur. A social worker being *present* at an interview with an alleged perpetrator may be defined by some SSDs as constituting a joint interview, whereas the police may categorise it as a sole interview with a social worker present. Most police and SSD respondents emphasised that a social worker who had been involved in interviewing an alleged perpetrator, and could thus be called by the court as a witness concerning the interview, would face problems in work with the family and offender in the future. This represents one clear limit on cooperation.

Whether to examine a suspected victim medically is a difficult decision, and one where the orientation of the police to gathering evidence for a prosecution seemed likely to produce different emphases. The expected differences were manifest, but not gross. Some 17 per cent of police forces but only 7 per cent of social services always medically examined, and 62 per cent of police forces but 55 per cent of social services usually examined. Examination was occasional in 21 per cent of police forces but 38 per cent of SSDs. While little difference was manifest when forensic evidence was likely (55 per cent of police and 57 per cent of social services saw this as an appropriate reason to examine), allegations of penetration (penile, digital or object penetration of the child's vagina or anus) was an appropriate reason for 13 per cent of police but only 6 per cent of social services. Examination in order to exclude the possibility of medical problems was seen as appropriate by 13 per cent of police but by 20 per cent of social services' respondents.

Difficulties with Joint Arrangements

Difficulties ranged across training, physical resources, human resources, organisational structure, roles, approach to investigation, procedures, application of joint procedures, managers, other agencies, and personality. These categories were common to both agencies' responses, and despite there being some variation in the frequency with which they were identified, there were remarkable similarities.

Table 9.1 shows the four most frequently cited categories of initial problems. Both agencies most frequently identified issues concerning police and social services' role in investigations, and the problem of stereotypical perceptions of each other, as causing early difficulties. Both also reported that this was addressed by training that included elements of role examination and reappraisal.

Table 9.1 *Four Most Frequently Mentioned* Initial *Difficulties*

Category of difficulty mentioned by respondent	Police (N = 47)		Category of difficulty mentioned by respondent	Social Services (N = 98)	
	n	%		*n*	%
Roles	20	43	Roles	42	43
Approach to investigation	13	28	Approach to investigation	36	37
Human resources	11	23	Organisational issues	14	14
Organisational issues	9	19	Procedures	14	14

Problems with approaches to investigation included issues of role. Social services felt police often wanted to move too quickly, whilst the police felt social services dragged their feet. Police respondents worried that social workers would ask leading questions in interviews and undermine judicial evidence. In contrast, social workers worried that police investigators would not be sensitive to the needs of the child. Both reported that these misgivings were resolved through joint training and experience of joint work.

Several organisational problems were cited, but most prominent were police working shifts while social workers did regular hours, and secondly, one agency specialising in child care activities and the other remaining generic. Working hours sometimes resulted in an investigator starting with one partner and having to work with another halfway through, exacerbating conflict over appropriate times to conduct interviews and so on. The problem of one agency being specialised, perhaps into a team, whilst the other worked generically, sometimes meant that trained investigators from the two agencies had few opportunities to work together on more than one occasion, hampering development of working relationships. This applied equally to both agencies.

The police more frequently identified the problem of human resources, possibly because they had to argue a case for redeployment of personnel into CSA specialist investigation to the chief constable, whilst social services could draw from within their staff, causing understaffing elsewhere.

When 'current' difficulties were explored the same categories were found to apply, as shown in Table 9.2. The four most frequently cited areas showed little change; clearly these are relatively intractable problems.

Table 9.2 *Four Most Frequently Mentioned* Current *Difficulties*

Category of difficulty mentioned by respondent	Police (N = 47)		Category of difficulty mentioned by respondent	Social Services (N = 98)	
	n	%		*n*	%
Organisational issues	11	23	Approach to investigation	25	26
Miscellaneous	10	21	Related to medical profession	24	25
Human resources	9	19	Miscellaneous	24	25
Role/approach to investigation/related to medical profession	9	19	Role	22	23

The persistence of 'role' suggests the limits of initial training. Some respondents worried about erosion of their role, and some said that over time investigators tended to 'revert to type'. This was often linked with a change of manager to one unfamiliar with joint work. The 'miscellaneous' category reflected local difficulties emerging as joint work developed.

A continuing theme was constraints imposed by limited resources. In one of our site visits to social services, designated workers reported that their work was inadequately resourced and supported by senior managers and union officials. They worried that, as reorganisation into specialist teams proceeded, all their colleagues would opt out of the hot seat into work with a lower profile, such as work with the elderly. While they tried hard to avoid tragedy, they felt this was probably the only way proper resources would be allocated.

Progress had been achieved but only against opposition from trade unions, senior managers and colleagues. There was conflict over restricting this work to female social workers, and to social workers on a certain grade. These respondents gave the impression that policy development had largely been determined by the police, who were seen as having organised earlier. The police team had been abruptly set up without consultation with social services in about 1986. They acknowledged that in some areas the police had managed to achieve progress in the interests of clients, citing the instance of restructuring the job of police surgeon on part-time lines, so that female doctors, previously missing (and preferred in work with children), had been attracted into the posts. There was nevertheless a continuing tension over the tendency of police to work on the basis of 'disbelief'. Some officers had different attitudes to those of social workers towards adolescent girls who made allegations; the social workers saw it as a matter of the officer's personality. But early problems in getting police to accept that they should have social workers alongside them had been overcome.

While we have been concerned with where police and social services stand on the care/control continuum, we will close with the views of parents whose children had been the subject of a CSA investigation. Although the sample of twelve is small, there is limited literature on parents. Generally, they were satisfied with the investigation and made many positive comments about both agencies. Criticisms mainly concerned the follow-up work by social services, and the response of the legal system. The small number who criticised the investigation cited receiving insufficient information or explanation. Where they had observed a joint interview with the child, they appreciated the sensitivity with which it was done. Where a prosecution occurred, concern was expressed by most parents about the lengthy process to the final court hearing, and the need for more protection for the child in court. But almost all appreciated the rationale for joint investigation. As one put it: 'they have to act together because there is so much that one knows and so much that the other knows, and it's a two-way thing, because the social services are used to picking people up and putting them back together, but the police are more used to picking up the information'.

To conclude, the differences in perspective of those police and social workers directly involved proved to be mild. There were more problems with those in their own agency who played only a peripheral role in CSA investigations. The practice of joint investigation better reconciled social services to control and made the police more alert to welfare considerations. It seems that change occasioned by the special and distressing case of CSA has already spread to child abuse in general – whether it will become more widespread remains moot.

Police often observe that the organisation functions well *in extremis*, when all involved 'pull together' because of commitment to some compelling goal, such as coping with a disaster. In such circumstances, difficulties of culture and bureaucratic organisation are temporarily overcome. Child sexual abuse was such an issue, and its investigation prompted the serious commitment of those involved. But it is one function among many competing for resources – of personnel, of management and supervision, of cash for equipment. The logical converse of 'pulling together' is that when there is not a 'crisis', the organisation functions less well, as routine tensions surface again.

We began by criticising simple bipolar distinctions and by suggesting that it was important to look at gradations of practice which fell between polar opposites. Evolving policy in the investigation of child abuse afforded a good opportunity to examine practice in an area which takes both police and social services some way from their prevailing brief, with the police significantly involved in 'caring' interventions and social services playing a significant role in social control. While there was tangible movement by members of both agencies away from their traditional posture, we found evidence both of continuing obstacles to new working practices within each agency and a tendency for members of each agency to revert to customary practices and attitudes over time.

The implication is that the process of organisational change is slow and the innovations are unlikely to become established through a single intervention or initiative. The finding will be unsurprising to students of the police. There is a long history of innovations in police work being stymied by resistance from front line officers. Yet the organisation is under unprecedented official and public pressure to change, and the balance of effort between control and care is at the heart of the debate. There are calls for greater sensitivity to the needs of victims, a reduction of 'techno-policing' in favour of a community-based style of patrol, greater responsiveness to the priorities of ordinary people (especially ethnic minorities), and a heightened orientation to the interests of other social agencies. The case of child protection suggests some of the practical challenges that face efforts to change the established balance of care and control in the police.

Bibliography

Bannister, A. and Print, B. (1989) *A Model for Assessment Interviews in Suspected Cases of Child Sexual Abuse*, NSPCC Occasional Paper Series, No. 4.

Blagg, H. and Stubbs, P. (1988) 'A Child-Centred Practice?', *Practice*, II, 1, 12–19.

Blyth, E. and Milner, J. (1990) 'The Process of Inter-Agency Work' in the Violence against Children Study Group (eds) *Taking Child Abuse Seriously* (London: Unwin Hyman) pp.195–212.

Browne, A. and Finkelhor, D. (1986) 'Impact of Child Sexual Abuse: A Review of the Research', *Psychological Bulletin*, 99, 1, 66–77.

Conroy, S., Fielding, N. and Tunstill, J. (1990) *Investigating Child Sexual Abuse* (London: Police Foundation).

Cornick, B. (1988) 'Proceeding Together', *Community Care*, 17 March, 25–7.

DHSS (1988a) *Report of the Inquiry Into Child Abuse in Cleveland 1987*, Cm 412 (London: HMSO).

DHSS (1988b) *Working Together: A Guide for Arrangements for Inter-Agency Cooperation for the Protection of Children from Child Abuse* (London: HMSO).

Fielding, N. (1984) *Probation Practice* (Aldershot: Gower).

Fielding, N. (1991) *The Police And Social Conflict* (London: Athlone).

Home Office (1988) *The Investigation of Child Sexual Abuse* Circular 52/1988 (London: HMSO).

Home Office, Department of Health, Department of Education and Science, Welsh Office (1991a) *Working Together Under The Children Act 1989* (London: HMSO).

Home Office (1991b) 'Circular 84/1991' (London: HMSO).

Hunt, A. (1981) 'Dichotomy and Contradiction in the Sociology of Law', *British Journal of Law and Society*, 8, 1, 41–52.

Jones, D. and McQuiston, M. (1988) *Interviewing the Sexually Abused Child* (London: Gaskell).

Metropolitan Police and Bexley London Borough (1987) *Child Sexual Abuse: Joint Investigation Project* (London: HMSO).

Ryder, R. (1991) 'The Cult of Machismo', *Criminal Justice*, 9, 1, 12–13.

Shapland, J. and Vagg, J. (1988) *Policing by the Public* (London: Tavistock).

Social Services Inspectorate (1988) *Child Sexual Abuse: Survey Report* (London: DHSS).

Stevenson, O. (1989) 'The Challenge of Inter-Agency Collaboration', *Adoption and Fostering*, 13, 1, 31–8.

Thomas, T. (1988) 'Working with the Police', *Social Work Today*, 20, 19–20.

Waterhouse, L. and Carnie, J. (1990) 'Investigating Child Sexual Abuse: Towards Inter-Agency Cooperation', *Adoption and Fostering*, 14, 4, 7–12.

10

The Matrix of Care and Control

Mike Stephens and Saul Becker

It is not that individuals fail to appreciate and perceive subtleties, nor to recognise interconnections; it is that in some areas of life we frequently prefer strong and clear messages. We form partial images of many types of activity, which seem to operate at times as a kind of social shorthand. These allow us to distil quickly what we perceive to be the essence of those activities. As far as the police are concerned, and with the image of the Dixon of Dock Green kind of bobby now fast receding from the public's direct experience and consciousness, there is perhaps an understandable tendency to view the activities of the police as primarily a controlling set of functions.

Personal experiences and the portrayal of the police in the media play an influential role in forming our perceptions of policing and the nature of the police organisation. When the public watch their television sets and witness scenes of unrest at which the police are dressed in paramilitary uniform, or when they see officers in cars with sirens wailing and lights flashing as they chase after criminals, it is difficult not to see them as the embodiment of agents of control. The stereotypical view of the police, which is most common among the general public, is one that emphasises the control aspects of police work. However, when we think of probation officers or social workers there is another broad stereotype, or form of social shorthand, that often comes to mind; one that focuses on the caring aspects of these two professions. When we stereotype occupations

213

and form images of their perceived essential characteristics in this way, we frequently forget or overlook actions that run counter to those stereotypes. Raynor (1985), for example, has questioned whether the probation service exists to help people who are in trouble with the law or to reduce crime. Similarly, Davies (1985, p. 30) has suggested that 'the social worker is contributing towards the maintenance of society by exercising some control over deviant members, by allocating resources, and by the provision of a wide range of supportive strategies designed to maximise self-respect and develop the abilities of individuals to survive and thrive under their own steam'. So it is with the police: they too are both agents of control *and* care.

Control

The police officer as crime-fighter or as a member of the thin blue line protecting society from violence and anarchy on the streets are the controlling images that frequently fill our imagination, as well as the pages of our newspapers and the screens of our television sets. Indeed, as Reiner in this volume has already shown, fictional portrayals of the police have, at different periods, focused on the control aspects of police work. In contrast, the picture of the officer providing a non-crime-related service remains at best a half-formed or half-remembered composition (Punch, 1979). Even if we *are* more conscious of the caring image of the police, it is still difficult to perceive of this function as the overriding purpose and rationale of the police organisation. Indeed, as several contributors to this volume have already suggested, it is difficult for most police officers themselves to conceive of their role primarily in caring terms. Moreover, given the strongly macho and crime- oriented culture of the police, particularly among the lower ranks and among many male officers, it cannot be said that the police have in recent times been adept at promoting the caring side of their activities in the eyes of the public. However, despite our own stereotypes and misunderstandings, despite the sub-culture predominantly of the lower ranks that still stresses 'real' police work in control terms, there is undeniably a significant care aspect in the work of the police. More importantly, there are many areas of police work where it is impossible to disentangle the elements of care and control. Indeed, not only are the two delivered together, they are interdependent at the pragmatic level, or at the point of delivery of police services. As the contributors to this volume show, it is often hard to disaggregate caring functions from controlling functions, especially in the police domains of community policing, working with juvenile offenders or the mentally ill, responding to domestic violence or sexual assault, and child sexual abuse investigations. In many of these activities the police are involved with other professions. At times, the police take on a social work role – caring functions – while social workers are themselves often involved in forms of *policing*. We must break away from the stereotypes and images that attempt to construct and define police roles invariably as care *or* control, when – as this volume clearly shows – modern policing in Britain is frequently both care *and* control. Indeed, police activities are often a *matrix* of both, in which a caring function may overlap, or reinforce, a controlling one, and vice versa.

Caring for Citizens

Indeed, not only can much of police activity be seen as simultaneously care and control at the pragmatic level; there are also good philosophical reasons for this. In the past, the police were often likened to citizens in uniform, a phrase designed to signify that the individual police officer had no greater powers at his or her disposal than the ordinary citizen. Over the years this position has been considerably altered, and the police now have substantial powers to arrest, to stop and search, etc., particularly since the passing of the Police and Criminal Evidence Act and the Public Order Act in the mid-1980s. However, if the powers of the police and the individual citizen are no longer comparable, the idea that the police are there to protect the citizenry has remained constant and has been an important influence over the police throughout their history.

According to T. H. Marshall (1976), each citizen enjoys certain basic rights associated with the nature of his or her citizenship.

Citizenship is a value-concept and implicit in its meaning are a number of value-judgements. As these value-judgements change, as they do in an open and democratic society, so our understanding of the term citizenship and the rights associated with it also change. Despite the ebb and flow of social forces that constantly modify the perceived meaning of the term citizenship, at any one time one or more substantial viewpoints about the essential elements of citizenship may co-exist. Indeed, much of Marshall's original viewpoint, written in the late 1940s, on the meaning of citizenship would still be accepted by many people today.

Marshall posited three basic elements to the concept of citizenship; the political, the civil, and the social. Put very simply, the political element was satisfied when adult individuals were accorded the right to vote and could also stand for election to democratic institutions. The civil element of citizenship was seen by Marshall as the most important element for it was the means by which one could assert and defend all the rights associated with the political and social elements of citizenship. However, for our analysis neither the political nor the civil element are overly important, and it is to the social aspects of citizenship that we must turn to provide a philosophical rationale for the matrix of care and control as delivered by the police.

The social element of citizenship dealt with the rights of citizens to enjoy minimum standards of welfare and security. The institutions identified by Marshall as being most closely associated with the fulfilment of this element were the social services and education. Marshall was essentially concerned with welfare issues and argued that the social element of citizenship was necessary in order to minimise the social and economic gap between the 'haves' and the 'have-nots' by underpinning the right of all citizens to enjoy minimum standards of living compatible with a civilised existence according to the standards of the day. However, we need not restrict ourselves to a 'narrow' definition of welfare. Welfare can also include a reasonable expectation that citizens may walk the streets of the land free from violent attack, from crime and from the fear of crime. In other words, welfare can also subsume the idea of security; security from crime, violence, and fear of crime. Moreover, since in all advanced societies crime and violence exist, this enlarged social element of citizenship also includes the right of citizens, who have had crimes perpetrated against them or against their fellow citizens, to have them properly investigated. In this scenario the police role is not just one of combating crime and quelling disorder – control functions – it is also about ensuring decent minimum standards of security – a caring function. On this level care and control are indissoluble and serve to provide a philosophical legitimation for the necessary interconnections of these two functions.

Some groups, however, have not always been afforded such security and protection. As a number of contributors to this volume have shown, many black people – especially Afro-Caribbeans – have often been at the sharp end of police interventions. Many have been denied, or have been excluded from, these elements of social citizenship. A draft statement on Ethical Principles for Police Officers (*The Guardian*, 9 December 1992, p. 4) – the first of its kind – set out the principles that should govern police interventions. These stress fairness, courtesy, respect and compassion – caring functions that if implemented would go some way towards protecting the social rights of all.

Certainly, the control of some is necessary for the protection of others. But control, subject to clear legal definitions of what is acceptable and what is not in terms of police activity, is simultaneously a caring function for *all* citizens, including potential and actual law breakers. By defining the legal (as opposed to moral) boundaries for behaviour, the law is a mechanism for both control and care. It allows all citizens to know the boundaries and rules of the game, and what might happen if the rules are broken and a wrongdoer is caught. It also assumes that ignorance of the law is no excuse.

While there are philosophical and pragmatic reasons for the interlinking of care and control in police work, it is by no means always the case that the two elements are equally combined. However, the preceding discussion does help us to identify three central issues, which require further consideration. These are as follows:

1) The extent to which certain police activities and policies are based on care *and* control elements.

2) The nature of the police's own identity and how they construct their own occupational roles that stress either care *or* control as the distinguishing feature.

3) The nature of the changing public perception and image of the police and what implications this may have for the police's future role and effectiveness.

Assessing Care and Control

In order to examine the first issue, the extent to which police activities are a combination of care and control, we must look at the policy making process within the police organisation. An examination of policy formulation will uncover the *degree* to which a particular policy and associated set of activities were intended to pursue a predominantly controlling or caring rationale. Here we will need to look closely at the stated objectives of the policy. For example, if we take an instance of large-scale public disorder, paramilitary policing can be seen *philosophically* as both care and control in terms of its objective to restore levels of public security necessary for a civilised existence. However, while the outcome of deploying paramilitary tactics may be to restore order (a care function), the behaviour of the police will clearly be predominantly influenced by the need to regain and reassert control. At the pragmatic level therefore and at the level of policy implementation the concern for both care and control has disappeared in favour of an overwhelming focus on control alone. Indeed, in a riot this is hardly surprising, but nevertheless the police should still remind themselves that there are care elements even in connection with quelling public disorder. For instance, if the police are seen to be overzealous in the manner in which they quell disorder, or if they are perceived to be indiscriminate in their use of violence against people at the scene of the disorder, public attitudes to the police may well become more critical so that it becomes more difficult for the police to do their job effectively in the period immediately following the disorder, and later.

Another example of the potential combination of care and control is the treatment of those who have been sexually assaulted, a policy formulated with a clear care objective. The police have come to realise that a more sensitive and caring approach is required when dealing with cases involving sexual assault or domestic violence. Such an approach not only benefits the victim, but as Edwards has suggested in this volume, it can also help to produce better evidence with which to prosecute the perpetrator. In this example, an emphasis on care also has important control aspects, namely the prosecution of those charged with domestic violence and sexual assault offences. However, whatever the original intentions of the policy behind the handling of such cases, it will not be viewed as a more sensitive and caring approach by victims unless those police officers dealing with these kinds of cases enjoy proper facilities and accommodation and have been adequately trained. Even when these aspects are in place, unsympathetic attitudes on the part of the police can undermine the original policy's goals. In other words, one must also look at policy implementation to discover the actual operational combination of care and control, since this particular mix may be entirely different from what was intended at the policy formulation stage. With all police policies the rank and file, the so-called street-level bureaucrats, are well-placed to alter the original policy goals and objectives. They are well-placed by virtue of their extensive powers of discretion, the low visibility of much police work, and the power of the police subculture – all of which may combine to subvert an originally caring initiative.

Moreover, we can form a further impression of the prime intention of a policy from evaluation studies. The increasing use of performance indicators, the emphasis on value-for-money, targeting, and quality of service all employ particular criteria that can be used to help us answer the question about the extent to which a police policy is based on care and control. The criteria used will indicate whether the policy is primarily one of care or of control. An analysis of the policy process (in its widest sense to include formulation, implementation and evaluation) would suggest that care and service is a predominant intention and aim of current police policies. There is considerable emphasis on care by chief constables, and this is increasingly reflected in the language of policy documents (see, for example, Her Majesty's Chief Inspector of Constabulary,

1992). Many performance indicators (for instance how fast the police respond to 999 calls) and quality measures are concerned to make police services fit the needs and demands of local communities. Regular surveys of 'customer' reaction and surveys of the public's responses to policing are now part of the movement towards the service philosophy. However, as this volume has shown, the rank and file, the subculture and organisational structure of the police still tend towards defining controlling functions as 'real' police work. This is, perhaps, hardly surprising – at least from the point of view of the junior ranks at the 'sharp' end of policing – when one considers that so much of their contact with the public is often tainted by or threatens to escalate towards aggressive or even violent behaviour. In such circumstances, officers value the idea of being in control and of controlling events since a failure to be in control may lead to personal attacks on the officers involved, or on others. Convincing constables that effective use of interpersonal skills and a proper understanding of cultural differences can help to defuse many potentially difficult encounters with the public has not been easy. This leads us to the second consideration.

Police Identity

The second issue is one concerned with an apparent riddle: if so much police work is a combination of care and control, why is it that so many police officers tend to define their role predominantly in terms of control? To some extent we have touched already on some of the answers. The subculture of the police, particularly in respect of the street-level bureaucrat, places great emphasis on the controlling aspects of police work (see, for example, Stephens, 1988, Chapter 2). Enforcing the rule of law and upholding the Queen's Peace figure prominently in the concerns of police officers. Moreover, the police as a whole do not take kindly to attempts to undermine their control, particularly their control over the territory they patrol. According to Holdaway (1984, p. 36), this territory, or 'ground' as the police call it, belongs to them; they control it and they are wary of any actions or groups that are perceived to be undermining that sense of control. One such group is young black people whom the police view, according to Hain (1980, p. 5), as a 'threat to social stability'. Holdaway's research in a particular subdivision noted that a hostel catering to homeless black youths was seen as a place of constant danger and challenge to the police and, therefore, was policed accordingly. For instance, even when an officer had to call at the hostel on a trivial matter, he would normally do so in company with other constables to ensure that any challenge to the nature and perception of police control would be less likely to succeed.

Moreover, the police are a quasi-military organisation with a hierarchical command structure premised not just on the basis of controlling disorder and crime among the public but also on controlling its own officers. While there have been recent advances in police management practices in respect of career development, stress counselling, and internal lines of communication and consultation, the rank structure is still exceptionally strong. Smith and Gray's (1985, p. 533) study of the Metropolitan Police suggested that, although there are caring aspects within the hierarchical structure, much of the supervision of junior officers tended to be rather negative, with supervisory officers criticising junior personnel more frequently than they praised them. Moreover, the gender and, to a lesser extent, the racial imbalance in the police service helps to preserve a male-dominated culture in which not only is control frequently elevated above that of care, but also the skills of female officers are not always as highly valued as they should be.

These and other factors create an organisational working identity and ethos that is heavily slanted towards the control element, particularly where policy implementation is predominantly in the hands of rank and file officers. Given the power of these forces, separately and in combination, serious questions must be asked about whether control can give way to care and service as the dominant working philosophy throughout the whole of the police organisation. It is not enough that chief constables want service. The demand for service, and the structures to support it, must be more widely accepted and developed. The police need to be more certain about what they are there to do, and they need to be far more rigorous and consistent in promoting their role and their image. This promotion must target not only the public, but also fellow police officers as the Metropolitan Police's *Plus Programme* has tried to do. This leads us to the third concern.

Police Image

The third issue addresses the question of whether and how the police wish to change their image of being predominantly controllers and what might be the implications of such a change. Public perceptions of the police are complex but the predominant one today is of the police as crime controllers. This image of the police is influenced by the contact that some members of the public have with the police, by the media, and by other experiences – whether real or assumed. The image that the police present to the public has always been of vital importance.

The creation of the very first police force in London over 150 years ago caused much popular anxiety; anxiety that had to be allayed by the politicians of the day in order to gain a measure of public consent for the new police (Reiner, 1992). Since that time public confidence in and consensus about the manner in which the police carry out their duties steadily rose, until it reached a peak in the 1950s. Throughout their history the police have taken primary responsibility for maintaining the Queen's Peace and for controlling crime (Bowden, 1978). When these functions were coupled with the traditional image of the police in the UK as a benign and generally even-handed organisation, the police were able to enjoy for many years impressive levels of legitimation and of public support. At this time the police enjoyed, for want of a better term, a 'good' image in the eyes of the public.

However, public consensus about the style and content of police operations began to decline more markedly throughout the 1980s. It must be said that the maintenance of public support is always easier the more homogeneous the society being policed and the less crime being committed. The 1980s, however, saw increasing disorder and division within society as a whole, and rapidly rising crime rates. The cosy, benign image of the police was coming under threat from the growing awareness of the public that the police were not stemming the increase in crime, nor maintaining acceptable clear-up rates. Moreover, the police's traditional image of unarmed 'citizens in uniform' was being severely eroded from another direction. Beginning in St. Pauls' in 1980, closely followed by the Brixton and other inner city riots of 1981, and continuing into the mid-1980s with disorder in Tottenham and the ructions of the Miners' Strike and the Wapping disturbances, the police were increasingly seen in their paramilitary role, and the image of the old-fashioned 'bobby' on the beat was fast being destroyed (Stephens, 1988). No police officer, certainly not senior ones responsible for planning the work and development of the police, could be satisfied with this image of the police as a para-military thin blue line, especially as allegations of unnecessary brutality began to emerge from the police handling of these events (NCCL, 1984 and 1986; McIlroy, 1985; East, Power and Thomas, 1985).

Fortunately for the police the 1980s ended with episodes of major disorder on the decrease, thus allowing them to reduce their paramilitary involvement with the public. Unfortunately for them the political spotlight focused once again on the in-creasing levels of crime and the falling clear-up rate, thus presenting yet another set of problems for the police. These problems were not simply operational ones – how does one go about containing the level of crime and catching more crim-inals? – they were also to do with the presentation of the police image in the eyes of the public. Here substance (police opera-tions) and image were coterminous. As the police struggled to improve their clear-up rates so their image as effective control-lers of crime began to suffer. Herein lies a vicious downward cycle for when public trust and confidence in the police fall so do the levels of co-operation and information, which, in turn, makes it harder for the police to detect and solve crime. A new response to rising crime, especially burglary, was required by the police at the start of the 1990s not only as a substantive operational set of tactics to try to reduce it, but also as a means of attempting to improve the police image. The need to forge a new approach and an improved image was the product of a number of factors: the growing difficulties for the police in dealing with a more heterogeneous society; official pressure on the police to become more efficient; the increasing crime levels and the declining clear-up rates; and the greater awareness of senior police managers that the police organisation had to face up to the fact that there were limits to what the police could achieve on their own in the fight against crime.

Although the 1980s had demonstrated once again that the constant historical mission of the police has been to maintain control over the 'dangerous classes', the 'lower orders', the new 'under class', and other groups in society deemed to require frequent police intervention, the benign image of the British bobby is still very powerful. Indeed, the public portrayal by senior officers of the even-handed and essentially trustworthy character of the police officer is an abiding article of faith. It was not surprising, therefore, that the new vision of the police put forward by the police themselves did not depart too far from the essentials of the traditional image.

Faced with the problems described above and with its image under threat and undergoing unwelcome change in the public's eyes, the police took the opportunity to reinforce its traditional image and legitimation. The message to the public was to stress that the police remain not only crime controllers, but also are 'carers'. The message emerged in the following manner.

The Police Federation, the Superintendents Association, and the Association of Chief Police Officers (ACPO) co-operated in the publication of the *Operational Policing Review* (Joint Consultative Committee, 1990). The review included a survey of the perceptions and expectations of the public, which highlighted the decline in the overall levels of confidence in the police and which was especially marked among black and ethnic minority groups – the very same groups that tend to have the most contact with street-level police officers. Moreover, the review pinpointed a mismatch in police–public expectations about the role of policing: the police valued law enforcement and crime control with all of its technological implications, while the public preferred a community policing-style of operation. The document concluded that what was required in the light of the review's findings was the restoration of the idea of 'traditional policing' to counteract the decline in confidence and to move somewhat closer to public expectations.

ACPO's response, which built on the pre-existing *Plus Programme* in the Metropolitan Police, was the *Strategic Policy Docu-*

ment (ACPO, 1990), at the centre of which was a 'Statement of Common Purpose and Values'. Soon adopted throughout the police forces of England and Wales, the message from this publication was one that set out the policing function as a form of public *service provision*, in which law enforcement and service roles are combined as opposed to being in conflict as was often formerly the case. In addition to crime control and maintaining the Queen's Peace, the policy document stressed the need for the police to reassure and to help the public, and to provide a sensitive service to vulnerable minorities.

The idea of providing a service to customers or consumers has been promoted by many police constabularies since the publication of the ACPO document. The various measures within this service philosophy are intended to bring about greater consultation between the police and the public; to improve on-the-street encounters between individual members of the public and individual police officers; to allow the police to forge a better and more effective 'partnership' with the public in the fight against crime; and, to some extent, to involve the public in police policy making. It is the police putting aside the term police *force* and stressing a more caring and service-oriented image and set of activities. However, while such ideas and their operational aspects will, to some extent, be reflected in police–public contacts, the police cannot depend on these alone to put across its new image. As Southgate and Crisp (1992) show, contact with the police is not evenly distributed throughout the population, and only a minority (40%) have any contact with the police in a twelve-month period. In particular, the contact of the wealthy and the middle class segments of society is much lower than that of working-class or other 'at risk' groups. Most people, therefore, depend for their image of the police not on direct contact (although this is an important source), but on media representations of the police and their work. Media representations include factual reporting of policies and events such as the Quality of Service initiative, the *Plus Programme*, and so on, but there are, in addition, fictional portrayals of the police, one of the most popular of which currently is *The Bill*.

Both the factual and the fictional influence the public's image of the police. The creation of a positive public image of the police is vital to the tenor in which officers can carry out their role. It also has an important impact on the public's level of trust and confidence in the police, the level of which affects the extent and quality of information flow to the police from the public and which, in turn, influences police effectiveness. Image and substance are interconnected, and if the aims of the *Strategic Policy Document* are to be fulfilled then the public must become more fully aware that the police are simultaneously attempting to alter aspects of their operations and to present a new image to the public. The issue for the police is not simply whether they can successfully incorporate this new emphasis on service and care into what has predominantly been a police culture predicated on order maintenance and crime control, but also whether the public will *recognise* and support the attempt. And it is here, in relation to this issue of recognition and of targeting the police message, that the role of the media and the way in which the police approach the media may prove to be vital.

However, it is equally vital that the police are not allowed to manipulate public attitudes and to present an image that is largely devoid of accuracy and truth. In respect of all police operations there should be a proper and effective system of police–public consultation and of accountability. Without such a system there is a danger that a powerful organisation like the police will become too autonomous and unresponsive to the wishes of the public it is supposed to serve. Where the police are promoting a more caring image there is perhaps a danger that the police will want to forge more working relations with other organisations. While the police may argue that such relations are in the interests of those groups that the new arrangements are designed to benefit, there may also be potential threats to individual freedoms and to the security of personal information in some inter-agency forms of co-ordination. Proper police accountability is required in order to ensure that a more caring philosophy does not run counter to the public interest nor undermine civil liberties.

While we have suggested that there are advantages for the police in enjoying a more caring image, such an image may not be without its dangers. For example, the image of caring may sufficiently disguise the actual legitimate power of the police so that their effectiveness is decreased as some people come to perceive the police as having gone 'soft' on crime control. One way forward to avoid such a danger, and subject to effective accountability procedures, may be for the police to stress their controlling function through their caring activities; that is to say, greater control through effective care.

Conclusion

Police rhetoric and the construction of their image, as well as the manner in which they communicate their policies, need to change. Such a change cannot rely on the discourse associated with *The Sweeney* and with cracking down hard on crime, any more than it can rely on the discourse associated with the comfy, avuncular *Dixon of Dock Green*. Instead, the police must promote an image of strength and purpose behind their caring activities. It is time that the police stood up and said openly and forcefully that caring is not only a vital and essential aspect of British policing, but also that it is often a means through which, legitimately and fairly, to pursue effective measures of control. Control measures, as well as caring activities, lead to a more secure existence for us all. The response by the police to the publication in June 1993 of the White Paper on the reform of policing and, more especially, to the Sheehy Report is an indication that the police are now prepared to voice more strongly their concerns about the service dimension of British policing. The Sheehy Report is an attempt to graft on to the police organisation a more efficient business ethos and, thus, its authors place great stress upon their recommendations to introduce performance-related pay and fixed-term contracts of employment, to flatten the hierarchical structure by abolishing the ranks of chief inspector, chief superintendent, and deputy chief constable, and to establish rigorous performance agreements against which to evaluate the work of the police (Sheehy, 1993). Mention is made of the need for performance agreements between chief constables and police authorities to focus on both quantitative and qualitative measures of success. However, unless the picture changes dramatically in the future, there will be a tendency to continue to concentrate on quantitative performance indicators, such as arrest and clear-up rates, and response times, since these are currently more amenable to measurement. There is a grave danger here that the qualitative indicators, more closely related to the service and care functions of the police, will be under-valued. Indeed, some of the recommendations in the White Paper may reinforce this tendency.

The White Paper notes the continuing increases in crime and argues that to combat this rise there must be not only a more effective partnership between the police and the public in the fight against crime, but also that the police themselves must place a much higher priority on combating wrong-doing (Home Office, 1993, p. 1). To fight crime more effectively, the Government proposes to set key objectives, which the police must achieve. These objectives will reflect the Government's view that fighting crime is the highest priority and, as such, the police's performance will be measured against these key objectives. The reform of police authorities proposed by the White Paper, coupled with the recommendations to devolve resources to local commanders and to consult the public about setting local policing priorities, will lead to the police becoming a more local and responsive service, argues the Government (Home Office, 1993, pp. 2–3). On the face of it such proposals might lead to the caring and service functions of the police receiving more prominence, but the main thrust of the White Paper's proposals is not in the direction of care, but towards control. And the major way in which the Government is determined to ensure that the police place further emphasis on their crime control role is through the setting of key objectives in crime-related areas. Performance indicators will add another 'encouragement' that the police deliver these objectives. Moreover, although it is presumably not impossible for police officers to secure an individual or group financial bonus, as recommended by the Sheehy Report, through involvement in typical service or caring functions, it will prove difficult to assess and measure these activities. It would appear, therefore, that one of the best routes towards achieving performance-related pay would be by feeling sufficient collars and by successfully pursuing other crime-related activities. We may speculate once again that non-crime-related issues in the caring and service areas of policing may carry less of an operational imperative. It remains to be seen whether the development of a more 'controlling' police organisation, as envisaged in the Sheehy Report and the White Paper in which the caring functions may be left to wither as a less and less important rump, will deliver a better police service to the public. In providing a service to the public, the police have a duty to ensure that citizens are able to enjoy the benefits of a secure environment. It is not a soft option to suggest that the interlinking of care and control may lead to a more effective policing system. Within the matrix of care and control there will be some police activities that accentuate the control element, others the care element, and at times a potent combination of the two. Neither the public not the police should flinch from the realisation that force is part of the service, and that service is part of the Force.

Bibliography

Association of Chief Police Officers (1990) *Strategic Policy Document. Setting the Standards for Policing: Meeting Community Expectations* (London: ACPO).

Bowden, T. (1978) *Beyond the Limits of the Law* (Harmondsworth: Penguin).

Davies, M. (1985) *The Essential Social Worker* (Aldershot: Gower).

East, R., Power, H. and Thomas, P. (1985) 'The Death of Mass Picketing', *Journal of Law and Society*, 12, 3, Winter, 305–19.

Hain, P. (1980) 'Introduction' in P. Hain (ed.), M. Kettle, D. Campbell and J. Rollo, *Policing the Police, Volume Two* (London: John Calder).

Her Majesty's Chief Inspector of Constabulary (1992) *The Inspectorate View on the Structure and Organisation of Forces* (London: HMCIC), 10 February.

Holdaway, S. (1984) *Inside the British Police* (Oxford: Basil Blackwell).

Home Office (1993) *Police Reform. A Police Service for the Twenty-First Century*, Cm 2281 (London: HMSO).

Joint Consultative Committee of the Police Staff Associations (1990) *Operational Policing Review* (London: Police Federation).

Marshall, T. H. (1976) 'Citizenship and Social Class' in T. H. Marshall *Class, Citizenship and Social Development* (Westport: Greenwood Press) pp. 65–122.

McIlroy, J. (1985) 'Police and Pickets: The Law Against Miners' in J. Beynon (ed.) *Digging Deeper* (London: Verso).

National Council for Civil Liberties (NCCL) (1984) *Civil Liberties and the Miners' Dispute* (London: NCCL).

National Council for Civil Liberties (NCCL) (1986) *No Way in Wapping* (London: NCCL).

Punch, M. (1979) 'The Secret Social Service' in S. Holdaway (ed.) *The British Police* (London: Edward Arnold) pp. 102–17.

Raynor, P. (1985) *Social Work, Justice and Control* (Oxford: Basil Blackwell).

Reiner, R. (1992) *The Politics of the Police*, 2nd edn (Hemel Hempstead: Wheatsheaf).

Sheehy, Sir Patrick (1993) *Inquiry into Police Responsibilities and Rewards*, Cm 2280.I (London: HMSO).

Smith, D. J. and Gray, J. (1985) *Police and People in London* (Aldershot: Gower).

Southgate, P. and Crisp, D. (1992) *Public Satisfaction with Police Services*, Research and Planning Unit Paper 73 (London: Home Office).

Stephens, M. (1988) *Policing: The Critical Issues* (Hemel Hempstead: Wheatsheaf).

Index